Richard
La Londe
and Friends

Fused Glass • Vitreous Enamels
and Other Techniques

Book II

Richard La Londe
and Friends

Fused Glass • Vitreous Enamels and Other Techniques

Book II
by Richard Parker La Londe

OZONE PRESS

Freeland, Washington

Richard La Londe and Friends
Fused Glass • Vitreous Enamels
and Other Techniques
Book II
by Richard Parker La Londe

www.richardlalonde.com

Published by

**OZONE
PRESS**

ozone-press.com
4651 Melody Lane
Freeland, Washington

First Edition

Library of Congress Control Number: 2009902191
ISBN-10 Number: 0-9779126-1-2
ISBN-13 Number: 978-0-9779126-1-2

Printed in China

contents

6   acknowledgements
7   introduction

Part 1: The Past
8   tektites, fulgurites, and obsidian
16   the invention of man-made glass
20   Pliny and wood stove glass
22   Egyptian faience

Part 2: Enamels and Slumping
26   the history of enameling on glass
30   vitreous enamels for sheet glass
42   the history of window glass
46   Rob Adamson & Fritz Dreisbach
     hand-made window glass demo
50   Glen Lukens - metallic oxides & window glass
54   textured ceramic-fiber molds
56   kiln shelf textures & shelf primer
58   hand-made clay & found molds
60   wet felt molds
64   Edwin Walter - sgraffito in-between the sheets
66   beach sand slumping mold
68   slump over an undercut mold
70   Maurice Heaton - enamels under glass
72   enamels under glass project
76   metal molds - La Londe style
80   Frances & Michael Higgins
     the "dropout"
84   ceramic fiber mold for the "dropout"
86   bubbles under glass
88   liquid enamel trailed glass
90   Margaret von Wrangel & Kyle Kinsey
94   Liz Mapelli - surface enamels
98   Paul Marioni - mixed media enamels
106   Meredith MacLeod - high-fire
      Sunshine enamels
112   plants and flowers
116   Avery Anderson - mica powder
119   mica techniques

Part 3: Glass Painting
122   the history of stained glass
124   Sherry Boyd-Yost - master glass painter
128   glass painting techniques
132   Peter McGrain - painting on fused glass
136   "Vitri-Fusáille" technique
138   Cappy Thompson - storytelling
144   Italo Scanga - art vs. technique
146   low-fire vessel painting

Part 4: Metals and Glass
148   the history of metallic luster on glass
152   metallic luster pen & halo luster
154   Edris Eckhardt - gold glass light box
158   precious metal foil
160   flatlight panel
162   window glass and metal inclusions
166   welded stainless steel slumping mold

Part 5: Other Techniques
168   John Luebtow - enormous slumped glass
174   Michael Dupille - "Castalot" mold mix
184   Craig Smith, Lawrence Jacobsen,
      Jayne Persico - "Colour de Verre" molds
188   Roger Nachman - crystal clear adhesive

Part 6: More Fused Glass
192   Richard La Londe - liquid glass line
196   artist's gallery - liquid glass line
202   botanicals: multi-layer technique
212   a public art commission

Part 7: Appendix
224   studio equipment & kilns
228   basic fusing - compatibility,
      volume control & annealing
234   bibliography
237   Richard's materials and suppliers list
239   index

acknowledgements

My gratitude to Vicki Grayson Liden of *graysondesign.net* for her graphic expertise in tweaking the final layout and images of my book. To Marian Blue of Blue and Ude Writers Services- copy editor; to Barry White - software support; and to iocolor - Seattle, WA and C & C Offset Printing Co., Ltd., Portland, OR/Hong Kong.

More grateful thanks to Jill Thomas-Clark (rights and reproductions manager of the Corning Museum of Glass) for providing the wonderful images of ancient and other glass, and to Elizabeth Hylen, Rakow Library, Corning Museum of Glass.

Not much has been written about Ed Walter, and it has been my good fortune to talk with his daughter Linda Walter, who filled me in about his life and techniques: thank you.

Thanks to all of the artists for their photographs and contribution of techniques. Thanks to June Fitzpatrick for studio help. Thanks to Fritz Dreisbach and Rob Adamson for recreating the various methods of sheet glass making.

I have tried my best to get the story right and to provide accurate information. Thanks to all who have helped me with this project. —Richard La Londe

Image on page 2: "Fire" by Richard La Londe, 1992, 23 in. (58 cm) x 20 in. (50 cm), fused Bullseye glass with gold leaf and dichroic glass.

Image on page 5: "Tree of Life," by artist Cappy Thompson, 2008, 29 in. (74 cm) x 89 in. (226 cm). Vitreous enamels reverse painted on mouth-blown sheet glass, laminated to brushed aluminum panels.

Photo Credits

Richard La Londe (RL) p. 2, 8 - 15, 20 - 21, 23 - 25, 32 - 40, 46 - 50, 52 - 62, 64, p. 65 "Owl," 66 - 69 except #5, 70 - 71 RL, except Heaton portrait from his studio pamphlet, 72 - 89, 91 "Kyle's portrait," 93, 98 - 99, 106 - 115, 121 except #1, 122 Rochester Window, 144 - 147, 150 - 162 except portrait on 155, 164 - 167, 175 portrait, 177 - 181, 189 portrait, 190, 193 - 195, 202, 204 - 240 except p. 223 #18
p. 5 Peter Mumford
p. 16 & 17 (CMOG) core vessels and enameled glass - Courtesy of the Corning Museum of Glass, Corning, New York, other shots, RL
p. 22 Vicki Grayson Liden
p. 26 - 29 CMOG
p. 30 Liz Mapelli surface enamel detail, others RL
p. 42 Used by permission of Pilkington, 2008
p. 43 Wikimedia
p. 51 Courtesy of the Glen Llukens papers, 1931-1983 Archives of American Art, Smithsonian Institution
p. 63 Roger Nachman
p. 65 "Portrait" courtesy of Linda Walter
p. 69 #5 courtesy of Linda Walter
p. 90 - 92 courtesy of Kile Kinsey, Kyle's portrait RL
p. 94 - 97 courtesy of Liz Mapelli
p. 96 Sarah Mapelli
p. 100 Mark Sullo
p. 101 RL except floating figure by Roger Schreiber
p. 102 - 105 Roger Schreiber, except kiln by RL
p. 116 - 117 Avery Anderson, portrait by Dianne Hunter
p. 119 - 120 Bruce Larion
p. 121 #1 Wikimedia
p. 122 Wikimedia
p. 123 Tiffany - Wikimedia
p. 124 Connie Crow
p. 125 - 127 Paul Yost, except "Roses & Lilies" by Sue Chartrey
p. 128 - 131 Paul Yost
p. 132 - 135 Rusty O'Toole
p. 136 - 137 Peter McGrain
p. 138 Michael Seidl
p. 139 "Portrait" James Cheng, "Eve" Michael Sidl
p. 140 "Lion" Cappy Thompson, "Queen" Lynn Thompson
p. 141 Peter Mumford
p. 142 "Muses" Spike Mafford, "Library" - Evergreen State College
p. 143 "SeaTac" Russell Johnson, fabrication shots- Derix Studio
p. 148 - 149 CMOG
p. 155 "Portrait" Henry P. Boynton, "Mother & Child"
p. 163 Roger Schreiber
p. 168 - 173 courtesy of John Luebtow
p. 174 Michael Dupille
p. 175 "Bench" Jim Gregory
p. 176 " Summer Triangle" & "Parliment" Michael Dupille, "Sea Turtle" Mike Seibel
p. 182 #9 Michael Dupille, #10, 11,12,13 Natalie Dupille
p. 183 #1 - 4 RL. #5-6, Michael Dupille
p. 184 - 187 courtesy of Colour de Verre
p. 188 - 189, & 191 Roger Nachman
p. 192 Roger Schreiber
p. 196 Alex Sutton
p. 197 "Owl" Alex Sutton, "Blaze" & "Animal Woman Dream" Martha Saly, "Capricious" Dan Urban
P. 198 "Fruits" Rebecca Gilad, "Abraham" Irene Sipel, "The Sprial" Gideon Shapira, "This One" Pat Walsh
p. 199 "A New Day" Rachel Shoham, "Mainly Red" Gideon Shapira, "Cock of the Rock" Paul Ahnberg
p. 200 "Dear & Moon" RL, "Navajo Blanket Wira" & "Serpentine" Bruce Durant
p. 201 "By the River" RL, "Steelhead" Jamie Rau
p. 203 Roger Schreiber
p. 223 #18 Don Larson

introduction

In the beginning there was natural glass and then man-made glass, and that has changed our world.

In 2006, I published my first book, *Richard La Londe: Fused Glass Art and Technique*. The basic idea for that book was to expose the reader to my artwork and techniques, but it evolved into a much larger story. I became intrigued with the glass artists who had come before us, and I began accumulating 1950's enameled glass and researching subjects like faience and enamels. This led to Book II, *Richard La Londe and Friends*. I want to share what I have collected, figure out how I think the artists made their work, and bring some of these techniques into the 21st century.

Since 1981 my focus has been fusing Bullseye glass, and so I thought that it was a good idea to bring other experienced artists into my book to share their techniques and artwork. Some are close friends, some are new friends, and some I am honored to have visited briefly like the Higgins. Others, are deceased, and I never knew them, but in researching their lives, touching their artwork, and re-creating some of their processes, I gained a sense of knowing them – I feel that they would also have been my friends.

If you are unfamiliar with glass fusing, I suggest that you take a basic fusing class, sometimes available through stained glass shops. You can also read an introductory book about fusing. I will not be talking about the basics or how to fire a kiln, but there is a section starting on page 228 that contains what I call "The Big Three" – compatibility, volume control, and annealing. You need to understand these concepts to be a successful glass fuser. That said, I believe all levels of glass enthusiasts and artists should find this book interesting. Since I reprinted 13 pages of very important information from my first book, I added 16 additional pages to make up for this.

It is said that the present generation discounts the preceding one. The exuberance of blowing glass overshadowed the kiln work that came before it. With the passage of time, we can look back and be amazed and appreciative of the artistic and technological developments of the artists from the 1950s and then all the way back to the ancient Egyptians. You can't know where you are going unless you know where you've been.

Why is there little exposure to the 1950's glass fusing artists? I asked my friend, Fritz Dreisbach, this very question. Fritz was one of the first students to study glass with Harvey Littleton at the University of Wisconsin at Madison. Littleton is considered the founder of the Studio Glass Movement, beginning with his Toledo Workshops in 1962. Harvey's students, "disciples," went out into the world and founded the early college glass departments – they taught the "gospel" of blown glass. Fritz told me, "that most of the 50's kiln glass artists didn't teach what they did, so they were forgotten." It is with this in mind that I write this book containing history, technique, and biographies. It is important to teach what we do.

Back in 1982, my time at the Bullseye Glass "Fusing Ranch" was very exciting. I felt like an explorer in a new world as we tried to figure out how to fuse glass and what to do with it after it was fused. Soon Bullseye Glass Company developed "tested compatible glass." The Bullseye Fusing Ranch marketed the "Stressometer" to test for compatibility and "Spray A" to prevent devitrification - which is a surface scum on the glass sometimes created during firing. The ranch sponsored fusing classes, and in 1983 I was one of their first fusing instructors. Later Bullseye adjusted their glass formulas, making many new colors of non-devitrifying compatible glass, stringer, frit and rod.

Why am I excited again? Window glass is a different animal, that devitrifies. Most vitreous enamels are not made for glass, not easily found at local fusing stores nor tested for compatibility to glass. I'm back at the "ranch" with unlimited possibilities, techniques to rediscover, and directions to pioneer – and you can join me. I foresee a renaissance for inexpensive window and recycled glass, with vitreous enamels and metals – a "green glass" revolution. In this book I have written about some of the glass techniques that I find interesting. There are many more to discover and invent, and that is up to you.

My recommendation: Get a kiln and do a lot of fusing and firing – experiment, try out your ideas, and learn from your mistakes.

Happy trails,

Richard La Londe

Part 1: The Past
tektites, fulgurites & obsidian

Glass is found in nature but is generally a rare occurrence.
Glass is a non-crystalline rigid material that for practical purposes acts like a solid. As it cools, the atoms in this viscous material can't organize into a crystalline structure and end up in an amorphous state. Glass fractures in a conchoidal or a curved cone-like shape. Most glass is geologically young, less than 35 million years, because with age it devitrifies and changes into other minerals. Natural glass can be formed by a comet or meteorite impact, and some of our earth's volcanoes erupt a volcanic glass called pumice and obsidian. I have also included fulgurites, which are made when lightning fuses silica rich sand particles together, so the walls of the center hole are sometimes glassy.

Humans have delved into the realm of the gods by channeling lightning to fuse sand and creating glass with an atomic bomb blast.

Tektites
Tektites are formed when the impact energy of a large meteorite or asteroid instantaneously melts the ground containing greater than 70% silica - for instance, quartz sand or soil with a composition similar to granite. This molten viscous material is flung into the atmosphere where it rapidly cools into a glass. When it falls back to earth it can be spread over an area of a hundred miles or more. Most impact craters do not produce tektites, and they are a fairly rare occurrence. Some transparent tektites can be faceted into gemstones.

Libyan Desert Glass
This glass is found in the Libyan Dessert and is transparent to opaque, and clear, amber, or white in color. A crater 19 miles (31 km) wide was recently discovered in satellite images of the Sahara Desert in Egypt near the border with Libya. The impact meteor was perhaps ¾ of a mile (1.2 kilometers) in diameter.

Moldavites
A large 15 million year old impact crater in the Bavarian area of Germany is probably the source for dark green tektites that were flung into the Moldau river valley in Czechoslovakia.

Indochinites
There are varied shapes for these black tektites. When the glassy material was ejected into the earth's atmosphere, speed and rotation froze the molten glass into either a round, disk, dumbbell, or tear drop shape. Rotating around its midpoint, the dumbbell shape was formed when material moved to either end. The teardrop shape was flung in one direction creating the aerodynamic shape or a raindrop. Formed by extraterrestrial impact or volcanic ejection, they are about 800,000 years old and found in the Thailand / Vietnam area.

Trinitite
The first atomic bomb explosion in the desert in New Mexico created a crater ½ mile wide (.8 km), which was glazed with a light green glass named "trinitite," proving that an impact can create glass.

facing upper:
Libyan Desert glass, 1 ½ in. (4 cm) x ½ in. (13 mm) x ¼ in. (6 mm) thick.

facing middle left:
Moldavite, 1 ¼ in. (3 cm) x ¾ in. (17 mm) x ¼ in. (6 mm) thick.

facing middle left:
faceted Moldavite, ½ in. (13 mm) across.

facing bottom:
Indochinite, left, is an example of a disk, middle is a tear drop and right is a dumbbell shape. The diameter of the Penny coins is ¾ in. (2 cm).

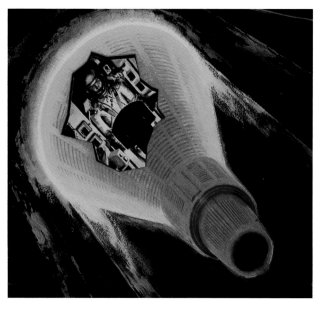

upper:
Three examples of Australites. The one on the left is ½ in. (1.25 cm) across, has its hot side pointing to the left and the backside has not spalled off yet. The middle example is a side view showing the heated surface on the left side and the button on the right side where fragments have conchoidally spalled off due to thermal expansion differences in the glass. The one on the right shows the conchoidal button side.

left:
This drawing shows the re-entry hot side and cooler backside just like the Australite undergoes during re-entry to earth.

The colored illustration shows a Mercury space capsule that is the same type in which John Glenn became the first human to orbit the earth in 1962. During his three orbits, mission control on Earth worried about whether he would burn up on re-entry. Notice that the space capsule is shaped just like the tektite in the upper left, but a heat shield is placed on the large hot end. This is also the same aerodynamic design as a rain drop shaped Indochinite, shown previously.

Just like the space capsule, a tektite is heated by friction as it passes through the earth's atmosphere. The tektite does not have a heat shield, and so this end heats up to incandescence and the trailing end cools as the air zooms by causing refrigeration. The difference in temperature produces thermal shock that cracks the tektite in a "conchoidal" shape. This is a typical fracture for glass and produces those interesting Australite buttons.

Australites
These glass tektites might be from extraterrestrial origin or were possibly thrown out of our earth's atmosphere and underwent a secondary melting upon re-entry. When they hit our atmosphere, friction caused the front surface to incandesce, and the trailing edge created a vacuum which chilled the backside. The hot front expanded and the cold backside contracted, causing thermal expansion cracks, which spalled off flakes and sometimes revealed a smooth, curved, button-like core that has the typical conchoidal fracture of glass. They never get much bigger than 1 in. (2.5 cm) because larger pieces probably explode during re-entry. These tektites are found in the northern part of Australia.

Fulgurites

Fulgur in Latin means lightning. When lightning hits the ground it can penetrate a few feet, about a meter. If it strikes sand that has a high silica content, such as a quartz sand beach, the instantly super-heated sand is fused into an upsidedown, tree-like structure whose branches decrease in diameter the deeper it goes. One fulgurite branch in Florida was measured at 17 ft. (5.5 meters) long.

It takes a temperature of about 3000° F (1650° C) to melt pure silica (SiO_2). Where the temperature is hottest, the sand grains melt instantaneously and create a tube, which sometimes has a smooth glassy inside. Fulgurites have a rougher, fused grain texture on the outside and can be transparent, white, or dark in color.

People who witness a lightning-sand strike can sometimes find an intact fulgurite and carefully dig it out, but usually we find pieces that have eroded from the sand. Lightning can also melt the surface of a silica rock into a glassy mess called a rock fulgurite.

Lightning has been artificially triggered by firing rockets with trailing conducting wires into the air. The lightning's energy creates fulgurites in buckets of silica sand to which the wires are attached.

upper:
Pieces of three "fulgurites" that were created when lightning struck silica sand and fused the sand grains together. Note the small black pebbles on the middle example; they were trapped by the fused sand. The longest piece is 5 in. (13 cm)) and about the diameter of the Penny coin which is ¾ in. (2 cm).

lower left:
Shows a hole in the fulgurites where the extreme heat from lightning fused the sand grains, creating a tube. Not all fulgurite pieces have this hole. The fulgurite segment on the right is 2 in. (5 cm) long for scale.

Obsidian and Pumice

Obsidian is volcanic glass, and pumice is a glassy froth filled with air bubbles. Pictured above is the awe inspiring obsidian flow in the volcanic Newberry Crater near Bend, Oregon. So what does this have to do with kiln glass? How about the fact that it is one mile (1.6 km) long and has and average thickness of 150 feet (45 m.); it is one of the largest piles of glass in the world.

I made a pilgrimage to the site of this pile of glass, redundantly named the "Big Obsidian Flow." I clambered out of my car in the parking lot right where the edge of the flow, about 60 feet high, stopped. Amazed, I climbed the stairs up to a trail that meanders around on top of the flow. If you visit, stay on the path; the pile consists of sharp broken glass and could cut you if you fell; it also quickly destroys shoes.

This flow is composed of 2 types of glass; about 90% is pumice, and 10% is dense black obsidian. Dark gray pumice is riddled with holes about a ¼ in. or larger and the lighter gray pumice is so full of minute air bubbles that it can float in water. These materials have been folded, sheared, shattered, broken, and left in a fractured heap of glass. At 1300 years old, it is Central Oregon's most recent eruption.

Glass fractures in a "conchoidal" pattern, which is cone-like and curved. Native Americans utilized this fracture effect to fashion (knapp) obsidian tools at this site and made arrowheads, spear points, knives, and scrapers. They also traded obsidian as a raw material throughout the Western United States. This site is now designated as the Newberry National Volcanic Monument, and taking pieces of volcanic rock is prohibited. There are other sites nearby, such

as the Glass Buttes area, where obsidian may be collected.

Most lava crystallizes into volcanic rock as it erupts, so glassy obsidian is a comparatively rare rock. It is occasionally found in the volcanic regions of our planet, such as the western United States, and is associated with the end phase of very recent eruptions. Obsidian does not occur in the eastern United States because it slowly breaks down when exposed to water and also tends to crystallize or "devitrify" into fine grained rock. This can be seen in the cristobolite crystals growing in "snowflake" obsidian. It is rare to find obsidian older than 20 million years.

A glass blower's classic formulation for glass contains about 70% silica. The Newberry obsidian is about 72% silica. When the granitic continental crust, which is about 70% silica, is melted, it usually erupts as volcanic rhyolite. If this lava is impaired by a disorganized web of atoms, it flows very slowly and this viscous material forms the natural glass called obsidian. Banded obsidian shows these flow lines. When the glass froths and foams and is shot full of air bubbles, it becomes glassy pumice. Some pumice is mined and used in concrete building blocks; it makes them 50% lighter than straight concrete.

above:
I photographed the "Big Obsidian Flow" from the 8000 foot high Paulina Peak located 30 miles south of Bend, Oregon. This flow erupted 1300 years ago and is 1 mile (1.6 km) long with an average thickness of 150 feet (45 m.). It is located in the Newberry Caldera (volcanic crater) which also contains two lakes. There have been many different obsidian flows at this site, and I found older pieces of obsidian on the top of Paulina Peak.

upper left: Richard is carefully sitting amidst a pile of broken obsidian in the "Big Obsidian Flow" at the Newberry National Volcanic Monument, 30 miles south of Bend, in central Oregon.

upper right: The 60 foot high, leading edge of the "Big Obsidian Flow." You are greeted with this wall of glass at the edge of the parking lot. Black obsidian makes up about 10% of the flow and 90% is bubbly pumice.

middle left: Three obsidian points or arrowheads and a small scrapper, found along the Columbia River near Portland, Oregon. The obsidian probably came from the "Big Obsidian Flow." Rough obsidian from this site was traded throughout this area.

middle right: Black obsidian mixed with dark gray, large bubbly pumice that has been rolled and folded.

lower right: A piece of light gray pumice floats in a wine glass of water. Cheers!

14

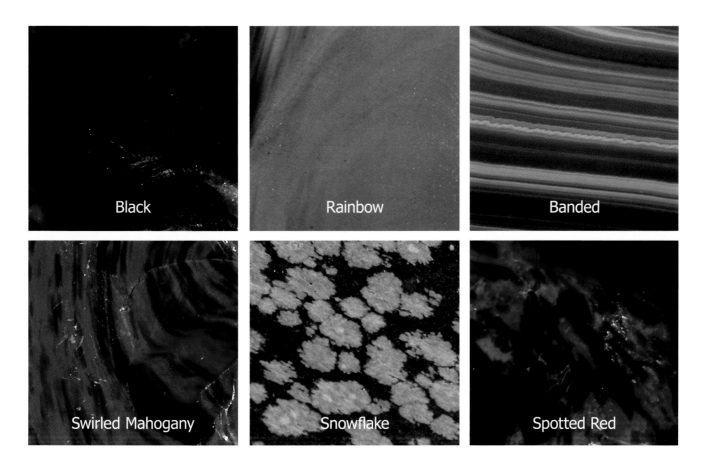

Black · Rainbow · Banded · Swirled Mahogany · Snowflake · Spotted Red

Colored Obsidian

Clear and lightly tinted transparent obsidian has been found, but it is very rare. Almost all obsidian is opaque black, which is colored by microscopic crystalline minerals suspended in the amorphous matrix of glass. Black obsidian's color comes from iron oxide, in the form of magnetite, Fe_3O_4. Uncommon colors include red and brown colored from other iron oxide, hematite Fe_2O_3 or limonite $FeO(OH).nH_2O$. Other colors include mahogany, pumpkin, and green. Some textures and swirl patterns are given fancy names, including midnight lace, flame, and spider web.

When light reflects off of a layer of tiny stretched bubbles that are oriented along a flow layer, it can produce a gold or silver sheen. Sometimes light reflects off of microscopic crystals in the obsidian glass, and green, blue, and purple colors are produced. This type is called rainbow or velvet obsidian. White or gray crystals in obsidian, which look like snowflakes, are cristobolite SiO_2, which has the same composition as quartz. They are formed by devitrification, and eventually when the glass crystallizes, it will disintegrate.

Sometimes an old obsidian flow absorbs water and changes into perlite, which is a white to gray glass with a high water content. Commercially, perlite is heated, and the expanding water causes it to inflate like popcorn; this is used in potting soil. Sometimes inside the natural perlite matrix are found small rounded nodules of obsidian know as "Apache Tears." They range in size from about ½ in. to 3 in. and look black from the outside, but when held up to the light, they reveal themselves to be transparent smoke gray to amber in color.

above: An "Apache Tears" nodule, 1 in. (2.5 cm) long, that was eroded from a glass matrix called perlite, which was created when obsidian absorbed water. The left view is in daylight and in the right view a halogen light shines through it.

TIMELINE (dates approximate)

Natural Glass	200,000 B.C.	Natural obsidian glass knapped into arrow tips, spear points, and knives. 200,000+ in Africa & 12,000+ in America.
Glazed Steatite	10,000 B.C.	Fired-clay vessels found in Northern Japan.
	6,000 B.C.	Fired clay vessels developed in Mesopotamia.
	5,000 B.C.	Copper smelting.
Egyptian Faience	3,000 B.C.	Glazed carved steatite and quartz rock.
	3,000 B.C.	Powdered silica faience developed.
	3,000 B.C.	Glass beads.
Egyptian Core Vessels	1,500 B.C.	Glass vessels made from sand cores coated with fused powdered glass, decorated with hot trailed glass threads, made in Egypt. Also fused crushed glass in molds.
	1,000 B.C.	Glassy faience developed.
Eastern Mediterranean Core Vessels	1,000 B.C.	Glass production decreases for about 500 years. Faience continues.
	500 B.C.	Core vessels produced in the Eastern Mediterranean area.
	200 B.C.	Lead glaze developed.
	200 B.C.	Lead bearing enamels developed.
Blown Glass	50 B.C.	Glass blowing invented.
	150 A.D.	Vitreous enamels on Roman blown glass.
	600–800 A.D.	Islamic metallic luster on blown glass.
	1,100–1,300 A.D.	Islamic enamels on blown glass flourished.
Enameled Glass	1,100 A.D.	Stained Glass in European Cathedrals begins.

the invention of man-made glass

The fascinating thing about ancient history is that it gets rewritten as new archeological discoveries are uncovered. From my research and also from some practical surmising, I have assembled a chain of events for the historical development of man-made glass, but in order to tell this story I need to begin with a simple definition of glass -- glass is a non-crystalline rigid material that for practical purposes acts like a solid.

Obsidian. When ancient hunters discovered obsidian, a naturally occurring glass rock, they were able to fashion very sharp-edged arrow points, spear tips, and knives. You have probably seen that when glass is chipped, it breaks outward from the point of impact, in a curved shape that leaves a very sharp edge. This is one of the basic properties of glass - conchoidal fracturing, and this property was exploited by early humans.

With the invention of agriculture, these early nomads were able to build stable communities. Early industries found in a few of these towns included copper smelting, manufacturing faience objects that had a glass-like surface, and glass making and shaping. All of these activities involved high temperatures in the process of turning raw materials such as copper and tin ore into bronze and turning sand, soda, and lime into faience and glass. Furnaces at that time were not hot enough to melt pure silica (quartz sand), so soda ash was added as a flux to lower the melting temperature; however, this made a glass that would deteriorate and dissolve in water, so lime was added to make glass stable and insoluble. These additives were discovered by trial-and-error over time.

The geographical genesis of man-made glass is usually attributed to the area called Mesopotamia, which means "land between two rivers" - the Tigris and the Euphrates. On today's map, this is the area of eastern Syria, Iraq, and western Iran. Here, a few small beads were found that date to the 3rd millennium B.C. about 5000 years ago. Analysis shows that they are close in structure to a true glass.

Man-made Glass. This then brings us to the question, "How did the invention of man-made glass happen?" The development of glass is probably associated with copper smelting, which began about 5000 B.C. in Mesopotamia and later spread throughout the Middle East. One of the first glass-like materials was probably accidentally found in a smelter oven, created when soda ash fluxed the surface of silica rich bricks or rocks used in the furnace walls. Some copper from the smelting process might have colored this glaze a greenish-turquoise color that was probably noticed and developed into faience and glass.

Both ancient metal smelters and glass kilns have been excavated, but none have been found with a closed top intact. It has been suggested that

"Glass is a non-crystaline rigid material that for practical purposes acts like a solid."

"What we do with glass today will be our legacy for the future."

below:
Eastern Mediterranean core vessel, 9 ½ in. (24 cm), 5th–1st century B.C. Courtesy of Corning Museum of Glass.

glass materials were worked over an open flame, possibly in a cone shaped oven with an open tip, looking like an Native American "teepee." An enclosed furnace probably would have evolved to conserve fuel and increase the temperature, aided by a chimney or bellows. When firewood was scarce, animal dung was probably also used as a fuel.

Glazed Quartz & Steatite. Glazed carved quartz has been found, but carving this hard silica is labor intensive. Many scarabs, beads, and amulets of glazed steatite, which is a soft carvable soapstone that hardens when heated, have been excavated in Egypt. These date from about 3000 B.C. and were produced during the ancient Egyptian period. The tradition continues today with fake antiquities.

Faience. Along the way, someone mixed crushed quartz rock, or silica sand, with soda ash and water. When heated and fused, this mixture forms a self-glazing paste we call Egyptian faience. The glaze creates a thin glass-like shell around a hard granular matrix. Pressing this paste into a mold was much easier than carving stone and adding a little copper turned it a turquoise color. The small amounts of calcium, a glass stabilizer, found in faience might have come from impurities in beach sand or from plant ash. Faience from this period usually consists of about 85 - 90% silica, 8 - 15 % soda ash, and a trace - 2% calcium. Faience manufacture also dates from about 3000 B.C. and continued throughout the ancient Egyptian period and into ancient Roman times. Faience beads are still made in Iran today.

Glass. Pieces of faience might have fallen to the floor of the kiln and sat there for an extended period of time, which might have produced a more vitrified glassy material. These bits of glass could have been bored or reheated and shaped. Glass beads wound around a removable copper core have been found, dating from the 3rd millennium B.C.

Purposeful melting of silica sand, plant ash, natron (mined soda), and calcium carbonate with coloring agents of metallic oxides and carbonates, lead to the creation of colored glass. Clear glass was rare during the ancient Egyptian period, probably due to microscopic bubbles causing a cloudy veil in the glass. The temperature of the furnace was not suf- ficient to decrease the viscosity of the glass, so all the bubbles could not escape. At first, quartz beach sand containing impurities of calcium carbonate as shells or limestone was probably used, and it was later discovered that additional calcium stabilized the glass.

Glass manufacture. Glass making was a two part process - making glass and shaping glass. Glass ovens were located in frontier areas, close to raw materials, and near abundant fuel - usually trees, plant material, or animal dung. The use of a chimney would draw more air and increase the kiln temperature. Glass manufacturing sites moved when the source of fuel was exhausted, and glass making was a major cause of deforestation - which probably also changed the local climate.

The glass manufacturers fused raw materials together, and this was fritted, crushed, and picked through to remove the impurities. This frit was reheated at a higher temperature and cooled into chunks and ingots of glass, which were exported and traded. Glass ingots have been found as cargo in ancient shipwrecks.

Core Vessels. At the glass-shaping site, usually at another location closer to a town, the glass was again gleaned for impurities and remelted to make glass objects. In Egypt and Mesopotamia, glass making was very active from 1600 B.C. - 1200 B.C. Objects made by fusing crushed glass in molds have been found, and core vessels of an exceptional high quality were also produced in Egypt.

Theories about these Egyptian core vessels all suggest that the core was made from sand, clay, vegetable material, and dung - which was formed around a metal rod in the shape of the desired vessel. The rod facilitated reheating the vessel between the different stages of glass application. Glass was applied to this core, and contrasting colored trails of glass were wound around this body and feathered, creating a zig-zag pattern. Handles and rims were added last, and the metal rod was either removed before or after the core vessels were annealed. After cooling, the core was removed, leaving a hollow vessel.

The Core Vessel Body. Here is where it gets interesting. Three theories try to explain how the body glass was applied to the core, before trailing.

(1) Early archaeologists first suggested that the core was dipped into molten glass, like a dipper in honey, to form the body. Today the idea of dipping is not accepted as ancient furnaces probably could not have produced a temperature hot enough to soften the glass so that one could dip into it.

(2) Another idea that some people believe is that the glass body of the vessel was threaded onto the core and heated to make it homogeneous.

(3) The third method, which I favor for early Egyptian core vessels, was proposed and demonstrated by glass artist Dudley Giberson from the United States. A damp core is covered with crushed glass, which is further moistened with water and tapped down. The wall thickness is built up by adding more layers of glass - water - packing. This is then heated over a vertical, open-topped, cone-shaped furnace to fuse the crushed glass into a homogeneous glass body. Early Egyptian core vessels viewed under a magnifying glass sometimes show a granular body. There seems to be the natural progression from glazed thin-shelled silica-sand faience to a thicker fused crushed-glass sand-core vessels.

After 1050 B.C. glass production declined until about 500 B.C. when a new renaissance of glass began in the Eastern Mediterranean area (Greece, Syria, Lebanon), producing new core vessels; not many were made in Egypt during this time. Core vessels were produced well into the Roman era, maybe as late as 300 A.D., and petered out when glass blowing, which created vessels faster and with less labor, took over. Core vessels continued to be made in Mesopotamia for a few more centuries.

The invention of glass blowing occurred about 50 B.C. The first blowers probably preheated chunks of glass which they picked up, heated further, and then blew with clay blow pipes. Dipping the pipes into hot glass that was melted in clay pots evolved later. Early blown glass was fairly small in size - mostly less that 3 inches (7.5 cm). The ingredient proportions varied in ancient glass, but a classic stable formulation for glass contains about 70% silica, 20% soda, and 10% lime.

Lead & Clay. The world's oldest fired-clay vessels date to about 10,000 B.C. from Northern Japan. They appear in the Middle East about 6000 B.C. and in China about 5000 B.C. A waterproof glaze was not developed for centuries, and one of the first was a soda ash glaze similar to faience, appearing about 1500 B.C. It tended to crack because of the expansion difference between the clay body and glaze. The addition of lead about 200 B.C. finally allowed pottery to be easily glazed. It wasn't until the Roman period that significant amounts of lead were used in some glass, which also lowers the melting point. Most of the early enamels were fused onto reheated glass vessels in a process similar to glass blowing, and a lower melting enamel would have been helpful, but not necessary. At some time they probably began firing enamels in a kiln or glass annealer.

Luster & Enamels. After the Roman empire disintegrated, the Eastern lands around the Mediterranean became the Islamic world. In this area during the 7th - 9th century, A.D. metallic luster was a popular decoration for blown glass. Multi-colored enameled glass flourished during the 12th - 14th century, A.D. During the renaissance in Europe, enameled glass decorated fancy blown glass. Today the tradition of enameling on glass continues.

Stained Glass. Islamic glass painting made its way to Europe, where about 1100 A.D., craftsman began painting on the colored sheet glass - that was made by opening and flattening blown cylinders. The vitreous paints probably contained lead which lowered the melting point and allowed them to be fused onto the stained glass without marking the backside. They were fired onto the glass surface in an oven/kiln, usually heated with wood.

We build our world with materials from the earth, and the evolution of man-made glass, from faience to glass, from core vessels to blown glass, is a tribute to the ingenuity of humankind. As we continue to develop new types of glass for the 21st century - such as fiber optics and composite glass materials - we must remember that what we do today will be our legacy that we leave for the future.

Pliny and woodstove glass

**Man-made glass dates
back to nearly 3000 B.C.**

Ancient Mythology

When stories about the discovery of glass making are told, the one most often repeated is by the Roman historian Pliny the Elder. He wrote a story about ancient Phoenician sailors building a fire on the sand during a windy storm. They propped their cooking pots on blocks of natron (soda ash) from their cargo, and the soda ash melted, "fluxed" the sand, which produced bits of glass. It's a fun tale, but we know the campfire would probably not have been hot enough to melt the sand sufficiently to make a recognizable glass, but natron fluxed sand could have been the idea for the faience industry.

After hearing this story I wondered just how hot a fire would have to be to melt glass. One day while walking on the beach near my home I discovered the flattened remains of a beer bottle that had been thrown into a beach fire. Could my wood stove be hot enough to slump glass?

On top of my wood stove, I warmed a piece of glass laying on the rim of a stainless steel bowl. I painted the inside surface of the bowl with a thin layer of separator (kaolin clay and alumina hydrate) so the glass would not stick. I placed this into my wood stove where I had built up a good bed of hardwood coals and watched through the stove window. I was really surprised when, within about two minutes, the glass began to bend, and in about five minutes the slump was finished. I let the fire cool down to anneal the glass and in the morning I retrieved my first piece of "wood stove glass."

The wood stove must have been around 1300° F (705° C) to slump my glass so fast. I know that I could have created a hotter fire by adding more air with a bellows or by opening the wood stove door and letting the chimney draw more air into the fire chamber. The ancient glass makers used similar methods to create a furnace hot enough to melt glass and deforested much of their environment in the process.

above:
A melted beer bottle that I salvaged from the remains of a beach fire.

facing upper left:
A ⅛ in. (3 mm) thick piece of dark adventurine Bullseye Glass that is sitting on the rim of a stainless steel mixing bowl on top of my wood stove. The bowl has a coating of shelf primer on the inside and a small hole drilled in the bottom.

facing upper right:
Using tongs, I am placing the preheated glass and bowl into my wood stove. To keep from getting burned, I am wearing "chili pepper" oven mitts. I have built a good bed of coals using maple, which is a hardwood.

facing middle left:
Shows the bowl and glass in the fire.

facing middle right:
Shows the glass that has slumped into the bowl and then I let the wood fire die down and anneal the glass.

bottom:
Shows the result of wood slumped glass.

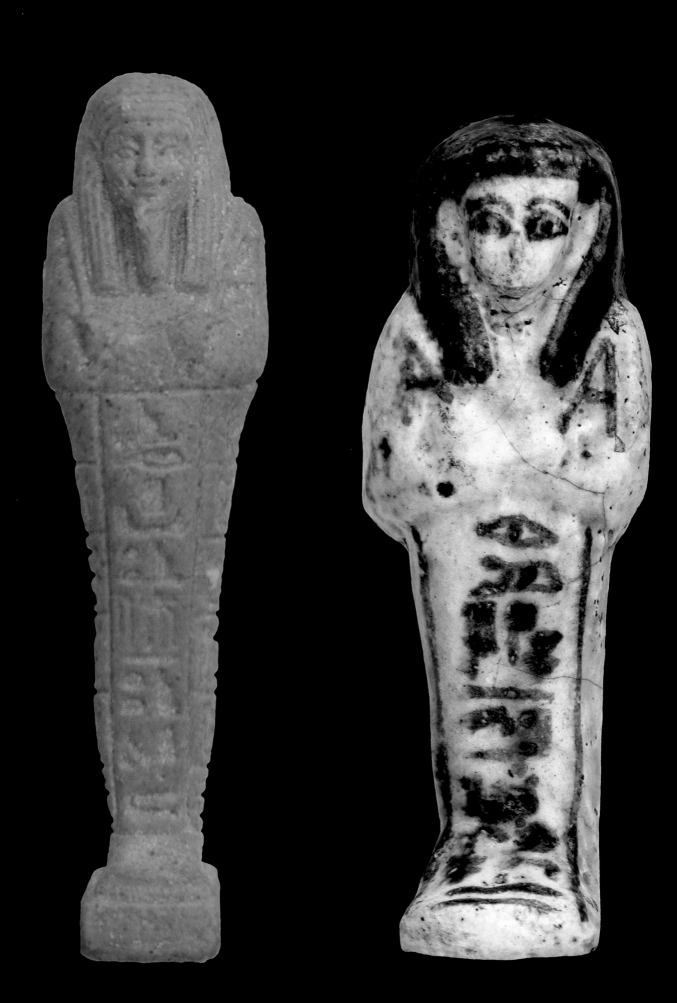

Egyptian faience

I am fascinated by the possible connection of Egyptian faience to the development of man-made glass. I use the term "Egyptian faience" to describe this ancient self-glazing, non-clay material that is generally found in Egypt, the Mediterranean (Minoan), and the near East (Mesopotamia).

The silica, soda, and lime self-glazing Egyptian Faience contains no clay and is probably where the idea of man-made glass originated.

The surface glaze of this proto-glass material is close to, but not considered a true glass. Soda ash fluxes the surface of the grains of silica just enough to create a glassy matrix that holds this material together. The picture above shows the turquoise colored shell and inner silica matrix. Early archaeologists thought that some of the Egyptian glazed artifacts looked like tin-glazed clay pottery made in Faenze and Northern Italy, where these clay bodied ceramics were developed during the middle ages and produced in the middle East and Europe. They are also called majolica and are still made today, but it is not the same as "Egyptian Faience."

Egyptian faience is sometimes called Egyptian paste and developed around 3000 B.C. Someone might have seen turquoise-green glazed rocks found in the walls of copper smelting furnaces. They replicated this process by purposefully glazing carved quartz, but shaping the quartz required a lot of work. Next was to carve and glaze steatite, a soft soapstone which hardens when fired. Later a paste of ground quartz, mixed with fluxing and coloring minerals, was tried. This could be molded, dried, and fired - which glazed the surface and held the object together. This was the beginning of Egyptian faience.

The best quality Egyptian faience uses crushed white quartz that enhances the colored surface glaze, but quartz sand was also used. Egyptian faience usually contains about 90% silica (quartz), 8% soda ash (the natural salt natron or burned plant ash), and a trace of calcium (maybe 2%); these percentages vary in different areas. A true silica/soda/lime glass that is stable contains about 70% silica, 20% soda, and 10% lime. It is also melted at a higher temperature than faience, around 2350° F (1290° C). The calcium in Egyptian faience might have been accidentally introduced when beach sand with shell fragments was used. A metallic oxide colorant such as copper produces the customary turquoise in an oxidation or neutral firing, and a light green color in a reduction firing, which was what most organic fueled kilns did at that time.

These ingredients were mixed with water and pressed into clay molds or hand built and carved. Set aside to dry, the salts "effloresced" or migrated to the surface. Quartz sand melts at 3100° F (1705° C). Soda ash "fluxes" or lowers the melting point, but ancient furnaces were probably not hot enough to do more than slightly soften the surface of the quartz grains and create a thin faience glaze.

facing left:
Egyptian Ushabti, 3 ¾ in. (9.5 cm) x 1 in. (2.5 cm) x ¾ in. (2 cm) deep, about 600 B.C. Egyptian ushabties were made to accompany a mummified person and serve as servants in the afterlife.

facing right:
Egyptian Ushabti, 3 in. (7.5 cm) x 1 ¼ in. (3 cm) x 1 ¼ in. (3 cm) deep, about 600 B.C. The black lines are painted with manganese or iron oxide pigment.

above:
Cross section of faience showing the turquoise colored, self-glazed shell and inner silica matrix.

bottom:
Fired clay mold for shaping an ushabti with Egyptian faience. This ushabti would have been 4 ½ in. (11.5 cm) H.

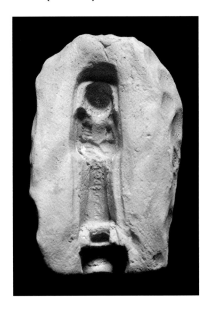

Make Your Own Faience

There are thought to be three methods used to create Egyptian faience. (1) molding or modeling of the faience paste - where the salts migrate to the surface, or "effloresce" during drying and then self glaze when fired, (2) dipping the molded piece into glaze and then firing, or (3) burying the piece in a pile of powdered glaze and firing in a closed container, which allows the material to adhere to the surface. A combination of techniques was also probably used.

Many objects were created from Egyptian faience including beads, amulets, ushabties, wall tiles, cups, plates, and jewelry. 10 in. (25 cm) is large for faience, and most pieces are 4 in. (10 cm) or less, including very small beads. Egyptian faience comes in all colors: yellow, cobalt blue, red, white, and black, but turquoise and light green are the most common colors. Many pieces are simple, but some contain multi-colored faience inlays and are very detailed. These items were made continuously from around 3000 B.C. and into the Roman period, where small amounts of clay and also crushed glass have been found incorporated into the mixture. Faience beads are still made in Iran today.

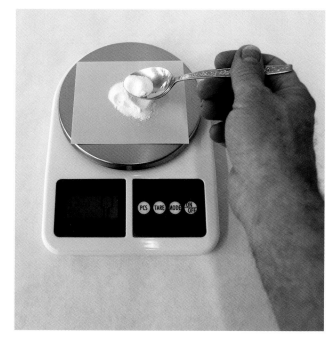

(2) Measure the ingredients by weight. I bought an inexpensive scale that weighs up to 1 kilogram at .01 gram increments. Using this I can make very small batches accurately. I used a mortar and pestle on the soda ash to make it into a finer powder.

calcium carbonate   copper carbonate

silica flour   soda ash

(1) **Faience recipe:**
>   87% silica flour - SiO_2
>   10% soda ash - Na_2CO_3
>   2% calcium carbonate $CaCO_3$
>   1 - 2 % copper carbonate $CuCO_3$

note: for this piece I used 2% $CuCO_3$ which makes a darker bead than 1% try different amounts.

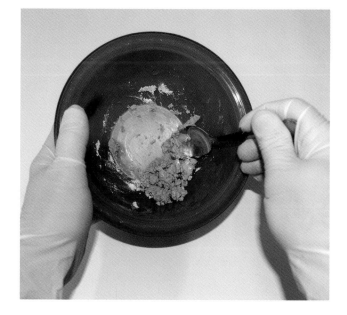

(3) I mix these ingredients in a bowl with a bit of water and add some CMC goop (see fusing section). I believe that the ancients used an organic binder, possibly gum arabic, to make the faience paste more moldable as it is somewhat stiff and crumbly without a binder. Chemical analysis of ancient faience would not show this binder as it burns out during the firing.

faience bead

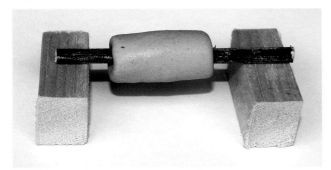

(5) I kneaded the faience paste in my gloved hands until mixed and smooth. For this bead, 1 ¼ in. (3 cm) x ½ in. (12 mm), I molded the paste around a dried hollow plant stem.

(6) The bead was air dried until it set, but you can use a hair dryer. It turns white from "efflorescence" of the soda ash and colorant.

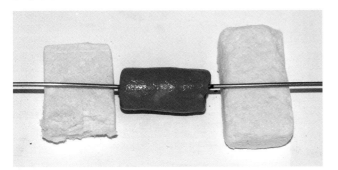

(7) I placed a piece of Kanthol element wire through the trimmed, hollow stem, and supported the bead in the kiln. The organic stem burned up and disappeared, and the bead glazed all the way around.

Firing Schedule:
1 minute (ASAP) to 190° F (88° C)
Soak 30 minutes

1 hour to 1550° F (845° C) - 1600° F (870° C)
Soak 15 minutes

Cool down in kiln. Faience is thermal shock resistant, but no need to grab it hot out of the kiln.

Slow down the firing and cooling time with bigger pieces.

molded faience

(8) I pressed an old, hippie moon belt buckle into a piece of clay, dried the clay for a week, and fired it to 1600° F (870° C). It has a small hole in the deepest area, the nose. I put olive oil inside the mold.

(9) I pressed wet faience into the mold and dried it in a warm spot for 1 hour. I ran a razor blade around the edge, tipped the mold upside down and it fell out. (Left) Just out of the mold (right) shows efflorescence.

(10) The 2 ¼ in. (6 cm) moon face was fired using the bead schedule. Spreading the wet faience from the center outward and further kneading might have produced fewer bubbles and pits.

(11) Other faience experiments, including a cobalt bead and white faience. I was surprised how durable and hard these faience pieces are.

Part 2: Enamels & Slumping
the history of enameling on glass

There are two types of vitreous enamels and they can be either transparent, translucent, or opaque. The first is one in which raw chemicals (batch) are melted in a furnace, and the resulting glass is then pulverized, usually by dumping the molten glass into water (fritting), and then refined by further grinding to a smaller size, including ball milling into powder. This type is a homogenous mixture throughout. The second type is an enamel where a combination of crushed clear glass (frit) is mixed with refined metallic oxides (colorants), and when fired, the clear frit traps the colorant particles in a glassy matrix. Enamels can be applied dry – one method is sifting, or wet – mixed in a liquid medium such as water or oil, and then fused with heat to metal, ceramics, or glass. There are both low fire enamels that can be fired onto a glass vessel without distortion and also high fire enamels that can be fused to glass usually supported by a ceramic shelf or mold during the kiln firing.

Fired vitreous enamels on blown glass began appearing during the Roman era, and an exceptional example is "The Daphne Ewer," but most examples are rare and usually only fragments. Also, there is one Egyptian core vessel that is purported to be enameled from about 1425 B.C. At first enameling on glass was part of the blowing process, where an object would be blown, cooled down, and glass enamel in a liquid medium painted onto the surface. This was then heated to just above the annealing point, picked up with a bit of hot glass on a metal rod, and reheated in a furnace - which fused the enamel onto the surface. Eventually enamels began to be fired kilns, probably wood fired.

Glass making continued after the Roman Empire declined, and with the advent of Islam during the 7th century, these glass makers incorporated Islamic design. Metallic luster painting (staining) was popular from 675 - 1000 A.D. Vitreous enamels reached their zenith from 1100 - 1300 A.D. in the Islamic World of Mesopotamia (Iran /Iraq), around the eastern Mediterranean, through Arabia and into Northern Africa. These techniques also came to Europe with the Moorish conquest of Spain and through interaction during the Crusades.

During the Renaissance, glass centers in Venice and Germany produced intricate enameled and gilt decorated glass pieces as seen in the Behaim Beaker and the Venetian Goblet on the next page. This tradition of decorating glass grew and after this time; glass was being decorated all over the world with vitreous enamels.

Kiln fired glass using opaque glass paints on stained glass windows began before the 12th century. The oldest leaded stained glass window with painting, which is still in its original location, is located in the Augsburg Cathedral in Germany where it was installed in 1140.

During the 1950s in the United States, self taught artists fused enamels made for steel and copper with window glass. For the most part they produced utilitarian dishes, bowls, and ashtrays. Today, a few glass artists use enamels in their artwork.

facing:
The "Daphne Ewer" late 2nd century to early 3rd century A.D. late Roman Empire, 8 ¾ in. (22.2 cm) H. found in a niche in a tomb at Kerch in the Crimea, Ukraine, about 1895. Translucent to opaque white, blown; enameled and gilded.
One of the gems in the Corning Museum of Glass.

below upper:
"Enameled Leg Fragment," possibly 1st century A.D., 1 ¾ in. (4.5 cm) H. x ¼ in. (6 mm) thick, Roman; possibly Egypt, blown and enameled. Courtesy of the Corning Museum of Glass.

below lower:
"Enameled Leaf Motif Rim Fragment," probably 1st century A.D., 2 in. (5 cm) H. Roman Empire: Near East or Italy, blown and enameled. Courtesy of the Corning Museum of Glass.

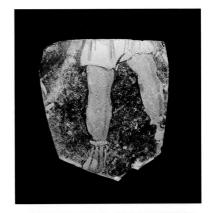

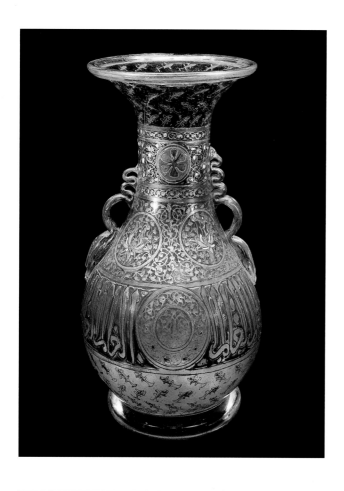

upper left:
"Vase" about 1300-1329, possibly Egypt or Syria (Islamic), 12 in. (30 cm) H. x 6 in. (16 cm) in diameter, polychrome enamel and gilded. Courtesy of the Corning Museum of Glass.

lower left:
"Candlestick Holder" about 1301-1399, 9 in. (22 cm) H. x 8 in. (20 cm) in diameter, probably Egypt (Islamic), polychrome enamel and gilded. Only two of these are know to exist and this is one of the gems in the Corning Museum of Glass.

upper right::
"Bottle with Apollo and Marsyas" 200 - 300 A.D., 5 ¾ in. (14.6 cm) H. x 4 in. (10 cm) in diameter. Enamels on blown glass, Roman, possibly decorated in Syria. Courtesy of the Corning Museum of Glass.

upper left:
"Perfume Sprinkler" ca. 1270, 2 ½ in. (6 cm), probably Aleppo, Syria (Islamic), blown with enameled and gilded decoration. Courtesy of the Corning Museum of Glass.

lower left:
"Decorated Goblet" about 1500 - 1525, 9 in. (23 cm) H. x 5 ¾ in. (14.5 cm) in diameter, Venice, Italy, polychrome enamel and gilded. Courtesy of the Corning Museum of Glass.

lower right:
"Behaim Beaker" 1495, 4 ¼ in. (11 cm) H. x 3 in. (8 cm) in diameter, Venice, Italy, blown, enameled, and gilded. An exported commissioned piece thought to be for a family marriage. The coat of arms belongs to the Behaim family of Nuremberg, Germany. This side depicts the archangel Michael killing a dragon. Courtesy of the Corning Museum of Glass.

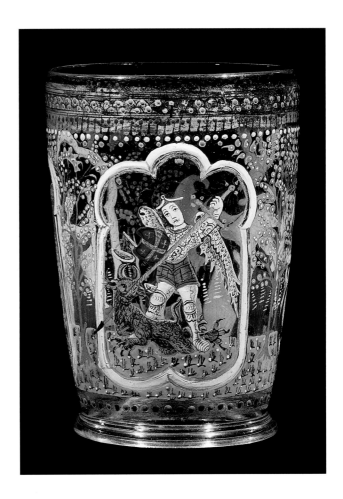

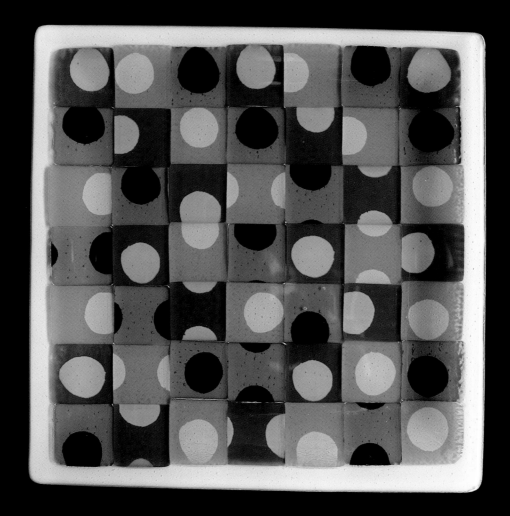

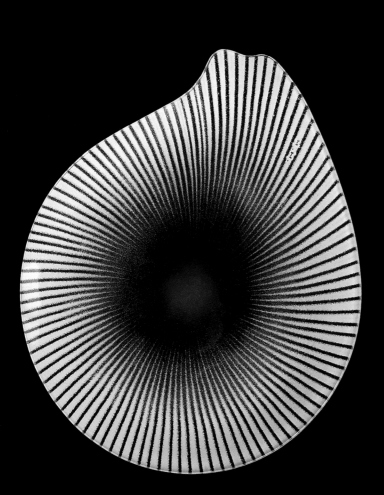

vitreous enamels for sheet glass

Compatibility

During the 1950s and 60s, kiln glass artists in the United States - such as Frances and Michael Higgins, Maurice Heaton, Harriette Anderson, Bill Sydenstricker, Earl McCutchen, Kay Kinney, and Ed Walter - used "trial and error" to figure out which vitreous enamels were compatible with window glass; and they eliminated those that cracked their glass. In the 1950s traditional glass stainers colors were available for painting stained glass, but most of the enamels used by these glass fusers were made for firing on ceramics, copper, or steel, and many had a different expansion rate (COE – coefficient of expansion) than window glass. In a studio pamphlet, Frances and Michael Higgins say, "We coat flat sheets of clear glass with micro-layers of color enamels." These thin layers of enamels were usually trapped between much thicker pieces of window glass, which helped these artists get away with more incompatibility than artists today, who fuse large amounts of colored glass together.

Color Density

Enamels are formulated as super dense colors, so they can be used in very thin layers. Stained glass used for fusing, such as that made by Bullseye and Spectrum, was originally formulated to be a certain color density at ⅛ in. (3 mm) and has to be fused in thicker layers than enamels to maintain the color and not be too light.

Lead in Enamels

In the past, one thing that helped enamels was the element lead, and many of the mid-20th century vitreous enamels contained it. Lead-silica glass melts at a lower temperature than window glass, and from my experience, leaded enamels seem to have a built in flexibility that spans a larger range of incompatibility. Lead also gave vitreous enamels more brilliance, clarity, and life, but it is also a health hazard to the artist, our environment, and the owners of these glass pieces. Some artists made their glassware safer by fusing the enamels between layers of clear glass, and Maurice Heaton put his enamels on the backside of his dinner ware. As for the artist's health, Frances and Michael Higgins and Maurice Heaton all lived into their 90s and never stopped creating art until they died. Ed Walter died at 82 with a loaded kiln ready to fire the next day.

So why get rid of lead? The companies that make these enamels probably didn't like the idea of litigation - being sued - and the EPA (Environmental Protection Agency) went after lead, and also asbestos, with a vengeance. In my opinion, these materials have their place when properly used, but then who guarantees that they

I see a renaissance in the use of inexpensive window glass and recycled glass with vitreous enamels and metals.

You have to act like a scientist - run tests, and experiments and keep notes - to understand how enamels work. Once you figure it out, then you can get on with being an artist.

facing upper:
"Polka-dots" Meredith MacLeod, 8 in. (20 cm) square x ½ in. (12 mm) deep, 2008, Sunshine enamels fused between window glass and then slumped on a second firing.

facing bottom left:
"Elliptical Platter" signed MH, artist Maurice Heaton, about 1960-1980, 13 in. (33 cm) x 11 in. (28 cm) x 1 in. (2.5 cm) deep, fused/slumped enamels under window glass.

facing bottom right:
"Surface Enamel Detail" artist Liz Mapelli, about the mid 1980s, Thompson enamels fused on top of sheet glass.

will be used correctly, and disposed of safely. In America we have so many laws to protect us that the individual doesn't have to take as much responsibility for his or her decisions and actions anymore! It is our duty to protect our children and our environment. Lead is a proven hazard to children's brain development and to our general health. So although I appreciate what it does for enamels, it is in our best interest to "get the lead out" and to handle it safely if we do use it.

There have also been a demise and consolidation of vitreous enamel producers and supplies. I suppose the "get the lead out" campaign didn't help them survive. Today, Thompson Enamels sells only non-leaded enamels. Versa Color dropped their leaded colors and now offers only a few dull colors. Drakenfeld and Paradise enamels are gone. This presents another challenge to the artist – finding a source for vitreous enamels to use with glass.

1950s Glass Fusing
In the United States there was almost no successful fusing of colored sheet glass before 1982, when the Bullseye Glass Company in Portland, Oregon, released its line of "compatible glass," which featured a complete color line of fusible transparent and opaque glass.

Before 1974, when Bullseye started making hand-rolled colored sheet glass, there were only three companies making stained glass in the U.S.: Kokomo, Wissmach, and Blenko. So in the 1950s and 60s those were the domestic glass choices for fusing. Blenko is a hand-blown cylinder glass and its compatibility between colors is not too good. If artists fused either Wissmach or Kokomo (but not fused with each other), they found that the blues and greens "sort of" stayed together and didn't crack and that the yellow and reds "kind of" worked together, but fusing the blues and greens with the yellows and reds was usually a disaster.

In 1949, Frances and Michael Higgins began producing fuse/slumped enameled window glass plates and bowls in Chicago, Illinois. They created very little fused stained glass pieces, as it was problematic. You will notice in the brown Higgins' example, that it contains only blues and greens and no yellows or reds. It also has air bubbles around the fused colored pieces, which are in minimal contact. Fusing the brown glass

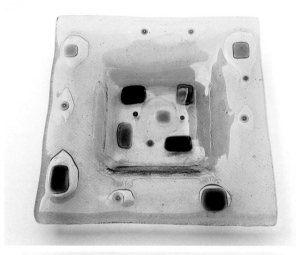

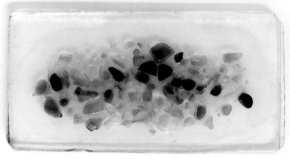

above:
"Fused Glass Dish," by Frances and Michael Higgins, made between 1951 - 1957 at their Wells Street Studio, 5 in. (13 cm) square x ¾ in. (2 cm) deep. On one of my visits to the Higgins' studio, I asked Michael about fusing stained glass. He told me something like this, "The colors weren't really compatible and it took too much experimenting to figure out which ones worked, so we only did a few pieces."

below:
"Fused Glass Architectural Sample", 1958, 2 in. (5 cm) x 4 in. (10 cm), fused window glass with chips from a broken beer bottle and yellow aquarium glass (probably Kokomo or Wissmach). There is a huge bubble surrounding these chips; nevertheless, they have bright halos of incompatibility when viewed under polarized light. My dad who was an architect, now retired, gave me this sample when I was 8 years old. I was fascinated by it, and somehow I kept if for all of these years - look where it lead me!

tightly to the colored glass could exaggerate any incompatibility and cause cracking.

For some of their projects, Frances and Michael Higgins wanted sheets of glass to fuse, so they applied enamels to the surface of window glass and ran them through a conveyor-belt decorating lehr to fuse and anneal. These sheets were covered with a "micro-layer" of enamel, so the compatibility problem was lessened. They cut pieces from these sheets, stacked, and fused them into plates and bowls. Fusing stained glass was very difficult and, for the most part, would have to wait for Bullseye Glass and 1982.

Cracking, Crazing, and Spalling
The early 1950's glass fusers became very creative with glass enamels and window glass. Not all experiments were successful, as enamels designed specifically for glass were not yet available. These artists usually had some ceramics or metal enameling experience, and so they turned to pigments, lusters, copper enamels, clay molds, and other ceramics related materials.

Some of the problems that they encountered were cracking - in which internal cracks developed within the enamels and glass - crazing - in which surface enamels crack - and spalling - in which pieces of the surface shrink more than the base glass and chip off.

Some of the early fusers encapsulated their enamels between glass sheets or covered them with a clear enamel to decrease cracking. Most enamels were of a higher expansion rate (COE) than the base glass, usually window glass, so after fusion, the enamels inside would shrink more than the base glass, pulling on the top and bottom glass which helped hold the glass together. This is similar to tempered glass results, in which a piece of glass is heated to above the upper annealing point, and then the surface is quickly chilled so that the surface molecules "set" or stop moving. As the interior cools, it shrinks and pulls inward, putting the surface of the glass in compression, which "tempers" or strengthens the glass. Marbles are not annealed for this very reason.

above: The rack in the Higgins' studio containing sheets of enameled window glass, photographed in 1992.

middle: Cracked enamel fused between window glass, actual size.

below: Various glass enamels, mediums, and sifters.

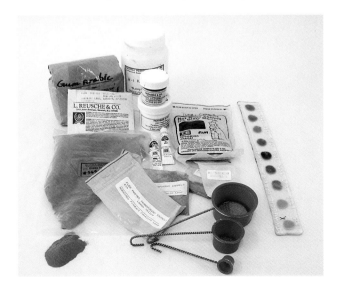

33

The "Stressometer" – Compatibility Testing

In 1982, along with its line of compatible glass, Bullseye introduced the "stressometer," an affordable "polariscope," consisting of two sheets of polarizing film and a flashlight lantern. The polarizing film takes random direction light waves and lines them up in parallel planes. When you put a piece of glass between two sheets of this film and place the polarizing sheets so that the parallel waves of light cross each other at 90°, you can see stress in the glass. This is a simple "polariscope" that has been used by scientists and engineers for many years, but what Bullseye did was to develop the "chip test" for compatibility. Basically if you fuse various pieces of glass to a clear strip of a glass, you can see the possible incompatibility by viewing the amount of halo around the chip. This tells you if the chip glass is compatible to the glass it is has been fused to. You can read about this test in detail, in the Appendix under "compatibility."

above:
My vintage 1982 Bullseye "Stressometer." This is a good device for checking compatibility tests and stress in glass. You can also purchase polarizing film from Edmund Scientific or search for "polarizing film" online and make your own over a light box.

Polarization Chip Test for Glass Compatibility

Test Glass Viewed Under Daylight	Test Glass Viewed Under Polarizing Light

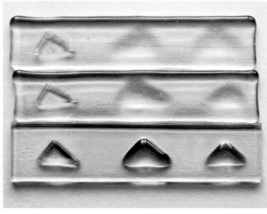

--Spectrum--
COE 96

--Bullseye--
COE 90

--Window--
Glass
COE 80 - 84

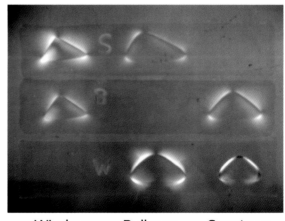

Window (1)	Bullseye (2)	Spectrum (3)	Window (1)	Bullseye (2)	Spectrum (3)

What this test shows:
Looking at Viewed Under Polarizing Light, column (1), at the bottom left corner, we see a chip of window glass fused to window glass and no "halo" of light. Window glass fused to itself is compatible.

Going upward in column (1) we see a medium halo for Bullseye on window glass and a very

large halo for window glass on Spectrum. Spectrum is less compatible to window glass than Bullseye, and both are not fusible to window glass. You can also see the compatibility differences for column (2) Bullseye and column (3) Spectrum. Basically I do not fuse glass that shows a halo. With this test, you can also see that Bullseye is not compatible with Spectrum.

Testing Enamels for Compatibility

You probably won't have compatibility problems if you stick to enamels rated for glass fusing and don't apply them too thick, but if you have problems or want to try something new, then use the Polarization Chip Test. You can also see the color and relative hardness. Make a square of enamels about ⅛ in. (3 mm) high and full fuse it to a strip of the glass that you will be using. For enamel application you will not use such a thick amount, so even if the test shows a little stress, a thin layer of enamel should work. I tested two overglazes, a clear enamel and a white glass, on strips of clear window glass, Bullseye, and Spectrum. I viewed them under polarizing light. For the overglaze tests I used glass powder that had settled to the bottom of the bottles. These clear overglazes when piled ⅛ in. (3 mm) high, turned white. The test for window glass is below.

This polarizing light tests showed me: Fuse Master "Super Spray" - tended to creep and ball up in my test but showed compatibility with window glass, OK with Bullseye 90, but not with Spectrum 96. As a thin surface overglaze "Super Spray" should work, even though this test shows incompatibility with Spectrum.

"Spray A" - showed compatibility with window glass, Bullseye, and Spectrum.

Reichenbach Enamel White - totally not compatible as it cracked the window glass.

Thompson 6000 Clear Enamel - window glass compatible, OK with Bullseye, but not Spectrum.

Annealing Test - the corner is cut off and fused on itself to show if the glass is annealed. Annealing stress can throw off all of your polarizing light interpretation.

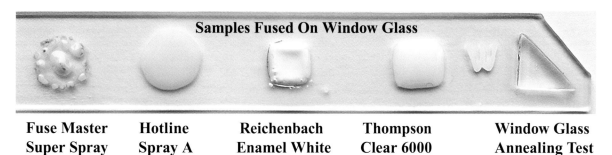

Samples Fused On Window Glass

| Fuse Master Super Spray | Hotline Spray A | Reichenbach Enamel White | Thompson Clear 6000 | Window Glass Annealing Test |

Testing Enamels for Color and Firing Temperature

It is helpful to fuse your enamels onto a test strip to see if they hold up when fired to the temperature that you want. You will also be able to determine if the enamels will change color and what the effect of firing on top of the glass or in-between two pieces of glass is. You can also check on firing against the tin or air side of window glass. The test strip below is Thompson 5000 series opaque enamels fired on window glass, and their style numbers were marked on the test glass with a paint marking pen, before firing. One

half of the test strip is covered with a top layer of window glass, and you can see this is where the enamels flair out. Thompson recommends firing these enamels between 1350° F (730° C) - 1450° F (790° C). These samples held up fairly well to a higher firing, both on top and underneath window glass, but the transparent colors thinned out a bit. Generally, but not always, transparent and red colors seem to be affected by higher firing temperatures. Window glass seems to devitrify more when fired to higher temperatures.

1600° F (870° C)

Fusing Compatible Stained Glass

Companies such as Bullseye, Spectrum, and Uroboros have done a wonderful job of providing us with a complete color line of almost non-devitryfing, fusible glass products. There might be some uses for enamels with these glasses, but I feel that it is limited because they have such good colors already.

Fusing With Window Glass

Modern window glass is sometimes called "float glass" because it is pulled across a molten tin surface as it solidifies so that the bottom side remains flat and shiny. Float glass was developed around the mid-1960s, so earlier window glass will not have a tin side. Worldwide the expansion rate ranges vary, from about 79 - 85 COE (Coefficient of Expansion), most being about 83. Use glass from the same sheet or manufacturer to eliminate compatibility problems.

Devitrification

Sometimes the surface of the glass puckers and looks scummy. This is devitrification, and is caused by crystal growth in the glass which usually appears on the surface and edges, but sometimes on the bottom that is against the kiln shelf, too. Air effects "devit," and I have seen it occur in a trapped air bubble. When using window glass frit, the "devit" can happen between the grains.

Devitrification can occur during firing and during cooling, and is aided by oil or dirt which gives the crystals a nucleus to grow around – oily fingers can actually leave "devit" fingerprints on your glass. For sheet glass, devitrification occurs with in a small temperature range, about 1350° F – 1450° F (730° C – 790° C), where enough heat, (kinetic energy) allows the molecules to move around and arrange themselves into a crystal lattice structure. Above this range, devitrification breaks down because the molecules are moving too much. Below this range the molecules don't have enough energy to move.

High temperature firing and soaking seems to increase devitrification, possibly by breaking down the glass and making "devit" prone surface molecules available for further devitrification. Calcium in glass, which is used as a glass stabilizer, is notorious for causing devitrification. For the volume of window glass sold, fusing is a very minor application, so replacing some of the calcium with a more expensive material has not been done. On the other hand, some of the Bullseye and Spectrum glass was prone to devitrification, and altering glass formulation has made them devitrify less.

When fusing window glass it is important to identify the side of the glass that was exposed to the molten tin bath. This is called the "tin side" and contains a minor amount of tin molecules embedded in this glass surface, which can react with some enamels, changing their color.

below:
Using a short wave ultraviolet light source you can find which side of the glass was against the tin. In a darkened room the tin side shows up as a white film and the non-tin side as pale purple light. Do not look directly at the short wave ultraviolet light as is harmful to your eyes.

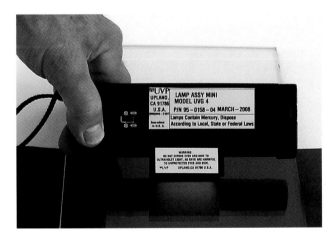

In my experience the tin side is less devitrifying than the other side of the glass, referred to as the "air side," but you should test your window glass to see which side "devits" less. You might want to try recycling old windows or salvage window glass from a glass supplier. A low temperature firing for glass painting should not devitrify window glass. When firing to higher temperatures or multiple times, you might need an overglaze to prevent devit.

Devitrification Prevention

1) Test fire different window glass from different manufacturers. Find one that doesn't devitrify too bad, and buy a larger quantity for future projects.

(2) Test fire the tin side vs. the air side for "devit" and use the side that works best, probably the tin side.

(3) Clean the glass and handle by the edges.

(4) Apply an overglaze or flux to the glass and edges, if needed.

(5) Fire and vent quickly through the "devit" zone, about 1350° F – 1450° F (730° C – 790° C).

6) Avoid prolonged firings, high temperatures, and multiple firings, if possible.

Overglazes for "Devit" Prevention

Whether on window glass or stained glass, the top surface and edges of the glass can be covered with a non-devitrifying glass called "over-glaze," which needs to be fired to almost a full fuse and can prevent surface devitrification.

Hotline "Spray A" - is a low melting lead glass overglaze that holds up to multiple firings and gives a durable crystal clear surface, but it has a slightly yellowish tint when applied to the tin side of window glass – so use it on the air side. It can also cause a color reaction with sulfur-containing glass. Use on non-food surfaces. **Look for the new re-formulated non-lead "Spray A" soon.**

Fuse Master "Super Spray" - is a super low-lead (rated at 99.98% lead free) overglaze that produces a clear surface, not quite as crystal clear as "Spray A," but can be used on dinnerware.

Flux for "Devit" Prevention

A "flux" can lower the melting temperature and a "surface modifier," such as boron, changes the make up of the surface molecules, inhibiting devitrification.

Fuse Master "Clear Coat" - does not contain lead or glass powders and is a fluxing agent that produces a shiny glass surface.

Fusing Farm is developing a non-lead product that gives a shiny surface. I have tried their experimental "Freedom Flux" with good results. Check out their new products.

Make Your Own "Devit" Stopper Flux
One of the formulas that has been floating around on the internet is a borax surface flux.

Dissolve 2 heaping tablespoons (90 grams) of 20 Mule Team Borax in 1 pint (500 ml) of hot distilled water. Add 2 drops of dish detergent (which helps it flow on the glass surface) and 1 teaspoon (15 ml) of Thompson Klyr-Fire.

There will probably be particles on the bottom of the container, which is good because this means that the borax has dissolved into a "supersaturated" solution, the water can't hold any more. Apply liquid to a clean glass surface and fire.

You might want to check your fluxed or overglazed glass for chemical weathering by running a sample in the dishwasher a number of times or putting it into hot vinegar for a few hours.

Use a cotton ball or foam brush to apply "overglaze" or "devit flux" to glass. I don't use an airbrush, which can put noxious dust into our air and environment.

Creating "Devit" on Purpose

This seems like a weird concept, especially after we go to so much trouble to get rid of devitrification, but now you can create different styles of "devit" with 4 different, non-toxic "Wrinkle Cream" surface modifiers for glass from Fusing Farm. Paint and comb for a great texture, or spray on to create a light frost, and then fire your glass to a full fuse. This product has unlimited possibilities. Don't get mad about "devit," get even with the new Fusing Farm Wrinkle Creams, **www.fusingfarm.com.**

Ed Walter, an early 1950s window glass and enamel fuser, observed that some customers liked "devit," so he called it a "satin finish."

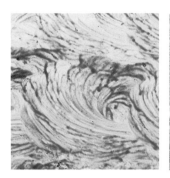 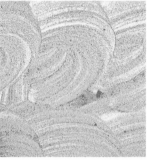

(1) above: Is a fired example of Fusing Farm "White Picket Fence" and to the right "Maximum Etch" Wrinkle Cream on window glass.

(2) I apply a "Maximum Etch" border with a cotton ball. "White Picket Fence" will be applied to the center of the glass, which is placed over the silver foil.

(3) below: Gold Rim Bowl, 1 in. (2.5 cm) H. x 9 in. (23 cm) x 7 in. 18 cm. The "Maximum Etch" Fusing Farm Wrinkle Cream produced a delicate matte surface above the silver foil that has turned golden in color. The "White Picket Fence" Wrinkle cream gave the center a mottled look.

Safety - Working with Enamels and Hazardous Materials

- **Wear a good dust mask -** vitreous enamels can contain finely ground glass and may contain harmful colorants such as selenium, cadmium, chrome, and lead.
- **Wear rubber gloves and safety glasses.**
- **Do not eat food when working with enamels** - you might ingest harmful chemicals.
- **Do not allow young children into the enamel area of you studio.**
- **Do not sweep your enamel area; use a damp cloth to wipe the area and rinse the cloth safely.**
- **Use a HEPA vacuum cleaner instead of a regular vacuum or shop vac.**
- **Wash your hands, change your clothes, and take a shower when done.**

Lead Poisoning & Hazardous Chemicals. The danger of lead poisoning for the artist shouldn't be taken lightly. Use non-leaded enamels if possible and handle enamels that contain lead very carefully. Follow the guidelines in the Safety section above. The only reliable test to check lead levels in your body, is a blood test, and if you have too much lead then you can go through chelation therapy - in which lead is removed by bonding to chemicals injected into your blood with a tube. It may take a few months and can make you feel ill. I handle my enamels very carefully to avoid this.

Some of the colorants in enamels are not bound in the glass until fired and are easier to absorb into your body than is a stable glass that has been melted and then crushed into a frit – such as fusible Bullseye or Spectrum glass. Some enamel colorants are hazardous metals such as cadmium, and chrome. This is another reason that enamels must be handled carefully.

Dinnerware. Make sure that the food surface contains no lead. You can purchase a lead testing kit at large hardware stores and pottery supplies. You wipe the surface with a test swab and see if the swab changes color – this tells you if lead is present. If possible, do not put enamels on the surface of the glass but sandwich them between layers of glass and use a non-leaded overglaze when dealing with devitrification.

Artwork. I use the Hotline "Spray A," which contains lead, on the surface of my fused glass wall panels and art vessels. I like it very much, and it gives the surface an incredible gloss. My art pieces are not designed for food and I handle the "Spray A" very carefully.

Other Hazardous Dusts. Wear a good dust mask when handling dusty materials in your studio, including sand for glass casting, fired thin-fire shelf paper and ceramic fiber paper and blanket materials and also when scraping shelf primer off of your kiln shelves.

Thin Fire Shelf Paper is a very hazardous material. Some people use this to keep the glass from sticking to their kiln shelves. It turns into a powder after firing and must be vacuumed off the shelf with a HEPA vacuum, which has a micro fine particle filter system, so the dust does not get back into your room. When removing your glass after firing on thin fire paper, always wear a good dust mask. I never use Thin-Fire Shelf Paper and find that I can get a much smoother finish on my glass with shelf primer.

My Philosophy. I sometimes use lead bearing enamels and overglaze, ceramic fiber materials, and encounter hazardous dusts in my studio. I do not freak out about these dangers or let them control how I make my artwork. I dispose of them properly, and I am conscientious about our environment and my studio space. I am knowledgeable about hazardous studio materials and take precautions to minimize the risk.

Getting Started with Easily Available Enamels

(Vitreous enamels work best when fired to the manufacturers recommended temperatures)

Glass Painting on vases and panels (low temperature)
I suggest that you buy a few basic colors in 1 ounce packets, of finely powdered "Fuse Master" low temperature transparent enamels (contains lead), and 4 ounces of "Fuse Master" water friendly medium,
www.fusionheadquarters.com

Sifting Enamels for fusing & slumping
I suggest that you try a few basic colors of "Thompson Enamels" (does not contain lead). Buy a few 2 ounce containers of various colors of 80 mesh, opaque and transparent enamels, for either window glass or for stained glass and a set of sifter screens.
www.thompsonenamel.com

Stamping, Rolling, & Painting for fusing & slumping
I suggest that you buy a few colors in 2 ounce containers of powdered "Ferro Sunshine Enamels" and a 4 ounce bottle of "Thompson" A-14.
www.warmglasselements.com

A Basic Firing Schedule For Window Glass

Window glass is a stiffer glass than Bullseye or Spectrum, and also needs to fire to a higher temperature for a full fuse and to round the edges. Above 1100° F (593° C), fire quickly up and down, to minimize devitrification, and to avoid a high temperature soak.

The firing temperatures for this schedule will vary with different kilns, placement of the pyrometer, and whether the kiln is high temperature fiber or brick. Learn your kiln and keep records of your firings. Below is a very basic firing schedule for some of the smaller projects in this book. Larger pieces need to warm up, anneal, and cool down over a longer period of time. For example, a 20 in. (50 cm) x 20 in. (50 cm) x ¼ in. (6 mm) piece of window glass might take 8 hours from room temperature to 1100° F (593° C). **hr. = hours   min. = minutes**

Shallow Plate – Fuse /Slump
6 in. (15 cm) x 6 in. (15 cm)
2 - 3 pieces of ⅛ in. (3 mm) glass stacked

500° F (278° C) /hr. to
1100° F (593° C)
1 min. soak

ASAP (as fast as possible) to about
1550° F (845° C) - 1600° F (870° C)
Look in your kiln and when the plate is done, vent your kiln to about 1050° F (565° C), then let the kiln cool to:

950° F (510° C)
45 min. anneal soak

250° F (140° C) /hr. to
600° F (315° C)
1 min. soak

Off
(the kiln cools down by itself)

A Bigger List of
Materials and Suppliers

(Work on the non-tin side of window glass
to prevent color reaction)

Low Temperature Enamels
1050° F (565° C) - 1200° F (650° C)
Reusche www.reuscheco.com Glass Stainers colors, opaque and transparent enamels that are finely powdered enamels that work well with a painting medium, 1050° F (565° C) - 1080° F (585° C).

Fuse Master www.fusionheadquarters.com
42 wonderful low fire transparent enamels that mature at 1175° F (635° C).

Medium Temperature Enamels
1200° F (650° C) - 1400° F (760° C).
Metallic Lusters - Reusche and Thompson
Fires between 1100° F (595° C) to 1400° F (760° C).

Versa Color www.amaco.com 8 lead free colors in an oil base 1325° F (720° C) to 1460° F (795° C).

Medium - High Temperature Enamels
1300° F (705° C) - 1550° F (845° C) +
Thompson Enamels www.thompsonenamel. com Lead free 80 mesh enamels.
80 COE (5000 opaque & 6000 transparent series) for window glass normal firing range 1350° F (730° C) - 1450° F (790° C).
90 COE (7000 opaque series & 8000 transparent series) for Bullseye and Spectrum glass, normal firing range 1550° F (840° C) - 1650° F (900° C).

Ferro (Sunshine Series) www.ferro.com
(click on decoration colors, find and click on "Sunshine")
19 colors, 24 opaque, mostly mixable enamels except the cadmium orange and red colors, 1420° F (770° C) - 1520° F (825° C)
small quantities: **www.warmglasselements.com**

Fuse Master www.fusionheadquarters.com
Lead free opaque 21 inter-mixable 1300° F (705° C) - 1550° F (845° C).

Float Dekor in Europe
www.creative-glass.com
Float Fire 82 in the United States
www.armstrongglass.com
A variety of various sized colored frit, stringer, confetti and colored sheet glass to fuse with window glass.

Mica Powder
www.seppleaf.com
www.glasscolor.com

Liquid Mediums
Thompson A-13 and **A-14**
Thompson A-1 Klyr-Fire
Fuse Master Water Friendly Medium II
Squeegee Oil Pine resin oil.
Liquid Gum Arabic

Overglaze & Flux
Fire to at least 1400° F
(760° C) for a glossy surface.
Fuse Master Clear Coat Overglaze
Hotline Spray A Contains lead, don't use for dinner ware. Look for the new re-formulated non-lead "Spray A" available soon.
Fuse Master Super Spray Non-lead flux.
Fusing Farm A new non-lead devit stopper is coming soon.

Devitrifying Agents
Fusing Farm Wrinkle Cream
www.fusingfarm.com

Silver Foil
Olympic Color Rod
www.glasscolor.com

Other materials and supplies are listed in the back of this book, beginning on page 237.

Pilkington Float Glass for Windows

Raw Material Feed

Inside the Melting Furnace

Sand	72.6 %
Soda Ash	13.0 %
Limestone	8.4 %
Dolomite	4.0 %
Alumina	1.0 %
Others	1.0 %

Float Glass Process

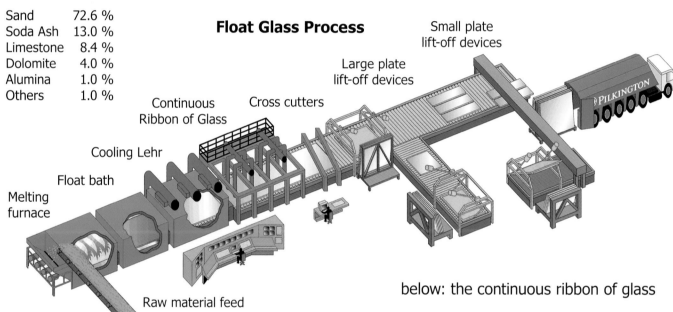

Small plate lift-off devices

Large plate lift-off devices

Continuous Ribbon of Glass

Cross cutters

Cooling Lehr

Float bath

Melting furnace

PILKINGTON

Raw material feed

below: the continuous ribbon of glass

FLOAT GLASS

The float glass process, developed by Pilkington in 1952, is now the world standard for high quality glass production. Float glass is often processed further before being fitted into buildings and vehicles. The process, originally able to make only ¼ in. (6 mm) thick glass, now makes it as thin as 0.4 mm and as thick as 1 in. (25 mm). A "batch" of precisely mixed raw materials is melted in the furnace. Molten glass, at approximately 1830º F (1000º C), is poured continuously from a furnace onto a shallow bath of molten tin in a chemically controlled atmosphere. It floats on the tin, spreads out, and forms a level surface. Thickness is controlled by the speed at which the solidifying glass ribbon is drawn off the bath. After annealing (controlled cooling), the glass emerges as a "fire" polished product with virtually parallel surfaces. Around 280 float plants are in operation, under construction, or planned worldwide. Pilkington operates 25 plants and has an interest in another nine. Used by permission of Pilkington, 2008.

the history of window glass

The History of Sheet Glass

When humans started creating dwelling structures, the need to see indoors became a problem. You could cut a hole in the wall, but this didn't work too well in colder climates and bath houses. Transparent materials found in nature were probably used to cover opening holes, such as tightly stretched animal skins (rawhide), mica, and cut stone such as alabaster. Glass, as a made-made material, began about 3000 B.C., and glass blowing developed around 50 BC. Once sheet glass was invented, it became a perfect solution for interior illumination. Minerals could also be added to create a transparent or opaque colored glass, such as stained glass.

Handmade Window Glass
Pre-79 AD Roman Glass

Window glass manufacture dates at least as far back as the Romans, where it was rare and used sparingly in bathhouses and villas. Found in Italy at Pompeii, buried under Mt. Vesuvius ash in 79 A.D., is a greenish-blue cracked window pane that is now on display at the British Museum in London. Other Roman window glass has been discovered, scattered all over Europe and in the Roman colony of Britannia (United Kingdom). It has been suggested that Roman window glass was cast into a mold or created by the successive reheating and stretching of a chunk of glass, into a rectangular shape. Later, window glass was made by blowing an elongated bubble, which was then cut open and flattened while hot.

1200 English Broad Sheet - Cylinder Glass

Early European window glass making was a continuation of Roman techniques. The cut and flattened bubble technique, now called "Broad Sheet," was first made in Sussex, England about 1200. These panes were smooth on both sides, rather small, and contained imperfections. Cylinder glass manufacture continued for centuries.

1330 French Crown Glass - Rondels

French glass makers spun hot glass bowls attached to metal rods into flat disks called rondels. These were first made in Rouen, France and later in London, England, beginning in 1678. The term "crown glass" may have originated from the crown-like punty button at the center of the rondel or because the bowl, before spinning flat, looked like a crown. By the early 1840s, crown glass was gradually superseded by hand-made, mechanically assisted, blown cylinder glass. You can tell crown glass from cylinder glass if you look at the ripples in the

The architecture of our cities changed almost overnight, with the availability of inexpensive float glass.

Sears Tower, Chicago, Illinois 1973. The distance to the roof is 1,450 feet (442 m), 108 stories.

glass. Crown glass ripples are curved and ripples in cylinder glass run across the sheet. These hand-spun disks were as large as 4 ft. (1.25 m.).

1688 Rolled and Polished Cast Plate Glass
The French made thick sheets of thick plate glass by casting glass on a table and moving a roller over it; the roller was set on guides to produce the thickness desired. The sheet was then polished by hand. These were mainly used for mirrors. By the 1800s in England, rolled glass was ground and polished using steam engine power.

1834 Improved Cylinder Sheet
Using a German process, Robert Lucas Chance Company began making large blown cylinder glass in England. This glass was hand-made by teams of men using mechanical support to hold the blowpipes and hoists to help swing the hot cylinders in pits. The cylinders were later flattened in a kiln. In 1851, glass for the Crystal Palace was made using this method. Chance Brothers made large, mechanically assisted cylinder glass as late as the 1920s.

1847 Rolled Cast Sheet Glass
James Hartley in England introduced rolled thin sheet glass in England.

Industrial Sheet Glass
The steam engine mechanized the handmade processes and ushered in the industrial revolution, which created mass produced affordable window glass. Technological developments also included the Siemens regenerative furnace (1863) which was more fuel efficient, the Bievez annealing oven (1870) which lowered an 8-hour annealing time to 30 minutes, and the Siemens continuous melt tank furnace (1873) which replaced the pot furnace. Between the steam engine polished glass in 1880 to the Pilkington float glass introduced in the early 1960s, many window glass technologies were developed.

1883 PPG (Pittsburgh Plate Glass Company)
By 1860, many store fronts in the United States used expensive machine-polished plate glass imported from Europe. By 1895 imports to the U.S. from Europe fell sharply, because PPG was producing 20 million square feet of mechanically ground and polished plate glass a year.

1903 Machine Drawn Cylinder Window Glass
The process for mechanically drawing cylinders of glass was invented in the United States (1903) and later manufactured in the UK by Pilkington (1910 – 1933). 40 ft. high cylinders of glass were drawn vertically from a tank of molten glass, cut into 7 to 10 ft. cylinders that were then cut lengthwise, heated, opened, and flattened.

1913 Flat Drawn Sheet
Sheet glass was drawn horizontally from a furnace first produced in Belgium and later manufactured in Kent, England (1919) and the USA (1925).

Early 1920s Horizontal Drawn Flat Glass
Continuous one sided grinding & polishing was developed in the United States and later adopted by Pilkington (1931) in the UK.

Glass was drawn from the furnace horizontally and then ground and polished on a conveyor belt.

1925 Vertical Flat-drawn Window Glass
Inexpensive window glass was produced in Mt. Vernon, Ohio (1925) and Clarksburg, West Virginia (1927). A continuous sheet was vertically drawn from a molten tank of glass, touching no rollers until it became rigid, which created a sheet glass that did not need to be ground and polished. Controlling the speed of the draw created different thicknesses of glass. This window glass was marketed by PPG.

1935 Pilkington Double Sided Continuous Grinding & Polishing
This glass was ground and polished on both sides.

Mid-1960s Pilkington Float Plate Process
The idea of pulling a horizontal continuous ribbon of glass over a molten bed of tin to produce a glossy two-sided glass that needed no mechanical polishing was invented by Alistair Pilkington in

1952. He announced this new idea in 1959, and it took 7 years to perfect. Virtually all of today's window glass is made by this method. The first float license was granted to PPG in 1962. Pilkington stopped making polished plate in 1967.

American Stained Glass
1880s Opalescent Sheet Glass
Opalescent glass contains both opaque and transparent glass swirled together. Kokomo Glassworks claims to be the oldest opalescent sheet glass producer, in operation since 1888 in the U.S. It is located in Kokomo, Indiana where natural gas was discovered and used to heat the glass furnaces. They make mechanically rolled transparent and opalescent stained glass.

John La Farge is generally credited with the invention of streaky opalescent glass and received a patent in February 1880. Not to be outdone, Louis Comfort Tiffany was awarded several patents for variations of LeFarge's glass in November of the same year. In 1892 Tiffany began making his own opalescent glass called "Favrile" - meaning hand-made - in Queens, New York.

By the early 1960s the only companies producing machine rolled stained glass in the U.S. were Kokomo and Wismach. Blenko Glass Company made blown sheet glass. They still do today.

1974 Stained Glass Revolution
With the revival of Tiffany stained glass lamps and windows and also the ensuing "Stained Glass Hobby Movement," numerous glass companies sprang up to make colored sheet glass.

In 1974 Bullseye Glass Company, makers of hand-rolled sheet glass in Portland, Oregon, was probably the first one of these companies to market its glass. Other companies setting up hand rolled operations in Portland were Genesis Glass (defunct) and Uroboros Glass. Spectrum Glass Company in West Seattle, Washington, modified the 1920s horizontal flat drawn - ribbon process. They soon moved to Woodinville, WA and built the largest stained glass factory in the world.

Many people jumped into this scene, starting companies and buying equipment from closing companies to start new companies. People moved and merged from one to the next like a "gold rush" turned "glass rush," and most went defunct.

There was some very interesting glass made, on a small and also on a large scale. Peter Morris manufactured very little glass, but his truly dichroic glass, which went from coral pink opal to steel blue transparent, was magnificent. David Ruth's transparent sheets containing silver and gold were unbelievable, Oceana ripple was cool, and Uroboros ring mottles are still great. When I helped Rob Adamson and Fritz Dreisbach roll some sheet glass as a demo for this book, I thought, Whidbey Island Stained Glass? Nah!

1970s - 1980s New Stained Glass Companies
(Red - defunct / Black - still going)
Advance Glass Company - Newark, OH
Armstrong Glass - Kennesaw, GA
Bullseye Glass Company - Portland, OR
Bulls Bridge Glass - Kent, CT
Canadian Art Glass - Calgary, Alberta, Canada
Chicago Art Glass - Elk Grove Village, IL
Colorado Art Glass - Denver, CO
Crystobol - Santa Ana, CA
Freemont Antique Glass - Seattle, WA
Genesis Glass Ltd.- Portland, OR
Hollander Glass Company - Stanton, CA
Lins Glass - Florida
Merry-Go-Round Glass, Fort Smith, AR
Oceana - Soquel, CA (Youghiogheny now manufactures Oceana ring mottels)
Optimum - Eaton, CO
Orient & Flume - Chico, CA
Peter Morris - Chicago, IL
Ruth Glass - Santa Cruz, CA
Scott Glass - Brooklyn, NY
Spectrum - Woodinville, WA
Stock Art - Chicago, IL
Uroboros Glass - Portland, OR
Wasser Glass (Glass Hues, Inc) - Sarasota, FL
Wheatoncraft - Millville, NJ
Youghiogheny - Connellsville, PA

Three Types of Hand-made Window Glass Demonstrated by
Rob Adamson and Fritz Dreisbach

Rob Adamson b. 1945   Fritz Dreisbach b. 1941

Rob Adamson, one of the early glass pioneers in the Northwest, began blowing glass in 1969 and was the technical director at the Pilchuck Glass School beginning in its third year (1973 - 1978). Rob opened his Glass Eye Studio in Seattle in 1978. At that time, it was the largest production glass studio in the U.S. Rob Adamson, known locally as "the godfather of glass," trained and employed many well known glass blowers, including Dante Marioni, Preston Singletary, Paul Cunningham, Joey de Camp, and Eric Lieberman.

Fritz Dreisbach was a student of Harvey Littelton's the second year of his glass program at Madison and graduated with an MFA from the University of Wisconsin. He went on to set up the glass studio at the Toledo Museum of Art in 1967. Considered "the teacher's teacher," he has given over 300 lectures, workshops & hot glass demonstrations all over the world during his 40+ years as a glass blower. Fritz was a founder of the Glass Art Society (GAS), president twice, and received the GAS Lifetime Achievement Award in 2002.

Both Rob and Fritz are of the first generation of Studio Movement glassblowers, and I am honored to have them as my friends.

Blown Cylinder Glass - glass is blown into a cylinder and the ends are removed. The cylinder is split, heated in a kiln, and opened into a flat sheet; both sides are smooth.

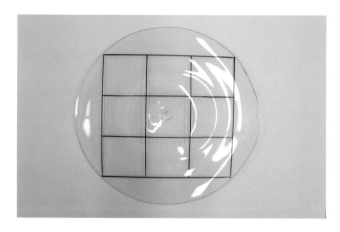

Crown or Rondel Glass - glass is fashioned into a bowl, heated, and then flattened into a disk by the centrifugal force of spinning; it's smooth on both sides. The lines show where window panes will be cut.

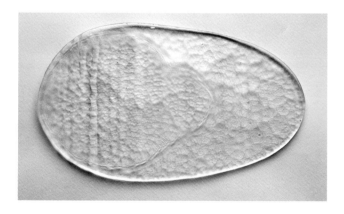

Rolled Sheet Glass - glass is ladled onto a metal table and then flattened by a roller. It has chill marks on one side and is smooth on the other and can be rolled with a textured pattern.

Blown Cylinder Glass

(1) In this photo hot glass is blocked in a wooden mold to create the beginning bubble shape. Glass is built up on the end of the blow pipe by gathering numerous times from the furnace. It is shaped and then blown into a small cylinder. This can be done on the marver table and with tools or in a cylindrical mold.

(2) Here the cylinder is blown and rotated in a wet wooden mold. This technique probably goes back to late Roman times and was known during the middle-ages in England as "Broad Sheet."

(3) The cylinder is released from the mold, broken off the blow pipe & placed into an oven where it is annealed & slowly cooled to room temperature. As late as the early 1900s, large cylinders were made by teams of men using mechanical hoists to help move & swing 6 ft. (1.8 m) hot glass cylinders in open pits to elongate them. Sometimes the bottom end is removed while still hot.

(4) The ends are cut from the cylinder that is then split lengthways with a glass cutter. This cylinder is placed into an oven or kiln and slowly heated to the softening point. When the glass is slightly soft it is manipulated open with wooden sticks and laid flat.

Rondel or Crown Glass

(1) Fritz Dreisbach is blocking hot glass that has been gathered on the blowpipe. This is then blown and shaped into a flat bubble.

(2) The punty rod is dipped into the furnace and a bit of glass is shaped on it's end. The hot punty is placed onto the center of the bubble which is on the blow-pipe, seen on the right side in the photo. The bubble is broken off the pipe and reheated.

(3) The reheated bubble on the punty is opened into a vase shape. Further reheating and shaping sets the vase up for opening flat.

(4) After the final reheat, the vase shape is spun flat using centrifugal force. This "rondel" or "crown glass" is broken off the punty and put into the annealer. The glass disk is marked into window panes and cut with a glass cutter. The cheaper center button piece is now much coveted for decorative windows. Disks about 4 ft. (1.25 m.) in diameter were made.

Hand Rolled Sheet Glass

(1) Molten glass from the furnace is ladled onto a warm, but not hot, casting table.

(2) The glass is rolled with a metal cylinder which runs on rails that controls the thickness of the sheet. This is the basic process that Bullseye and Uroboros use to produce their hand-rolled glass.

(3) The glass cools until it becomes rigid, but above the upper annealing point, and is slid onto a wooden paddle.

(4) The rolled sheet glass is loaded into the oven for annealing and a slow cool down so that it does not crack.

Glen Lukens 1887 - 1976

Metallic Oxides and Window Glass

As a ceramic artist and teacher, Glen Lukens developed many new glazes and glaze techniques. He taught courses in ceramics, metal-work, and jewelry at the University of Southern California in Los Angeles during the 1930s. His emphasis was on form and surface treatment, and he trained many of the next generation artist-teach-ers, who would go on to establish the Studio Pottery movement in the 1950s – 1960s. His students included F. Carlton Ball, Laura Andreson, Barbara Willis, Vivika Heino, Myrton Purkiss, and Beatrice Wood.

Right after World War II, in 1946, through the Inter-American Edu-cational Foundation, then with UNESCO, and finally through the Haitian Government, Lukens made three extended visits to Haiti. He found a very poor population with many sick and dying people, the result of eating from gourds which were hard to sanitize. Glen helped by establishing a small school, teaching pottery. They pressed native clay into gourds which they glazed and fired. This gave the people safe dinnerware. He also helped the locals establish a busi-ness selling pottery. It became his mission and passion to help the Haitians. On April 10th, 1955, he is quoted in an LA Times article, "If I stay here, in America, all I can do is turn out more pottery and glassware. But over there I can help people who sorely need it to raise their standard of living - even if it's only a little."

Glen probably began exploring the use of glass during the mid-1930s, and by the early 1950s, after retiring from USC, he was creating glass vessels and dinnerware which were smooth on the inside with a rough texture on the backside. Glen applied metallic oxides and carbonates to the window glass surface to give his pieces a subtle hint of color. These were fuse-slumped into his rough clay molds.

Lukens was a great humanitarian and a pioneer in ceramics and glass.

facing: "Three Vessels" This is a representative grouping of artistic and functional glassware by Glen Lukens. A metallic glaze has been applied to the surface of window glass and slumped into a textured clay mold. The mold has been coated with "kiln wash" so that the glass does not stick and fired to a temperature high enough to pick up some of the mold details.

"Yellow Bowl" circa 1950, 2 ¾ in. (7 cm) deep x 11 ½ in. (29 cm) in diameter. Signed Glen Lukens on the backside foot rim.

"Turquoise Bowl" circa 1950, 1 in. (2.5 cm) deep x 7 ½ in. (19 cm) in diameter. Signed Glen Lukens on the backside foot rim.

"Pale Aqua Plate" circa 1960, 2 ¼ in. (6 cm) deep x 20 in. (51 cm) in diameter. Not signed, attributed to Glen Lukens.

bottom: Glen Lukens in Haiti.

California Desert Glass: written by Glen Lukens

Transcribed from the Glen Lukens papers 1931 - 1983, courtesy of the Archives of American Art, Smithsonian Institution.

Although glass was first made about 3200 years ago it continues to be made of the same three earth materials -----Sand; Lime; and Sodium Carbonate. Sometimes borax and potash are added to give it toughness.

The sand is pure quartz, the lime is purest limestone or calcium carbonate and sodium carbonate is the same as old fashioned "saleratus" or "washing powder". When borax is added to the basic materials it is the pure variety known as Twenty Mule Team, and the potash is in the form of potassium nitrate.

There are thousands of uses for glass and there are thousands of formulae or recipes for each type of glass manufactured yet glass is always just a variation in the amount of each of these five named earth materials. My glass is made of only lime, soda, and silica. Each must be free of even the faintest trace of iron or other impurity so that the finished glass will be crystal clear before the metallic oxides are added to color it with. Rose color is obtained by adding manganese and cobalt carbonate, Green is obtained by adding copper carbonate, Blue comes from cobalt oxide, Yellow and Yellow Green is the result of adding chromium oxide and Ruby Red is made by adding pure gold to the glass.

After searching the deserts and mountains of California for many years for the materials with which to make ceramics and since the work in glass began with that search also, it seemed appropriate to call the finished glass - California Desert Glass. In it's colors it reflects every mood of the changing lights over the deserts and mountains.

How the glass is made.
First, the glass is a sheet or a pane of glass three sixteenths of an inch thick.

To make a service plate a circle of glass is cut eleven inches in diameter. Second, A mold for the plate is made from clay because glass can be shaped only while it is red hot, then the glass will sag or bend into the mold and conform to the contour. The interior of the molds are made rough so that the underside of the bowls will have a rough surface and the top surface will be quite smooth. This texture on the underside will give brilliance to the glass.

Third, The surface of the flat circle of glass is stained with oxides and carbonates of metals before heating begins. Cobalt oxide produces varying tints and shades of blue. Copper carbonate makes turquoise, chromium makes yellow color and pure gold is used to make the best pink, rose, and ruby red. Fourth, the glass with its color on it is then placed on the mold and the mold is set in the kiln. The kiln holds from fifteen to sixty pieces at each firing depending on the size of the pieces. The kiln is heated slowly to 850 degrees Fahrenheit. After that temperature there is no danger of breakage in firing and the kiln can be speeded up until 1400 degrees has been reached. At that temperature the glass has softened enough to conform to the walls of the mold. After 14 hours of slow cooling it can be removed from the kiln.

It is the rough rugged texture on the underside of the glass that gives the brilliance to the color. Rays of light entering the surface are stained, then they are channeled through the interior of the glass. When a ray of light strikes the curved surface of the underside it is reflected in another direction continuing that direction until another transparent surface is encountered. This is the theory as well as the practice used in making the glass.

After working for almost eight years the glass received first prize in the 1942 America Design Award given by Lord and Taylor Company in New York City. The prize was $1000.00. The award was stated as follows.

"Awarded to Glen Lukens of Los Angeles California the 1000 dollar America De-

facing: "Two Bowls" attributed to Lukens, circa 1960, Clear Bowl, 2 ¾ in. (7 cm) x 9 in. (23 cm) and Turquoise Bowl, 2 in. (5 cm) x 6 in. (15 cm).
above: "Blue Canyon" signed Glen Lukens, 3 in. (7.5 cm) x 11 ½ in. (29 cm) circa 1960.

textured ceramic-fiber molds

(1) Glen Lukens used clay molds, but I like fiber which requires no drying time. Save used ⅛ in. (3 mm) fiber paper and rip it into pieces. Place them onto a pre-fired sheet of fiber paper on a kiln shelf. Wear a good dust mask and rubber gloves as the airborne fibers are really dangerous to breathe. Use a mixing bowl for the inside shape and place fiber around it.

(2) Brush Hot Line "Spray A," which is a leaded glass frit in a liquid medium, onto the air side of a 10 in. (25 cm) circle of 3/16 in. (4.5 mm) window glass. I added a very tiny bit of cobalt oxide to produce a dark blue color. You can also use a non-leaded frit such as Fuse Master "Super Spray." Place this upside down in the mold, so the oxide is on the back of the bowl.

(3) Oxide Plate #1, 10 in. (25 cm) in diameter x 1 in. (2.5 cm) deep. The tin side up did not devitrify because I dropped the temperature from full fuse to 1050° F (565° C) quickly by venting my kiln. Here the oxides and "Spray A" (flux) formed a thin glass coating on the back of the piece. The cobalt area shows the brush strokes.

 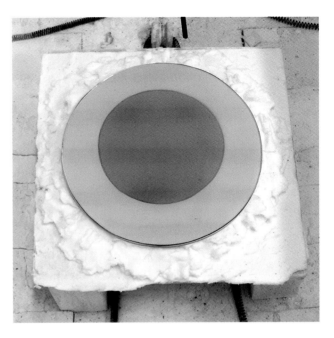

(4) Airbrush "Spray A" with cobalt oxide onto a ⅛ in. (3 mm) piece of window glass. I dry the cobalt and place a circular piece of paper over the center area and then spray the rim with copper carbonate. Cobalt is a very strong colorant, and I need to use about 3 times as much copper carbonate to produce a decent turquoise color.

(5) I have covered the dried "Spray A" / oxide mix with a second piece of ⅛ in. (3 mm) piece of window glass, tin side up. Glen Lukens applied his metallic glazes to the top surface, but I want to put them in between or underneath to keep them away from any food that might be put into this bowl. This is the same fiber mold as the piece on the left.

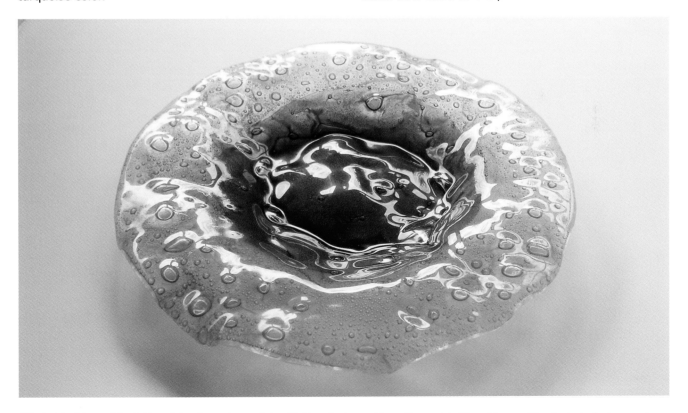

(6) Oxide Plate #2, (25 cm) in diameter x 1 in. (2.5 cm) deep. Here the oxide/flux (Spray A) mix is in-between two pieces of window glass. The bubbles in the turquoise are produced when the carbon dioxide gas is released from the copper carbonate, creating a great bubble effect.

kiln shelf textures and how to make shelf primer

(1) I mix powdered Bullseye kiln wash with enough water so that it takes about 6 - 8 "criss-crossed" coats to cover the shelf so that I can't see it. With smooth adjacent stokes, I apply shelf primer to a clean kiln shelf with a foam brush. Always wear a good dust mask when mixing powdered kiln wash or scraping a kiln shelf.

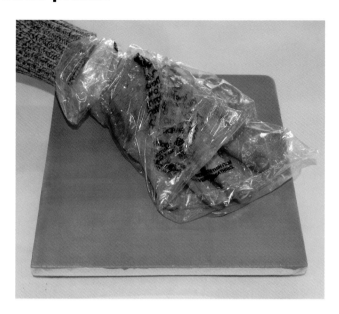

(2) Let the shelf primer partially dry and then burnish with your hand in a soft plastic produce bag. If you look at the surface, catching the light just right, it should really shine. You can make your own shelf primer – in a closed jar, dry mix 70% alumina hydrate (buy the finest size you can) with 28% powdered kaolin clay and 2% powdered bentonite clay.

(3) I photographed a garden gnome through a fully fused piece of ¼ in. (6 mm) window glass - note the rounded edges and corners. It was fired on a burnished shelf-primered kiln shelf and is pretty smooth.

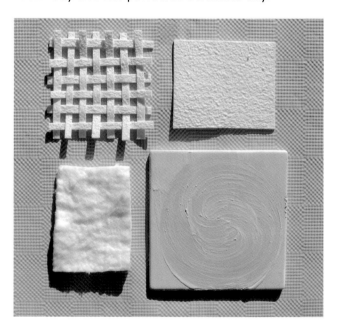

(1) Glass can be fused on ⅛ in. (3 mm) ceramic fiber paper to create texture. The binder must be burned off by firing to 1200° F (650° C), or it will haze the glass. You can achieve texture by weaving strips of fiber paper, using the rough side, firing on a piece of ceramic fiber blanket, or using a coarse brush to create a rough texture or pattern with shelf primer.

(2) Clear glass that has texture moves the light around and makes the glass more interesting! This is a piece of ¼ in. (6 mm) float window glass that was fired to 1550° F (845° C) over woven fiber paper. Pre-fire the fiber paper to drive off the volatile organic binder that can haze your glass. Ventilate the room.

(3) This is a piece of window glass fired to pick up the texture on the rough side of a piece of ceramic fiber paper. It is also a way to disguise the marks made when firing on a kiln shelf.

(4) Here window glass was fired on a piece of ceramic fiber blanket.

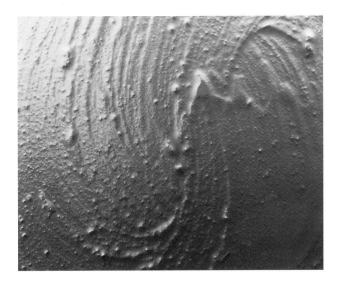

(5) This interesting swirl was made using a coarse paint brush and thick shelf primer. Window glass was fired to a hot enough temperature to pick up the texture.

Hazardous Dusts. Wear a good dust mask when handling dusty materials in your studio, such as glass casting sand, fired thin-fire shelf paper, ceramic fiber paper, and fiber blanket, as well as when scraping shelf primer off of your kiln shelves.

A very hazardous material in your studio is thin fire shelf paper. Some people use this to keep the glass from sticking to their kiln shelves. It turns into a powder after firing and must be vacuumed off the shelf with a HEPA vacuum, which has a micro fine particle filter system – so the dust does not get back into your room. When removing your glass after firing on thin fire paper, always wear a good dust mask. I never use thin-fire shelf paper and find that I can get a much smoother finish on my glass with shelf primer.

hand-made clay and found molds

If you are looking for simple plate and bowl molds for slumping then I suggest that you check your fusing supply sources for slip cast ceramic molds, and there are many special molds made just for glass slumping.

Hand-made clay molds are not my favorite. I lean toward stainless steel or rigidized ceramic-fiber molds because they can be made and used quickly. Clay molds shrink a bit and can warp during the drying process, and they need to dry slowly, or they will crack. Now if you happen to be a potter and can throw shapes on a wheel, then clay might be the perfect thing for you. With clay it is easy to make dropout rings. You can also create organic shaped molds that would be hard to make with other materials.

(1) First, go to a pottery supply and buy a block of "high grog" or "raku" clay. These clays are more shock resistant to temperature variations but more course in texture. Cut a piece of clay off the block with a knife or use a wire that has two wooden dowel handles, one for each hand, and saw off a piece.

(3) When completely dry, I fired from room temperature to 1600° F (870° C) in 6 hours and then cooled 6 hours down to room temperature. Paint shelf primer on the mold before slumping your glass.

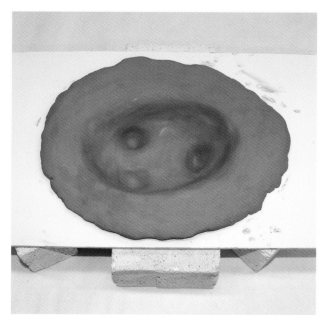

(2) Knead the clay like a loaf of bread (called wedging) and beat on it with the heel of your palm. This gets the air out. I hand formed it into an oval bowl shape, put dimples with vent holes, for tripod legs, and dropped it through a hole in foam core board to form a flat rim. Dry in a warm place. **The clay needs to be completely dry.** It should feel warm when you touch it.

(4) "Frog Bowl" 2 in. (5 cm) deep x 10 in. (25 cm) x 8 in. (20 cm), fused Thompson enamels and silver leaf in-between two sheets of ⅛ in. (3 mm) window glass. On the top surface is Thompson enamel for the eyes and Spray A overglaze to prevent "devit." This large rim mold holds the glass for fuse/slumping and keeps it from sliding unevenly into the mold.

found molds - ceramic and stainless steel

(1) Using a diamond bit, drill a vent hole in your slumping mold to let the air out. You can purchase ceramic molds designed for slumping glass or go to a ceramics shop and buy "bisque fired" slip cast clay pieces. If you buy "greenware," make sure that it is "bone dry," and fire to 1600° F (870° C) before using for slumping glass.

(2) Heat the pre-fired slumping mold to 300° F (150° C) and then airbrush or paint shelf primer onto the surface. Return to the hot kiln to dry quickly. You can smooth the brush lines with your fingers or sand lightly with a fine mesh such as pantyhose. Clean out the vet holes.

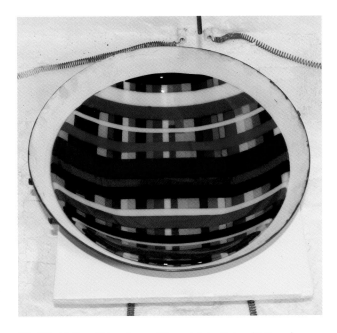

(3) You can find inexpensive stainless steel bowls and plates at thrift stores. Really steep-sided vessels do not make great slumping molds. Stainless steel is heavier than aluminum and is non-magnetic. Beware of chrome plated brass ware. Drill a vent hole in the bottom, heat in a kiln, and airbrush shelf primer onto the surface for a glass release.

(4) "Plaid Bowl" by June Fitzpatrick, 3 in. (7.5 cm) deep x 13 in. (33 cm) in diameter, 2008, slumped in a 15 in. (38 cm) stainless steel wok.

wet felt molds

The 1950s glass slumpers used clay to make molds, and Glen Lukens pressed clay into a form to create his molds. He could wait days for it to dry before being able to fire it. Today commercial ceramic slumping molds are readily available from your local stained glass and fusing supplier.

The advent of humans into outer space spawned the development of high temperature alumina fiber materials to replace asbestos. By adding colloidal silica to this fiber blanket, we can create a moldable wet felt that can be formed over or into curved objects. Back in 1979, the first wet felt mold that I ever made was over a giant zucchini squash that I grew in my garden. The squash wasn't drying fast enough, so I put the whole thing in my kiln and baked it. I scooped it out with a spoon - what a mess. I don't recommend this. Either use a material that can go into the kiln for a form or wait until it dries. Wet felt tolerates thermal shock, does not need to air dry, and can be fired as fast as your kiln will go. It's also flexible, so it won't crush the glass in the mold if it gets trapped.

I have been thinking about the donut mold for a long time. It is a shape that works well for wet felt. I wanted a lumpy surface because clear glass looks good with a slight texture that moves the light around. You can also make a smooth mold by sanding and filling with shelf primer.

(1) Use ½ in. (12 mm) thick high temperature ceramic fiber wool to make wet felt that will end up being ¼ in. (6 mm) thick. If your fiber blanket is too thick, then you can carefully tear a thick piece into the appropriate thickness.

(3) Roll a pipe or rolling pin to squeeze the fiber down to about ¼ in. (6 mm). Flip it over and make sure that the colloidal silica soaks through and that it is completely soaked all over with no dry areas.

(2) Lay the fiber blanket on a sheet of plastic and pour colloidal silica, sometimes called "mold hardener," onto it. It takes about 2 quarts (1 liter) for 4 square feet (²/₅ meter).

60

(4) Spray vegetable oil onto your form as a release. If your form won't burn you can put it directly in the kiln with the wet felt. Aluminum works but can get soft and thin when it is fired.

(5) Lay the wet felt onto your form and press it in place. Metal bends one direction, but wet felt can make shallow compound curves before it wrinkles.

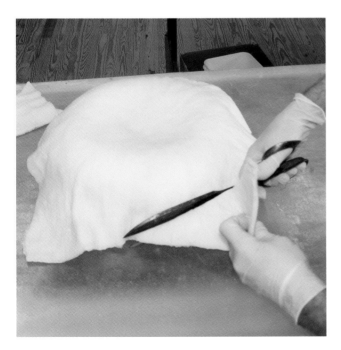

(6) Cut the excess wet felt off with scissors and save the scraps in a plastic zip-lock bag for later. As long as it doesn't dry out or freeze, you can use it again.

(7) Put the wet felt and the metal form on a kiln shelf that is protected from the colloidal silica by aluminum foil. Vent the kiln and the room, then leave the area as noxious fumes are produced during the firing. You can turn your kiln on high and go to about 1300° F (705° C) to dry and harden the mold.

 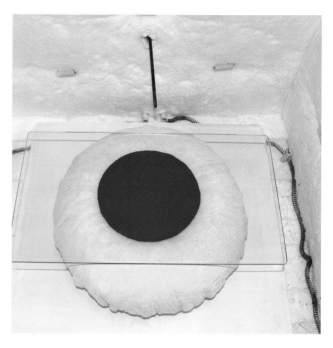

(8) Tap the mold with your finger; it should be rock hard. You can glove it out hot and paint on the primer, or after it has cooled, sand it for a smoother finish and then apply shelf primer.

(9) Window glass that is 3/16 in. (4.5 mm) x 10 in. (25 cm) x 18 in. (45 cm) is placed on the mold. There is a painted red Paradise enamel circle underneath the glass. I previously dried the enamel in a kiln.

"War of the Worlds Bowl"
2008, 15 in. (38 cm) x 10 in. (25 cm) x 4.5 in. (11 cm)
Paradise enamel red circle on the underside of 3/16 in. (4.5 mm) glass.

Roger Nachman - a large wet felt mold

(1) Roger Nachman making wet felt by pouring colloidal silica onto a huge piece of high temperature ceramic fiber blanket.

(2) Rolling the colloidal silica into the fiber with a big rolling pin. Note the rubber gloves.

(3) Placing the wet felt into a mold that happens to be an old satellite dish. This air-drys enough to hold it's shape and then it is fired in a kiln.

(4) A fused glass nautilus design is placed in the fiber mold, which is supported by bricks on the bottom of his kiln. The kiln lid is lowered and the piece is slumped.

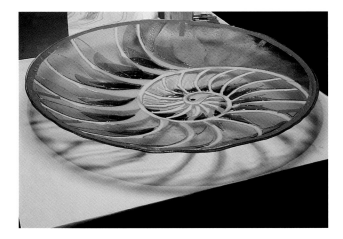

(5) The nautilus design after slumping. The edges are smoothed with a hand held wet grinder so that it will fit into a metal ring for installation.

(6) The nautilus skylight installed in a multi-million dollar yacht.

Edwin D. Walter 1918 - 2001

Sgraffito In-Between the Sheets

Edwin D. Walter received a Master of Arts from the University of Missouri at Columbia in 1948 and went on to teach for over 50 years, 38 of those at Troy State in Troy, Alabama. As a faculty member of the art department, he taught art, design, pottery, art history, and a crafts course - which included kiln formed glass.

Ed began fusing and slumping glass in 1948, and he signed his work, "WaLᴛer" with a capital "L" and long "T". His studio had two electric kilns, and was located in his home in Troy, and it is here that he created his "WaLᴛermelon" plates, "Fernware," ginkgo leaf plates, fish platters, windchimes, and wall pieces. Walter exhibited and sold in galleries and museum shops, which included the High Museum in Atlanta, Georgia and the Montgomery Museum in Montgomery, Alabama. Beginning in the mid-1950s he would pack his family and glass into their car and travel to craft shows around the Southeastern United States – where he sold glass art in his booth. Ed created kiln formed glass until the day he died, and left a fully loaded kiln ready to be fired. His artwork is in the collections of the Walter Chrysler Museum and the Smithsonian.

Walter was very experimental, fusing enamels with scratched designs (sgraffito), stenciled enamels, and metals in-between single and double strength window glass. He carved his first slumping molds from soft firebrick and later formed glass in handmade clay molds that contained vermiculite and sawdust – which made them lightweight and porous. Ed invented a special sagging mold that allowed for undercuts. He fused all sorts of glass, including old eyeglasses, electrical insulators, tinted plate, and textured bathroom glass. Some people liked the "satin-finish" of devitrification, but he sought out window glass that didn't devitrify, tossing out many bad sheets, and finding that the best was imported from Japan or Russia. The early enamels that he used were made for ceramics, but later he used Thompson vitreous enamels for glass, and he also used some Bullseye. Walter wrote about his glass techniques in the magazine *Ceramics Monthly*, during the 1950s and continued to share his knowledge with those who were interested.

Sgraffito is one of the techniques that Ed Walter used. I really love the wonderful word "Sgraffito," which sounds like the process - to scrape, scratch, and scruff away material. The technique is simple: sift a thin layer of powdered enamel onto a piece of glass, take a stylus - such as the sharpened end of a paintbrush, old dental tools, or a comb - and draw in the powder, and then fire. For these pieces, Walter used ¹/₁₆ in. (1.5 mm) window glass and placed a sheet of glass on top of his sgraffito enamels – fuse/slumping his creations in clay molds in one firing.

facing upper:
"White Fish Platter" 1970-1980's
1 ¾ in. (4 cm) x 9 ½ in. (24 cm) x 7 in. (18 cm).

facing lower:
"Blue Fish Plater" 1970-1980's
1 ¾ in. (4 cm) x 10 ½ in. (27 cm) x 7 in. (18 cm).

below:
"Blue Owl Bowl" 1 ¼ in. (4 cm) x 8 in. (20 cm) x 7 in. (18 cm).

making a beach sand slumping mold
Walter and Glen Lukens would have loved this quick sand mold!

(1) The ingredients for a sand mold are sand, powdered clay (preferably bentonite clay, found at your local pottery supply), and water. You can buy olivine sand, which works great, but local beach or dune sand is worth experimenting with. Vent your kiln area as sand might contain nasty organics that burn off. Bagged playground sand might work, too.

(2) Mix the dry ingredients, sand with about 5% bentonite; wear a dust mask. Slowly add water and mix with your hands until it firms up into a ball. If your beach sand is a bit coarse, then you might need to add close to 10% bentonite. With this mix, you can make a smooth mold such as Edwin Walter used or one that has a rough texture such as Glen Lukens.

(3) Plop the sand ball onto a kiln shelf and sculpt the shape that you want with your hands. You can make a depression and smooth it out with a little water and the back of a spoon. Pierce the mold several times with a thin wire to create vent holes for steam. With this sand technique, you can create a quick slumping mold.

(4) Put the sand mold into a kiln and turn the heat onto high, firing quickly to 900° F (480° C). Vent your kiln because a lot of water is driven off during the heating process. Take the shelf and mold out of the kiln with gloves, let it cool a bit, and paint it with shelf primer. Small cracks can be filled with the primer.

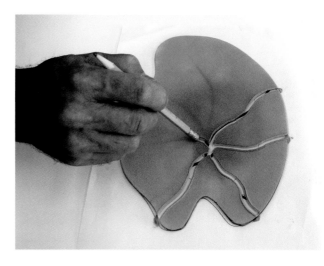

(1) I cut three pieces of ⅛ in. (3 mm) window glass. Onto the bottom layer I sift Thompson enamels. These will be seen through the vein lines of the lily.

(2) On the middle glass sheet, I sift a thin layer of green enamel with a darker enamel in the center. I draw large "sgraffito" vein lines with a rounded pencil eraser.

(3) The window glass is tin side up. To assure no devitrification, I apply a clear overglaze or borax "devit" stopper to the top.

(4) The three layers are stacked onto the primered mold and fired to full fuse. The finished Lily is 1 in. (2.5 cm) x 9 in. (23 cm) x 6 ½ in. (16 cm).

Fuse-slump Water Lily In The Sand Mold

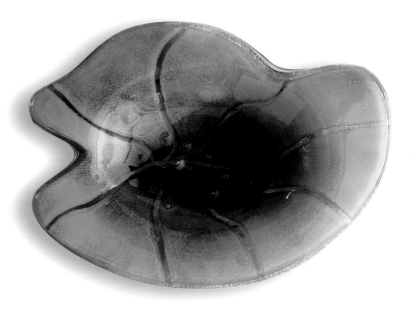

above: "Blue Bowl" signed WaLTer, 1970's-1980's, 5 ½ in. (13 cm) tall x 6 in. (15 cm) in diameter.

Shaping glass over a form goes all the way back to the Romans. In the early 1980s I used to drape glass over clay flower pots and now many people slump over commercial stainless steel forms that look like they came from old milkshake mixers. What intrigues me about this Edwin Walter piece is that it has a rounded vessel wall that would have trapped a mold inside. I experimented to make a piece like this including the tripod legs, which I also like.

slump over an undercut mold

(1) I place disks of "wet felt" over the ends of ¼ in. (6 mm) steel rods put into holes drilled completely through a soft kiln brick. Three tall ones will create tripod legs, a center disk keeps the bottom from dropping too far, and 3 shorter ones to keep the sides from collapsing. The wet felt is fired to 1100° F (595° C) and then shelf primer is applied.

(2) I fused two ⅛ in. (3 mm) window glass, 14 in. (35 cm) diameter disks with scraps of silver foil, and sifted Thompson enamels and baking soda for bubbles in between. This fused disk is placed on my tripod mold.

(4) The finished piece 6 in. (15 cm) H. x 8 in. (20 cm) in diameter.

(3) The piece has sagged over the form. Notice in figure (1) the rods are set at an angle so the vase can curl under. It is important that the holes go all the way through the brick and not be too tight. After cooling the rods will just fall through the brick, and the piece is released. The primered wet-felt pieces should easily come out, but a bit of prying will release the stubborn ones.

(5) After my experiment, I found out from Walter's daughter that he used plaster molds for sagging, and she sent me this photo.

Maurice Heaton 1900 - 1990

Enamels Under Glass

Maurice Heaton was born in Switzerland and came to America in 1914 to work with his father, Clement Heaton, on stained glass church windows, which included kiln fired glass painting. In 1937 he began fusing enamels onto window glass, sometimes utilizing stencils, making ceiling light fixtures and glassware. By 1947 he was sifting enamels onto glass and inscribing (sgraffito) the enamels with his designs. He fused the enamels to stick to the window glass and during a second firing, fuse/slumped his pieces in steel molds that he made.

A 1980s studio pamphlet stated, "The kilns are still housed in the 200-year old grist mill on Old Mill Road, long a dirt road bordering the pond that supplied the power for the firing. The adjoining barn, also a landmark, which contained the atelier, workshop and display room, burned to the ground in April 1974. The entire contents were destroyed. A small new studio has been erected on the ruins of the historic old one." Maurice lived and worked in rural Rockland County, New York and actively pursued his art until 1990. He signed his work simply with his initials M.H.

facing upper: "Flounder Plater" circa 1960, ¾ in. (2 cm) H. x 8 ½ in. (22 cm) W. x 14 ½ in. (37 cm) L., enamels on the back of ⅛ in. (3 mm) window glass.

facing lower: "Fish Plate" circa 1950, 2 in. (5 cm) H. x 7 in. (18 cm) W. x 12 in. (30 cm), enamels on the back of ⅛ in. (3 mm) window glass.

upper: Photo of Maurice Heaton sifting enamels onto glass, in his studio, from the cover of a pre-1974 studio brochure.

lower: "Supper" a large plate, circa 1950, 17 in. (43 cm) in diameter, enamels on the back of ³/₁₆ in. (4.5 mm) window glass.

Enamels Under Glass Project

Maurice Heaton's main technique is enamel under the glass, and he worked in reverse, sifting enamels onto window glass. In the June 1954 *Craft Horizons Magazine* (the precursor to *American Craft Magazine*), I found an article in which Heaton describes working on a light table, sifting enamels onto window glass, sgraffito drawing in the enamels, fusing the enamels in the first firing, flipping the piece over, and slumping into a mold during a second firing. The following section explains my attempt to create a fish, similar to Heaton's, but of my own design. Do not copy another artist's ideas and techniques. Honor them, by creating your own direction, modifying and building on the art that came before you.

(1) During a 1981 lecture, I heard Maurice Heaton say that he used metal molds for slumping. I hoped that this open bottom, stainless steel mold will work.

(2) To test my mold, I slumped a piece of double strength, ⅛ in. (3 mm) window glass. The mold worked great, but the glass wrinkled.

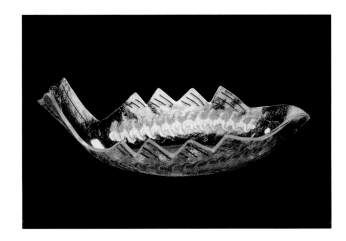

(3) Next I tried thicker glass to stop the wrinkling. I use a piece of ¼ in. (6 mm) Bullseye with frit. It didn't wrinkle, but the frit didn't stick too well.

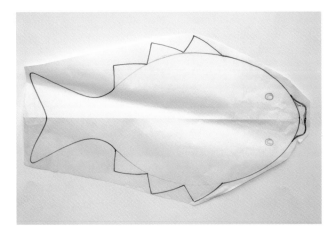

(4) The shape wasn't quite right, so I refined my design, making it fatter, so it would have enough glass for the sides after shaping.

(5) I used colored markers to lay out a pattern, loosely based on Japanese fish kites.

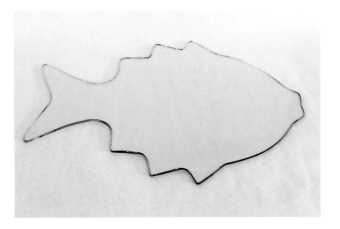

(6) I attempted to recreate the technique that Heaton might have used, and I make a 6 in. (15 cm) experimental tile. Using Thompson enamels, I sift cobalt onto a piece of window glass, draw lines in the enamel, and sift on red and white enamels. I fuse this to 1250° F (675° C) to stick the enamels to the glass. For a second firing I flipped it over, coated with a "devit" flux, and fuse/slumped it into to a mold to 1550° F (845° C). It worked! Temperatures will vary in different kilns.

(7) I cut 3/16 in. (4.5 mm) window glass using a glass cutter. A diamond saw removed the tight curves; edges were smoothed on a fine 200 grit wet belt sander.

(8) I sifted Thompson enamel to make red dots. Maurice Heaton's fish plate provided inspiration and was a springboard into new artwork.

(9) Sometimes I use a bit of odor-free hairspray to stick down the enamels. You need to ventilate the room and try not to breath it.

(10) Wear a dust mask when sifting enamels. I sifted turquoise Thompson enamel onto the tail and fins and then lightly covered the design with cobalt Thompson enamel.

(11) I read somewhere that one of Heaton's neighbors observed him making lines with the eraser end of a pencil. It works great!

(12) Hairspray is optional. Start by misting the spray onto the enamels so that you do not blow them away and then spray more directly as they become wetter. Use enough to hold the enamels. You can probably also use an airbrush and a enamel medium such as Klyrfire. Experiment to find out what works.

(13) I fused the Thompson enamels to 1250° F (675° C), just hot enough in my kiln to stick the enamels to the glass and not leave kiln shelf marks on the backside of the glass. Experiment to find the right temperature for your kiln.

(14) The enamel side is flipped down and placed into the open-bottom mold on a shelf-washed kiln shelf.

(15) "Fish Dish" 3 in. (7.5 cm) H x 18 in. (46 cm) L x 9.5 in. 24 cm) W, 2008, artist R. La Londe.

Metal Molds - La Londe Style

Molds for shaping glass can be made from any material that won't burn, melt, or give off poisonous fumes. You can use clay flower pots, stainless mixing bowls, refractory fiber blanket, or you can make molds from clay, plaster/silica mix, kiln bricks, kiln shelves, metal, and other materials. You can bend glass over or into molds.

I prefer stainless steel for my molds! Stainless steel can be very thin, 24 - 22 gauge, .03 in. (.075 mm) or less, and unlike mild steel, it doesn't flake at slumping temperatures of 1250° – 1450° F (680° - 790° C) . Thinner molds allow glass to heat and cool faster than do thicker, denser molds. Stainless can be bent into a curve such as a half-cylinder, but resists bending into a compound curve such as a hemisphere; spinning stainless on a lathe will stretch it into shape without wrinkles.

I slump my vessels into molds that I make myself by bending and fluting sheet stainless steel. To give vessels a flat bottom, leave the mold open to the kiln shelf. Molds can be fastened together with pop rivets. Heat the metal molds to 250° F (120° C) in a kiln and brush or spray shelf primer onto them as a release. If you use a mixing bowl, drill a small hole in the bottom to let the air out.

You can usually slump into clay and over metal. A metal mold shrinks more than the glass and can crush it unless the glass can move and slip upward as it does in a tapered metal mold.

Slumping bends glass into a mold without a noticeable change in thickness and in **sagging** the glass thickness changes. Francis and Michael Higgins invented the "dropout" mold technique for sagging, in which multiple layers of glass are placed on a ring mold. With heat and gravity the glass drops through the hole and stretches. Glass for sagging must be thicker to provide material for stretching and thinning of the wall.

My vessels are quite recognizable for their fluted shape and the following images illustrate how to make my mold.

(1) Remember from grade school how to make a paper cone. Take a section out of a circle (blue) and then match up the two edges forming a cone (yellow). If you cut a piece from the top of the cone, it will stand up like a bowl (red).

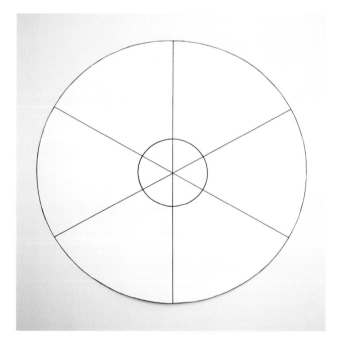

(2) To make a sheet stainless steel mold, mock up a paper pattern. To give you the basic location for ribs and valleys, mark the circle into 6 parts and cut out the center. This pattern is 24 in. (61 cm) in diameter with a 7 in. (18 cm) diameter center cutout. After a section is taken out to create a cone, you will have to recalculate where the ribs and valleys go.

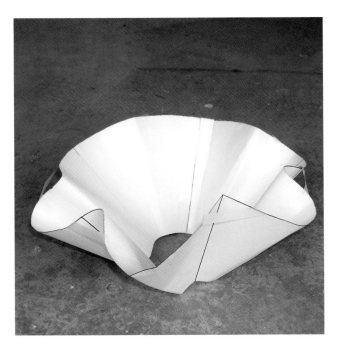

(3) Fold the paper to resemble the mold that you want. Use pieces of tape to hold the bends in place. You will have to remove a section from the circle to create the slope that you want (see picture #6).

(4) I use a uni-shear to cut the 24 gauge stainless steel.

(5) You can also use a pair of compound metal shears to hand cut the thin 24 gauge metal. Stainless steel is a hard material and takes some muscle to cut. Wear gloves, as the metal is sharp as a knife and can cut you. Carefully sand the sharp edges with a file or sandpaper.

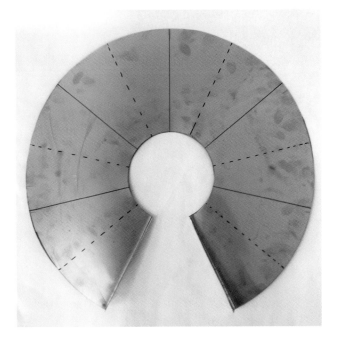

(6) Cut the 24 gauge stainless steel and leave extra material to make a flanged seam where the two pieces will join. Bend the flanges up, 90°, over the edge of a table with a soft mallet. Measure again and divide the circular area into 12 sections, 6 for the ribs and 6 for the valleys. Put the flange joint in the bottom of a valley.

(7) Clamp the two flange ends together with lock-nose pliers. Drill and pop-rivet the flanges together, creating a cone.

8) Bend and form the cone into 6 ribs over a pipe that is clamped to the edge of a workbench. Use feltpen lines as guides for bending. The flange joint is in the valley and not on the ridge where the glass will drag when it slumps into this mold.

(9) The finished 24 gauge stainless steel mold.

(10) Heat your metal mold to 350° F (180° C) and glove it out of the kiln. Wearing a dust mask and out-doors, spray shelf-primer onto the hot surface until it begins to look wet. Dry it in a kiln and repeat spraying primer until you no longer see the metal surface. The primer is tender until fired.

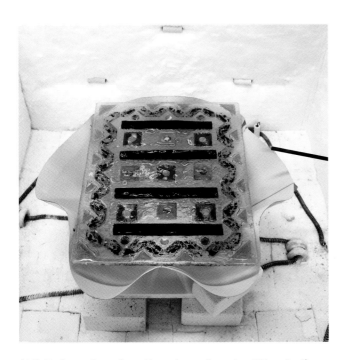

(11) Before slumping, the glass piece is sitting in the metal mold. The black thermocouple is midway on the right side, with the point just over the mold edge. The mold is sitting on a ⅝ in. (15 mm) mullite kiln shelf raised 2 in. (5 cm) off the bottom of my kiln to minimize uneven cooling between the thin sides of the metal mold and a thick kiln floor.

(12) Slumped in the mold. The release primer should last for several slumps before a touch up is needed. Reheat and spray the spots that have been worn off. Some primer will slightly stick to the glass and can be removed with glass cleaner. Sometimes I apply a light coat of Armorall (silicone) to the back of the piece, which disguises some of the mold drag marks.

The vessel is 5 in. (13 cm) H. x 12 in. (30 cm) x 10 in. (25 cm), fused window glass with metals.

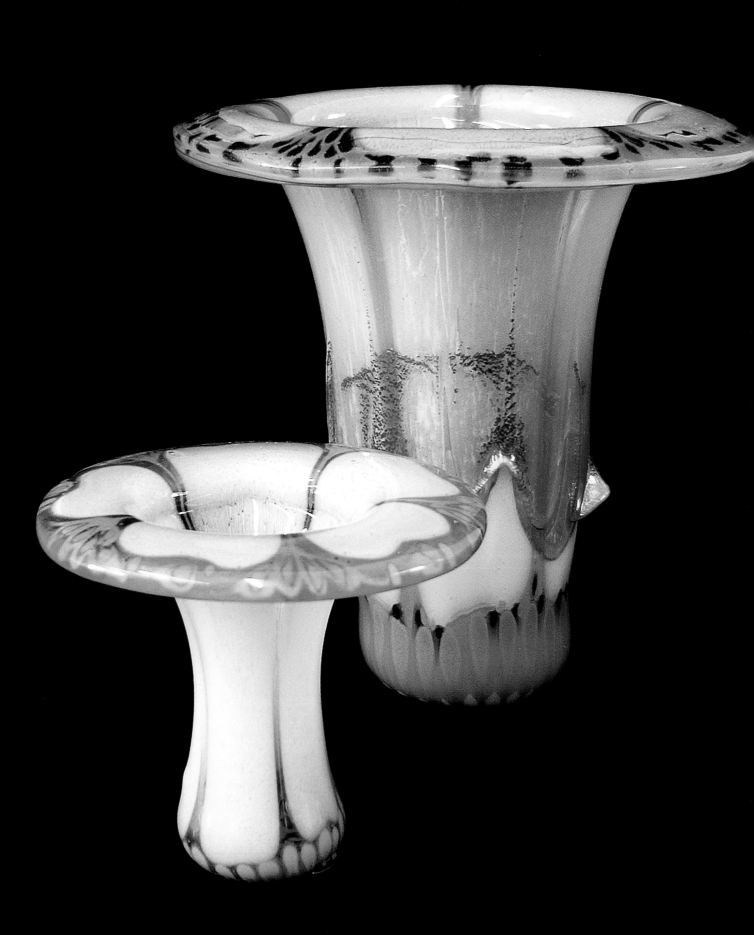

Frances Higgins 1912 - 2004
Michael Higgins 1908 - 1999

The "dropout"

In 1948, Frances and Michael Higgins set up their first studio and began making kiln-fired window glass and enamel decorative ware - plates, bowls, ashtrays, and vessels - eventually selling in department stores. From 1957 - 1964 they designed glass pieces that were made by the Dearborn Glass Company and, in 1965, briefly by Haeger, both located in Illinois. Thousands of pieces of "Higginsware" were produced. Some of these are readily available on the internet today.

In 1966 they set up their own studio again, this time in a storefront building they purchased in Riverside, just west of Chicago. Here they created their utilitarian ware and "one of a kind" pieces in the back art studio, sold them in the store front area, and lived in an apartment above. They signed their pieces jointly as "higgins" and were quite famous for their "Christmas Sale" which they held every year. Customers lined up and waited in the cold for a chance just to get inside the door. Frances and Michael Higgins both lived and created artwork into their 90s. Their studio continues today making "Higgins" style pieces, www.higginsglass.com. There are two wonderful books **Higgins: Adventures in Glass** and **Higgins: Poetry in Glass** by Johnson and Piña, that present a nice history and contain many color pictures.

Frances and Michael Higgins constantly experimented with ideas that became new techniques for their artwork. They fired "micro-layers" of enamels onto sheets of window glass, which they later cut into pieces that were assembled and fused again. In this way, they created a complete color palette of glass that was "practically" compatible. They made bubbles with soda and created bubble traps. Frances applied enamels in a liquid medium with a device similar to a very large eyedropper, creating flowing designs. One of the many techniques that they developed is the "dropout," and for this they made their own clay ring molds.

When I get an idea in my studio, I usually want to make it as quick as possible. I don't want to wait for a week for clay to dry and then to slowly fire it before it is ready to use. I will either cut a hole in a kiln shelf with my diamond saw and smooth it with a rasp, or I will cut a piece of fiber board, soak it with colloidal silica, fire it in a kiln, and be able to sag glass through it within ½ hour.

Frances and Michael Higgins were innovators, and I want to give them credit for developing the "dropout." Many of you have made "dropouts," and I encourage you to push this idea and create new forms with it. There are also many new techniques for you to invent.

above: Frances and Michael Higgins, Riverside Studio, 1995
www.higginsglass.com

facing: Two window glass and sandwiched enamel dropouts signed "higgins," circa, 1995. The left beige dropout height is 6 ½ in. (16 cm) with a lip 6 ½ in. (16 cm). The right blue dropout is 3 ⅜ in. (8.5 cm) H. with a 4 ³⁄₁₆ in. (11 cm) lip.

81

window glass dropout

(1) I placed three ⅛ in. (3 mm) pieces of glass onto a ⅝ in. (15 mm) kiln shelf, in which I cut a 4 in. (10 cm) diameter hole in the center. I placed this ring mold, 3 ½ in. (9 cm) above a second kiln shelf that is elevated above the bottom of the kiln. Clay rings do not warp like a fiberboard ring at the higher temperature used during a dropout firing.

(2) The sag is beginning. Placing the kiln posts close to the center hole helps support the drop ring, especially if it is made out of fiberboard. **You need a wide rim of glass, so that the glass does not fall through the hole!** The finished piece will be 5 in. (13 cm) high with a 6 ½ in. (16.5 cm) lip and a 3 in. (7.5 cm) diameter body.

(3) I visually check the drop, and when I find it to be where I want it, I then open the door of the kiln, all the way open and quickly vent heat to slow down the sag. I close and open the door until the temperature is stabilized at about 1050° F (565° C). I then engage my annealing program.

(4) The finished dropout. The bottom layer of window glass is a single piece of ⅛ in. (3 mm) with the tin side down against the drop out ring. On this I placed stripes of sifted Thompson enamels. I covered this with a second piece of window glass upon which I placed a layer of silver foil. This is covered with a third piece of window glass, tin side up. The silver turns golden yellow during the firing.

Bullseye Glass dropout with a veil

(1) I am using Bullseye Glass for this dropout. It sags about 50° F (28° C) lower and acts less stiff than window glass. Here I placed 8 triangular sections, ⅛ in. (3 mm) thick, which extend over the dropout hole on the ring mold. They will fall down and be dragged, creating a textural veil on the vessel.

(2 Next I place a layer of black, a layer of blue, and some orange triangles, which do not go all the way to the edge, but will add extra glass for the vessel wall, a total of ½ in. (1.5 mm) thick. The material for the wall comes from the area of glass right on the edge of the hole to about ¾ in. (2 cm) in, toward the center. The wall ends up about ⅛ in. (3 mm) thick.

(3) I answered the telephone at the wrong moment and returned to vent the kiln just a little too late, so the dropout collapsed a bit at the bottom, but I really like the look. The Bullseye Glass sagged quicker than window glass. The rim and bottom of the vessel are the original thickness and the wall has thinned. Allow enough thickness to create the stretched wall.

(4) You can see how the stretched triangles look on the outside of the vessel. The finished piece is 5 in. (13 cm) high with a 6 ½ in. (16.5 cm) lip and a 3 in. (7.5 cm) diameter body.

ceramic fiber mold for the "dropout"

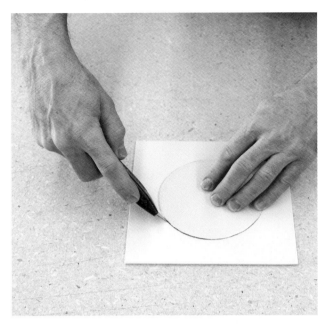

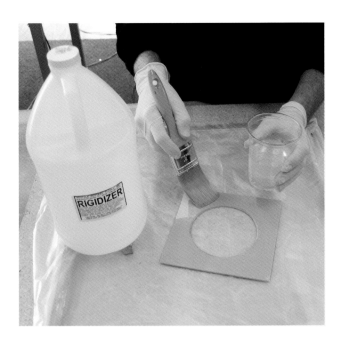

(1) Cut a ⅛ in. (3 mm) fiber board with a matte knife, held on an angle to make a sloping edge. This thickness works well for a small ⅛ in. (3 mm) piece of glass used in a sag. Wear a dust mask when cutting and handling fiber board. **For a larger diameter drop ring or one that will fire to a hotter temperature, use thicker fiber board.**

(2 Using a paint brush, soak "colloidal silica" rigidizer into both sides of the fiber board. Wear rubber gloves and do this on a piece of thin plastic sheet. Do not use the less expensive sodium silicate (water glass) as this will not work as well.

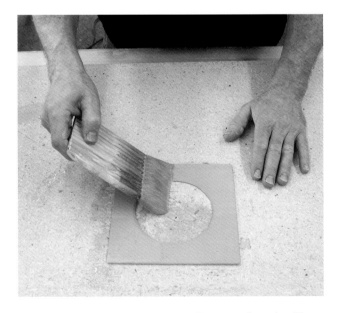

(3) Place the wet rigidized fiber board onto a kiln shelf that has been covered with aluminum foil. If not protected, the "colloidal silica" will soak into and ruin your kiln shelf. Turn the kiln on high, leave the vents open, and fire quickly to about 1250° F (675° C). Ventilate and leave your kiln area as the fumes given off are very noxious.

(4) Peeking into the kiln, you will notice that the fiber board will turn black at about 1000° F (540° C) and then, after the organic binder has burned off, will go back to a lighter color. You can remove the hot mold from your kiln and apply a few coats of shelf primer which will quickly dry. Fiberboard molds can sometimes warp slightly but will not thermal shock.

84

beyond the "dropout"

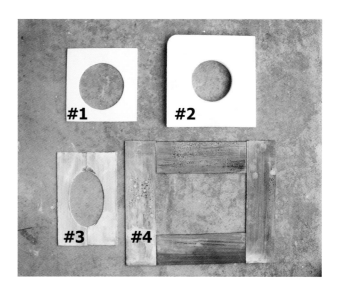

Be creative with your mold materials! With sagging you can make a piece that is smooth on both the inside and the outside. Create sculpture or cut the rim off and see if your kiln work is mistaken for blowing.

upper left: "Green Pagoda" R. La Londe 2002, 8 in. (20 cm) H. x 10 in. (25 cm) square. In one firing I sagged four dropouts through removable stainless steel rings, supported by soft firebricks, see mold #4 in upper right hand photo.

upper right: Molds for Dropouts:
#1, a ⅛ in. (3 mm) fiber board ring mold for thin glass, shallow sags.
#2, a ⅝ in. (15 mm) mullite kiln shelf ring mold.
#3, a two piece stainless steel oval ring mold.
#4, a 4 piece ⅛ in. (3 mm) x 3 in. (7.5 cm) stainless steel flat bar sagging mold used for "Green Pagoda." Stainless steel molds need to be cut into sections or they will crush the glass during cooling.

below: "Golden Bowl," 3 in. (7.5 cm) H. x 9 in. (23 cm) x 6 in. (15 cm). Dropout sagged and then the rim was cut off and the edge polished.

Bubbles Under Glass

You can create random bubbles under glass by fusing baking soda (sodium bicarbonate) between two sheets of glass and trapping the released carbon dioxide gas. Vitreous enamels mixed with baking soda can be sifted, stenciled, or painted directly onto glass and covered with a top piece of glass. Some fusing supply stores sell a variety of colored enamels called "bubble powder." The greater the depth of enamel, the more you will trap huge bubbles along with smaller ones. It's fun to use this technique to create a partially controlled, organic look in fused glass; you never really know what will happen until you open the kiln. In a studio pamphlet, Frances and Michael Higgins said, "Naturally, some gases escape from the enamels, and are then trapped between the glass sheets as they fuse. These are deliberately accepted, controlled, and used to enhance the vitality of the work."

upper left: Purple Ashtray, 7 in. (17 cm) x 7 in. (17 cm) x ¾ in. (19 mm) deep, signed Higgins, 1957 - 1964 Dearborn Glass Factory, Bedford Park, Illinois.

upper right: Higgins Turquoise Ashtray, 4 in. (10 cm) x 4 in. (10 cm) x ½ in. (12 mm) deep, signed Higgins, 1957 - 1964 Dearborn Glass Factory, Bedford Park, Illinois.

lower left: Powdered baking soda (sodium bicarbonate) sprinkled between two pieces of ⅛ in. (3 mm) window glass was fused, trapping the released CO_2 bubbles.

lower right: Too much baking soda and too high a temperature can create huge bubbles.

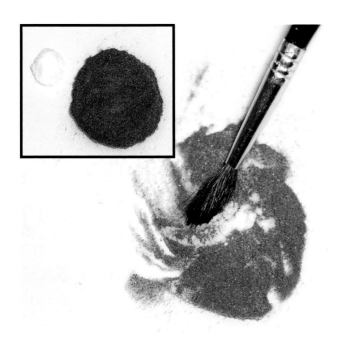

(1) Wear a dust mask and mix 5 - 10% baking soda (sodium bicarbonate) with 95 - 90% enamel powder. Just eyeball the mix. Experiment with different amounts of baking soda to create various bubble effects.

(2) Mix this "bubble enamel" with some CMC Goop and water, thinning it so that it flows easily. Apply it to the glass with a squeeze bottle. You can also sift the "bubble enamel" directly onto the glass.

(3) 3 layers of 3/16 in. (1.5 mm) window glass are stacked onto a shallow 1/8 in. (3 mm) fiber board ring mold that is lifted 1/8 in. (3 mm) above the shelf. This creates a 1/4 in. (6 mm) drop circular center depression with a lip. Between glass layer 1 and 2 is a 6 in. (15 cm) x 6 in. (15 cm) sheet of copper foil and between layer 2 and 3 is the "bubble powder" trailing.

(4) Fused Bubble Plate, 6 in. (15 cm) x 6 in. (15 cm) x 3/8 in. (4.5 mm) thick. The background turquoise bubbles occur when thin copper foil is fused between two sheets of glass. Perfect control of fused copper leaf is difficult, and the copper center is a happy accident. You can see the bubble pattern in the cobalt trailings. More baking powder, more bubbles.

upper left: "Blue Flower Bowl" 9 in. (23 cm) in diameter x 2 ¼ in. (6 cm) deep, signed Higgins, circa 1990, enamels fused/slumped between window glass.

lower left: "Pink, Blue, and Orange Bowl" 8 ½ in. (21 cm) in diameter x 2 ¼ in. (6 cm) deep, signed Higgins, circa 1990, enamels fused/slumped between window glass.

For many centuries potters painted their clay vessels with colored liquid clay called "slip." 20th century ceramicists used a "slip trailer" which is a tapered glass or plastic tube similar to a huge eye dropper. In the early 1950s, Earl McCutchen, a ceramics instructor at the University of Georgia, used a "slip trailer" to apply low temperature clear glaze frit that was mixed with ceramic colorants. He squeezed designs onto window glass that he fuse/slumped into ceramic plate and bowl molds. Frances Higgins was friends with Earl McCutchen while at University of Georgia in the late 1940s. The wonderful pieces on the left, signed Higgins, are probably made with a modified "slip trailer" with a small hole in the rubber bulb that can be covered and uncovered with a finger, allowing gravity flow of liquid enamels through a tube with a small tip hole.

liquid enamel trailed glass

(1) Pill containers make a perfect place to mix and store a small amount of very finely powdered enamels. Here I mix "Fuse Master" - Lead Free Opaque Enamel with water and add about 25% "Fuse Master" - Water Friendly Medium or liquid gum arabic. Mix in the container with a paint brush. It should be about the consistency of tomato juice or slightly thicker.

(2) I slurp up some enamel slurry and drag the tip of the "slip trailer" on the non-tin side of a piece of ⅛ in. (3 mm) window glass to create a flowing design. Unlike the "liquid glass line," where you want the line to stand up, here the densely colored enamel will spread out a bit.

(3) I sift Thompson Transparent Enamel onto the non- tin side of a ⅛ in. (3 mm) sheet of window glass.

(4) I flip the air-dried trailed design upside down with the enamels trapped in-between the two sheets of window glass. You will trap a few small bubbles.

(5) Here I brush on a light coat of Fuse Master "Super Spray." Other Devitrification Preventatives are described on page 37. It is then full fused in a kiln.

(6) The fully fused piece, which does contain some trapped bubbles in the design, is placed over my "La Londe metal mold" (page 76) and slumped.

(7) The slumped trailed glass piece, titled "Chop Suey," is 5 in. (13 cm) H. x 12 in. (30 cm) x 10 in. (25 cm).

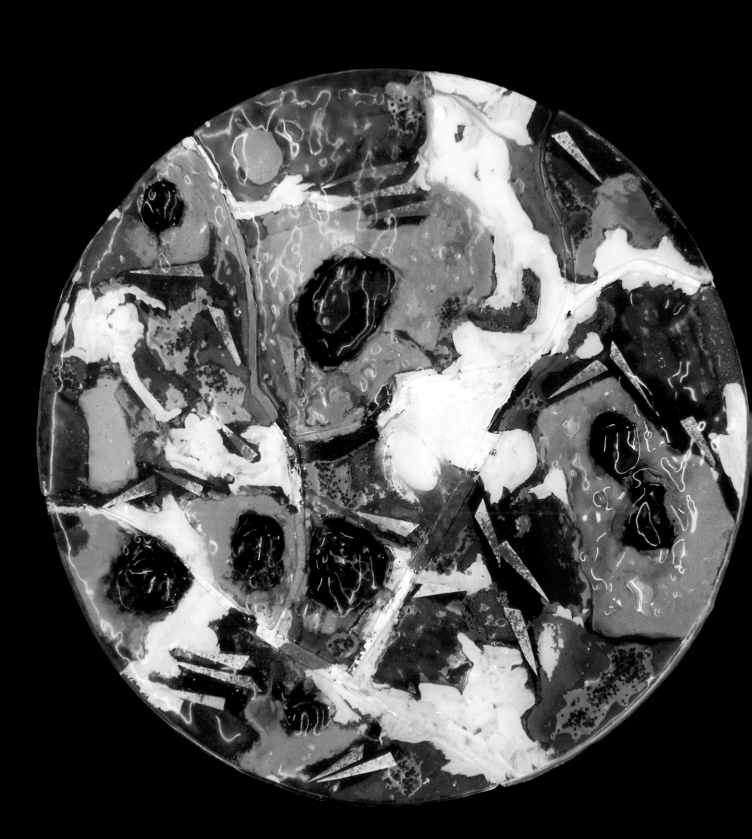

Margaret von Wrangel 1919 - 2005
Kyle Kinsey b. 1977

Self Taught Glass Enamelist

Margaret von Wrangel was born and lived in Estonia where she created ceramics and illustrated children's books. After surviving World War II in the early 1950s she emigrated to the United States with 3 young children and her husband. While living near Seattle, Washington she moved a kiln into her garage, where she slumped orange Blenko glass into lamp shades, which she sold. In 1961 at the age of 41, she attended the University of Washington in Seattle and earned a Masters (MFA) in art. Soon after, she was hired to start the ceramics program at Green River Community College.

Margaret retired from teaching and in the early 1980's developed an art business creating fused and slumped plates made with window glass and colored with Versa Colors, Mason stains, Reusche, and other enamels. She slumped these into molds, which she contracted a metal shop to make by spin-forming sheet steel on a lath. Margaret exhibited and sold her glass creations in galleries in Alaska, Arizona, Washington, and on Canyon Road in Sante Fe, New Mexico.

facing: Margaret von Wrangel, "Poppy Plate" 1989, 20 ½ in. (52 cm) in diameter x 2 ½ in. (6 cm) deep.

lower left: Margaret von Wrangel, platter, 20 in. (50 cm) in diameter x 2 ½ in. (6 cm) deep.

above: Margaret in her studio, and Kyle Kinsey holding one of his platters, 2008

www.fusioninglass.com

Kyle von Wrangel Kinsey, as a child, played with glass in his grandmother Margaret's studio, and as a teenager, he made a few pieces. Kyle earned a BA at St. John's College in Sante Fe, New Mexico, lived in Portugal, traveled in Europe, and stayed with the von Wrangles in their 800-year old castle in Estonia. In 2002 the art bug called, and Kyle moved in with his grandmother to help her continue to live in her home and to work under her tutelage. He experimented with enamels, Mason stains, and mica fused with window glass and soon exhibited his large platters and bowls on Canyon Road in Sante Fe, New Mexico. In 2004 Kyle began selling his artwork in his booth at the Pike Place Market in Seattle, Washington, making his living as a glass artist.

Margaret von Wrangel passed her scientific exploration and artistic creativity of enameled window glass from one generation to another.

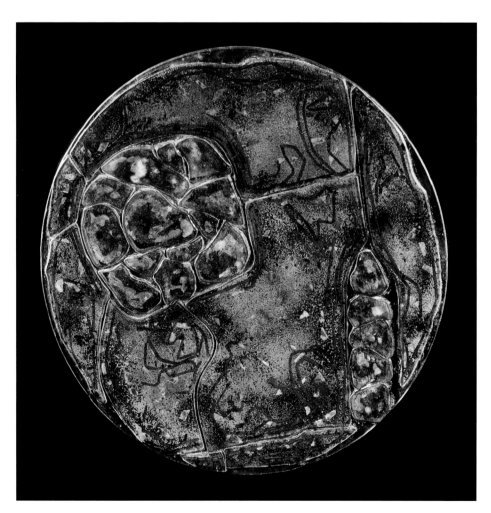

Margaret von Wrangel

upper left:
plate, 12 in. (30 cm) square, glass enamels, Versa Color, sheet brass, and window glass.

lower left:
platter, 20 in. (50 cm) in diameter x 2 ½ in. (6 cm) deep.

Kyle Kinsey

facing upper:
"Bowl" 2004

facing lower:
"Mica Platter" 2004, 12 in. (30 cm) x 16 in. (40 cm), glass enamels, Mason Stains, sheet mica, window glass.

Liz Mapelli b. 1948

A Pioneer with Surface Enamels In Architectural Glass

Liz Mapelli received a BFA in 1970 from the University of Colorado in print making and sculpture. Beginning in 1971 she blew glass with Dan Schwoerer and Ray Ahlgren at their Water Street studio in Portland, Oregon. Dan and Ray, along with Boyce Lundstrom, went on to found Bullseye Glass Company in 1974, where Liz managed the office briefly and experimented with fusing in electric kilns.

Mapelli's foray into public art came, in 1981 when she won a competition to create artwork for the new Justice Center in Portland, Oregon. Fusing large Bullseye glass tiles and surrounding them with smaller Italian mosaic tiles, she created her 5000 square foot (465 square meter) tiled ceiling. Liz Mapelli's ceiling was the first major public commission ever made, using fused Bullseye glass.

Since 1981 Liz has created over 60 major public and private installations in the U.S., which include: tile murals at the Central Square Subway Station in Cambridge, Massachusetts; a mural for Kaiser Permanente in Denver, Colorado; a suspended glass panel wall for the Argyle Library in Jacksonville, Florida; and a mural for the Honolulu Police headquarters, in Honolulu, Hawaii. Her work uses many techniques for fusing and enameling on window glass, Bullseye, and salvaged Vitrolite - which is no longer made but came in large sheets of opaque glass and was used on building facades in the 1920s - 1950s. Liz has also designed terrazzo floors.

By trial and error, Liz figured out which enamels worked. She used Reusche enamels mixed with water for spraying and Thompson enamels with a clear enamel cover-coat for sifting. Not all colors worked. Liz told me that lead in the enamels seemed to help bridge some of the incompatibility and that about 15 years ago when they took the lead out, the colors seemed to loose their virbrancy.

facing upper:
"Sumner Arts Center," 1994,
30 ft. (9 m.) x 4 ft. (1.22 m.),
Sumner, Washington.

facing lower:
Detail of the Sumner Arts Center, showing enamels applied with stencils and the use of sgraffito, fused onto Bullseye glass with hot lines, glass pieces and dichroic.

upper portrait:
Liz, with a Vitrolite tile that includes iridescent Bullseye and other glass additions, in front of her installation at the University of Colorado. For scale, find the man in the lift on the right side of the picture.

lower:
"Kaiser Permanente Lobby," 1986, back-lit vitreous enameled glass mural, 24 ft. (7 m.) x 3 ½ ft. (107 cm.), and fan-shaped wall sconces, 3 ft. (91 cm.) high, enameled window glass, Portland, Oregon.

surface enameling with Liz Mapelli

(1) Painting with Versa Color enamel pre-mixed with an oil based medium.

(2) Loading the airbrush with Reusche enamel in water as a medium for spraying.

(3) Liz wears a respirator and eye protection against the very fine enamel mist containing silica, lead, and other toxic pigments. Ventilation is important, too.

(4) Liz airbrushing Reusche enamels in water.

(5) Liz loading enameled window glass into her electric, top-fired, fiber kiln.

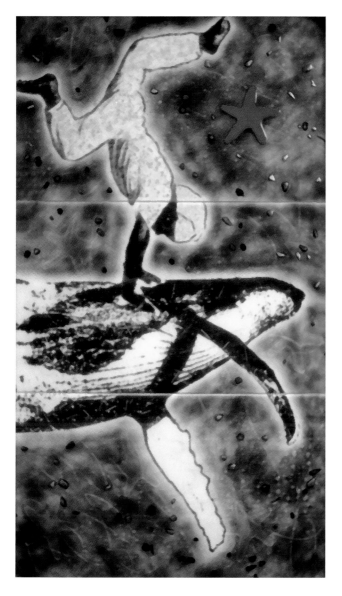

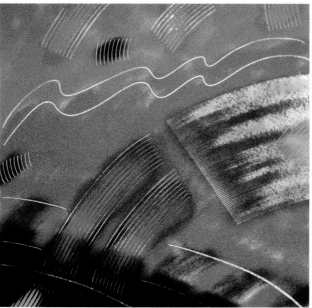

upper left:
Larson Elementary, 2003, Wassila, Alaska, for the Alaska Percent for Arts Program, enameled glass, one of eight panels portraying native stories.

upper right:
Detail of tile, airbrushed and sgraffito enamel with hot glass trails, stringers, and dichroic pieces fused on Bullseye glass.

lower:
Detail of a large tile, vitreous enamel on Vitrolite, painted with a brush, sifted, and airbrushed, with combed sgraffito.

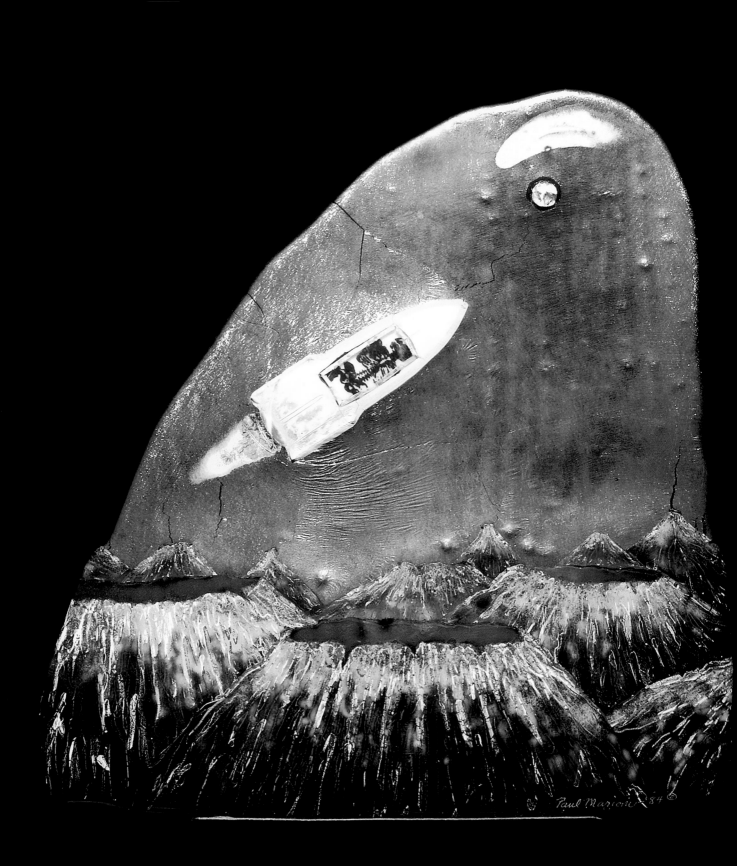

Paul Marion '84

Paul Marioni b. 1941

Mixed Media Enamels

I first became acquainted with Paul Marioni in the book, *New Glass,* by Otto Rigan published in 1976. I taught myself stained glass in 1974, was about to create Tiffany inspired windows, and fortuitously Paul appeared: the first technological explorer in glass that I had ever encountered. He was making 3-D glass panels, adding all sorts of things such as: X-rays, auto headlights, Fresnel lenses, and mirrors. He basically changed the way I thought about glass and took stained glass from decorative fluff to personal statement.

Born in Cincinnati, Ohio in 1941, he earned degrees in philosophy and literature, and then migrated to Mill Valley, California where he worked on cars as a "body-and-fender" man. He raised two children on his own, Dante and Marina, who have both become artists. Two of his brothers are also artists, inspiring him to seek the artist's life, which may not have lead to riches but certainly allowed him to pursue what he did best. Paul is a gentle human spirit and has a dark sense of humor. A few of the influences on his work are: politics - as a stage for human nature - death, skulls, skeletons, pacifism, Hiroshima, Mahatma Ghandi, and "the human condition."

Mr. Technique with a flair for spontaneity!

For his flat panel, "Peace Will Be Attained When The Last Of Man Is Gone," Paul used one of the curved ends of an irridized sheet of Bullseye glass; these sheets used to come with curved ends and were oval like a bulls eye. He quickly defined mountains with Thompson enamels and highlighted them with a white paint marking pen, cut out a glass rocket, placed a hand-made Versa Color decal of a skeleton under a clear glass window, and painted the rocket with gold luster. The moon is a piece of sheet mica.

Paul contacted me early in 1984. At that time, only a few people were fusing glass, and I was teaching for Bullseye. I came over to his studio where he had 5 of these pieces laid out on a table, all cracked. He told me that he had cut the pieces out of Bullseye glass. The compatibility test using polarizing light was just beginning to be used, and compatible Bullseye glass had only recently become available. I took one of the panels home and tried to fuse it again, but incompatibility was the culprit, and it cracked. He had used some old Bullseye that was not compatible. Paul let me keep it, and I treasure it today in my collection. This piece showed me the possibility of working quickly and spontaneously with numerous glass materials, something I have tried to do in my artwork for many years but have not yet achieved to my satisfaction.

"The studio glass movement is a result of cooperation and education, not competitiveness."

P. Marioni

"To say that Paul Marioni is one of the most extraordinary artists that I have ever met doesn't really give him the credit that he deserves."

R. La Londe

facing:
"Peace Will Be Attained When The Last Of Man Is Gone," 18 in. (46 cm) H. x 17 in. (43 cm) W. 1984. Fused irridized Bullseye glass, white paint marking pen, gold luster, Thompson enamels, mica, and Versa Color enamel hand-made decal of a skeleton.

portrait: 2008

Early on, Paul Marioni figured out how to balance technique with art and spontaneity. His unique glass was noticed by other glass artists in the studio glass movement, and he soon met Dale Chihuly, Fritz Dreisbach, Marvin Lipofsky, Richard Marquis, and Rob Adamson. Paul began teaching at the Pilchuck Glass School in 1974 and returned to teach there many years; he also taught numerous workshops at other schools and studios. Paul has been called "Mr. Technique" and "the Glass Artist's Glass Artist" - high praise for his talent, teaching, and generosity.

In 1978 Paul moved to Seattle to be available for art jobs from the newly founded Seattle Arts Commission, one of the first "Percent for Arts" programs in the country. Since then, he has created over one hundred large public and private commissions, many in collaboration with Anne Troutner.

For his creativity, Marioni garnered 3 national Endowment of the Arts Fellowships (which no longer are awarded, thanks to the conservatives in congress), and in 2004, he was awarded a Lifetime Achievement award by the Glass Art Society. Paul continues to work on personal art and architectural commissions. He splits his time between his large studio and apartment in an old telephone building in Seattle, Washington and a home in Guanajuato, Mexico.

Paul is a real technological innovator!
He saw the 1932 cast glass facade at the Radio City Music Hall in New York City - no one had done anything like that in the United States since then. An opportunity to create one of the first public commissions in Washington State came along for the Delridge Community Center in West Seattle, home of the State Golden Gloves Championships. Being a pacifist, Paul originally designed a window with dancers, and tried to convince the committee that boxing was a type of dance - but they wanted pugilism, with a knock-out blow depicted. A compromise was reached: a right jab to the stomach.

Paul experimented with ladling hot glass into CO_2-set sand molds, and produced the "Boxers Window," which was cast at the Spectrum Glass Company.

One person who read about "The Boxers" in a national magazine, was Paul Gardner, the Professor Emeritus in glass at the Smithsonian Museum, and he arranged to visit Marioni. Paul Gardner had been the assistant to Fredrick Carder, who was one of the founders of Stuben Glass Company. He told Marioni that he had helped Carter cast the Radio City Music Hall facade using Pyrex Glass. Gardner said that it was so difficult that Carder didn't want to have anything to do with a piece like that again.

When it came to creating spectators for the window, Marioni ladeled glass into a cast iron mold. The figures were designed to interlock, shoulder to shoulder, and the piece was held together with clear silicone. Paul told me "he felt like his brain was running out of his nose" by the time he finished cleaning up excess silicone with solvent.

Years later, the community center was turned into a battered woman's shelter, and Paul was asked if he wanted to move the window to another location. Paul exclaimed - you'd better! You can view this piece at the Washington State Convention Center, floor 4, in Seattle.

Floating Figures
Paul took the mold from the boxers window to Bullseye Glass Company in 1981, sifted Thompson enamels into it, ladled hot glass into the mold, dumped it out onto the casting table, and rolled a sheet, creating his "Floating Figures" series.

facing: "The Boxers," 1980, 6 ft. (1.8 m.) H. x 13 ft. (4 m.) W., weight 900 lbs. (375 kg), for the Delridge Community Center, Seattle, Washington, the Seattle Arts Commission. CO_2-set sand and steel mold, cast at the Spectrum Glass Company in Woodinville, Washington. "The Boxers" has been relocated to the Washington State Convention Center in Seattle.

above left: Cast iron figure mold.

upper right: One of Paul's favorite floating figures, 1981,

bottom right: "Floating Figure," 1981, glass monoprint, 14 in. (35 cm) H. x 24 in. (61 cm) L., made at the Bullseye Glass factory.

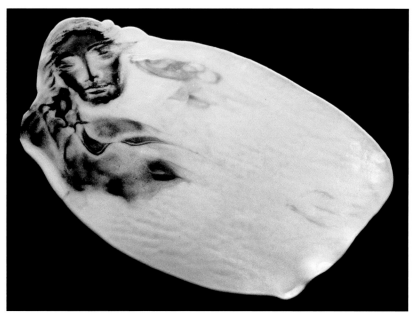

Later, he put various colored Thompson enamels in the mold and laid a bubble of hot glass that was on a blow pipe into the mold, picked up the face and blew it out into vases and sculptures. The "floating figures" and "face vases" are wonderful examples of a creative use of enamels in a very inventive way.

facing:
"Rocket Man" 1983, 12 in. (30 cm) H.

upper left:
"Face Vase" 1981, 12 in. (30 cm) H.

right:
"Head" 1983, 14 in. (35 cm) H.

Paul Marioni
Paradise Enamels

Paradise Enamels were high-fire vitreous enamels mixed in a squeegee
oil base that came in black, white,
brown, red, blue, green, and yellow
and were blendable to create many
different colors. They were marketed
by David Hopper from Paradise,
California. Ferro Sunshine Enamels
are a similar substitute today.

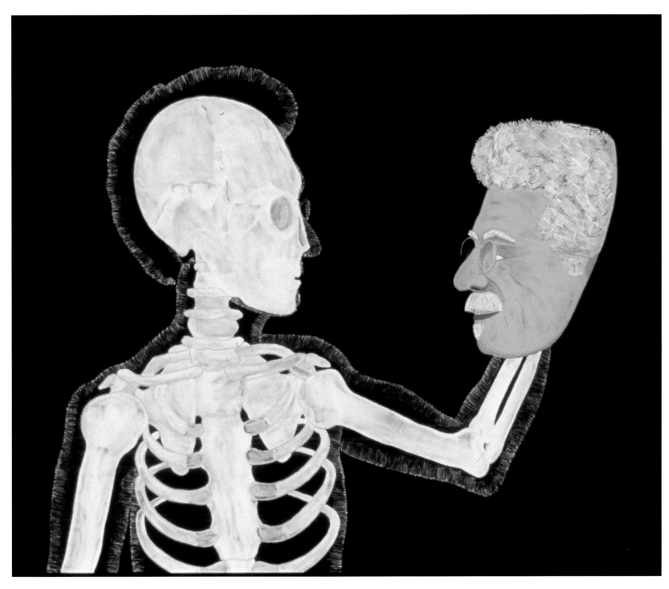

facing upper:
"Albino Jaguar," 1999, 26 in. (66 cm) H. x 23 in. (58 cm) W., Paradise Enamels on window glass.

facing lower:
"The Come On," 1993, 20 in. (51 cm) H. x 22 in. (56 cm) W., Paradise Enamels on window glass. Silver Leaf has also been fired on the figures.

above:
"Looking Back," 23 in. (58 cm) x 26 in. (66 cm), Paradise Enamels on window glass.

below right:
Paul Marioni with his Vintage Marathon Kiln, 2008. These kilns were the first top-firing, high temperature fiber-blanket kilns ever marketed for glass fusing and were sold by the Bullseye Fusing Ranch, circa 1982.

Meredith MacLeod b. 1957

High-Fire Sunshine Enamels

Meredith MacLeod attended Tyler School of Art in Philadelphia, learned to blow glass, spent one Spring at Penland School of Crafts in North Carolina, and graduated with a BFA from Massachusetts School of Art in Boston. She focused on flat glass, stained glass, and sandblasting because the furnaces always seemed to be out of order. In 1980, as a teaching assistant at the Pilchuck Glass School in Washington State, she was exposed to the ambience of the maritime Northwest. Meredith and her husband John Dewit built an art and glass blowing studio on Whidbey Island, near Pilchuck, in 1986.

Meanwhile, John's friend David Hopper discovered a high fire enamel that held up to the riggers of blowing and marketed it as Paradise Paints to other artists. Meredith began experimenting, fusing these paints onto window glass; she started an art and glass tile business in 1990. Hopper was selling paint manufactured by Cerdec, which was later bought out by the Ferro Corporation. That paint line began to be phased out, so in 2002 Meredith switched over to Ferro "Sunshine Enamels" - china paints designed as low fire glaze decoration on fired whiteware and porcelain.

Today Meredith MacLeod exhibits in galleries, pursues commissions, and makes tiles. She uses hand-carved rubber stamps and paints with brushes for glass and also printing on paper. She is influenced by 1950s illustrations in bird books, old textile patterns and 1930s fabric and color. Meredith says that her hand-printed and hand-painted artwork, "evokes an interest in something old that recasts itself as new." In the following pages, she generously shares some of the techniques that she developed and uses today.

meredithmacleodartist.com

facing:
"Stellar Jay" 2008, 8 in. (20 cm) square, ¼ in. (6 mm) thick. Sunshine Enamels, surface applied to window glass with a brayer, brush, and hand-carved rubber stamps. The enameled Jay's head is covered with a piece of clear glass. This piece is an example of both surface fired enamels and enamels fired under glass.

lower:
"English Sparrows" 2008, (female on left, male on right), 6 in. (15 cm) x 9 in. (23 cm) x ¼ in. (6 mm) thick. Sunshine Enamels applied with a brayer, brush, and hand-carved stamps, fired onto window glass.

(1) Meredith's tools consist of brushes, a pallet and pallet knife for mixing enamels, a rubber roller "brayer," and hand-carved stamps that she made.

(2) Meredith works in her studio and wears a respirator that can filter organic fumes, such as the noxious pine resin "squeegee oil" that she uses as a paint medium.

(3) Adding "squeegee oil" to the Ferro Sunshine Enamel powder on a piece of window glass that acts as a palette for mixing. Notice the gloved hands.

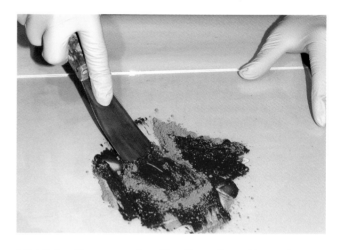

(4) Mixing the enamels with oil medium. Enamels contain toxic chemicals and the "squeegee oil" fumes can give you a headache. Ventilate the room with a fan.

(5) Rolling white enamel that has been mixed with oil onto a piece of glass with a brayer. Meredith puts the enamels against the non-tin (air-side) of the glass.

(6) Meredith heats the glass and enamel to 300° F (150° C) in her fan vented "burn-out kiln" to drive off the organic fumes. You can use your regular kiln and be sure to ventilate the room with a fan.

surface enameling with Meredith MacLeod "Sunshine Enamels"

(7) Meredith has hand cut a leaf into ³⁄₈ in. (10 mm) "Safety-Kut" rubber used for print making. With a brayer she applies green Sunshine Enamel that has been mixed with "squeegee oil."

(8) An ⅛ in. (3 mm) piece of window glass has been coated with white enamel using a brayer, and the fumes volatilized in a kiln. Transfer of the green enamel leaf pattern is accomplished by placing it on the white enameled glass and pressing with your hand. Here it is being lifted from the glass.

(9) Meredith signs her work with a hand-cut stamp, a decorative M. This piece is placed in a kiln and fired to 1550° F (845° C), using an appropriate firing schedule so as not to break the glass.

(10) This fired leaf piece is an example of surface enameling.

"Sunshine Enamel" under clear glass with Meredith MacLeod

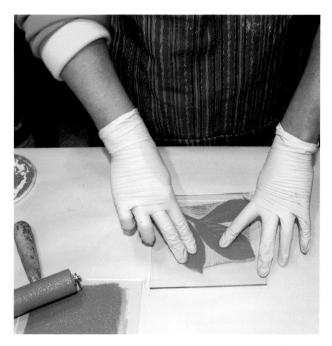

(1) Meredith has coated her hand cut leaf stamp with green Sunshine Enamel using a brayer. She places the enameled stamp up and puts a piece of ⅛ in. (3 mm) clear window glass over the stamp. Pressing with her hand transfers the enamel to the clear glass.

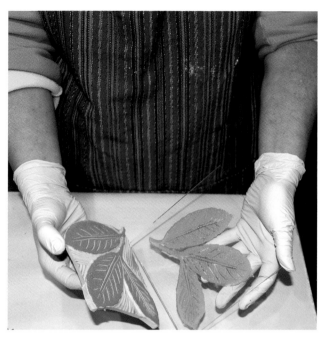

(2) Removing the stamp from the glass. The green enamel is dried in a kiln at 300° F (150° C).

(3) The stamp, glass palette, and brayer are cleaned using paint thinner, which is kept in an old paint can for this purpose.

(4) The green enamel was dried in the burnout kiln and now a layer of black "Sunshine Enamel" mixed with oil is painted onto the leaf pattern as a contrast for the leaf veins. The black enamel is dried in the burnout kiln.

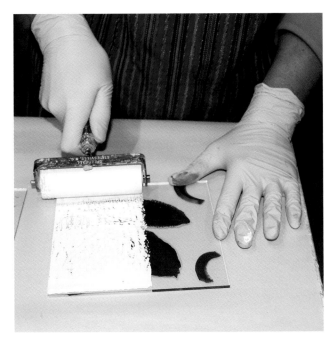

(5) A white background of "Sunshine Enamel" in oil medium is rolled on with a brayer, over the dried black enamel.

(6) This is again dried in the burnout kiln. The dried piece is then backed with a piece of ⅛ in. (3 mm) clear window glass and placed in the kiln. It is fired to a full fuse, which is 1550° F (845° C), in her kiln. Use an appropriate firing schedule so as not to break the glass.

(7) Meredith opens her kiln to load for a firing.

(8) Shows the fired piece, an example of enamel under clear glass.

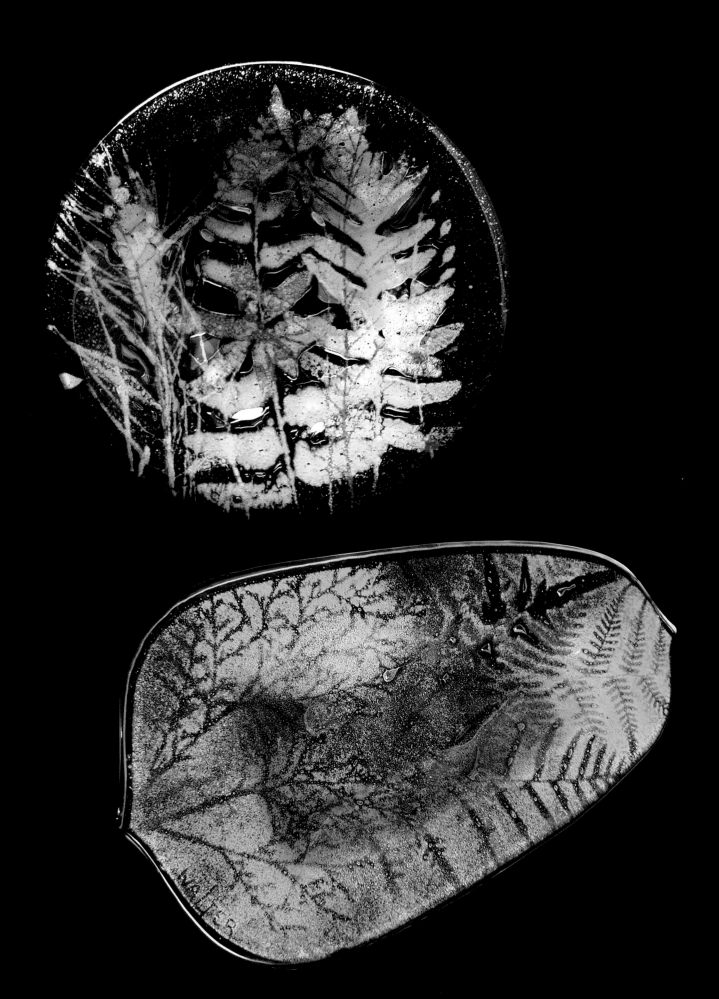

Plants and Flowers
Positive & Negative Design

Plants lend themselves to a recognizable but abstract form and provide a nice inspiration for enamel on glass. For this project I will use both Thompson and Paradise enamels. Sunshine enamels are similar and can be used as a substitute for Paradise enamels, which are no longer available. You can make a colored sheet of glass by rolling finely ground enamel mixed in a paint medium onto inexpensive window glass. This project is an example of enamel between glass.

facing upper:
"Ferns and Grass on a Black Background" bowl, engraved on the back - Higgins, 5 ½ in. (14 cm) in diameter and 1 in. (2.5 cm) deep x 3/16 in. thick, enamel fused in-between two pieces of double strength window glass, probably created by Frances Higgins with her "flip art" technique, sometime between 1970 - 1990.

facing lower:
"Ferns" plate, signed "Walter," 5 ½ in. (14 cm) x 9 ½ in. (24 cm), x 1 in. deep, x 3/16 in. thick, enamel sifted over plants as a stencil, fused in-between two pieces of double strength window glass.

(1) For this project I selected leaves from my garden and pressed them between two thick sheets of absorbent watercolor paper that I sandwiched between a flat table and a weighted plywood board. 2 weeks later they had dried and were flat. For this project you can also use fresh leaves, but they tend to curl, and I now have a stash of leaves for the wintertime.

(3) I cut a 6 in. (15 cm) x 6 in. (15 cm) x ⅛ in. (3 mm) piece of window glass and checked it with a short wave UV light, placing the non-tin side up. I place the leaf onto the glass, back with a piece of paper, and roll with a brayer - rubber roller. This transfers the paint to the glass; sometimes I can get two images from one leaf painting.

(2) I paint Sunshine enamel that has been mixed with squeegee oil onto the topside of a leaf. I will transfer the enamel to glass, creating a positive image of the leaf.

leaf plate - positive and negative

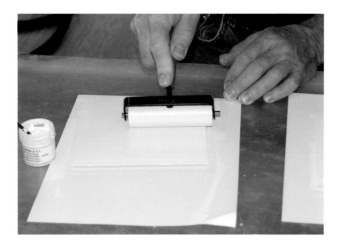

(4) I roll white enamel mixed with squeegee oil onto the non-tin side of the glass. You can see this in the previous Meredith MacLeod section.

(6) A duct tape lifting handle is put onto the dried leaf. This is placed on the dried enamel surface, and sifted Thompson enamels make a negative image.

(8) More sifting creates a negative leaf pattern.

(5) The positive leaf prints and the white enameled glass are placed onto a wire screen and ramped up in 15 minutes to 300° F (150° C) to burn off the oil.

(7) While holding my breath, I grab the lifting handle and remove the leaf carefully.

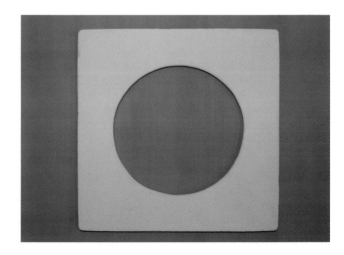

(9) An ⅛ in. (3 mm) thick, rigid fiberboard ring mold is placed on ⅛ in. (3 mm) broken pieces fiber board, creating a shallow dish mold on a primered kiln shelf.

(10) The sifted Thompson enamel negative leaf pattern on window glass.

(11) The dried Sunshine enamel positive leaf impressions on window glass.

(12) I flipped the positive print over and placed the glass on top of the other piece of glass, enamel to enamel. The painted and sifted enamels comprise thin layers but can still trap a few bubbles. This is placed over the fiberboard ring mold and fused to 1550° F (845° C).

(13) This plate was fired to the recommended temperature for Thompson enamels. The edges are very slightly rounded but still straight, and there is no devitrification on the tin-side up surface. The red enamel lost a bit of color, but overall I am pleased with this piece.

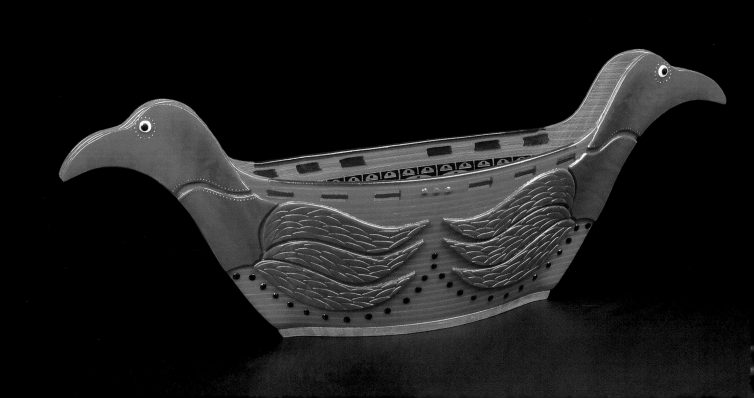

Avery Anderson b. 1945

Avery Anderson has a deep love for animals and nature. To express this passion with her artwork she uses many techniques, such as sandblasting, airbrushing, silk-screening, and photo resist. She also incorporates glass enamels, precious metals, lusters, and micas. Her fused glass pieces echo her philosophy: to live in harmony with Earth and all of her life.

Avery learned stained glass from her artist father in 1984 and went on to create commissioned glass panels and lamps. By 1987 she was experimenting with fusing, which in 1989 led to a glass fusing session at Camp Colton in Oregon. Soon after, a trip to the Southwest inspired a series of fused glass platters that included mica. Gallery shows and invitational exhibitions followed in the United States, including New Mexico, Florida, Oregon, Hawaii, and in Canada. Her work has been published in numerous books and magazine articles. Anderson traveled and taught techniques unique to her artwork - with Brock Craig, 2001 – 2004 - and later she taught in her own studio.

About Micas - an article by Avery Anderson

The word "mica" is thought to be derived from the Latin word micare, meaning to shine. Mica is an abundant mineral found all over the world and its size ranges from powder to large sheets. In 1963, a group of enterprising Dupont chemists patented a product that consists of very fine particles of mica with very thin layers of fused titanium dioxide and/or iron oxide. The thickness of the metal oxide layer determines the color; the level of iron oxide determines the opacity and earth tonality. The pigments are essentially non-toxic and they are widely used in eye shadows, lipsticks, nail polishes, paints, and "sparkle" toothpastes. For the glass industry, they are marketed under various names including, Pixie Dust, PearlEx Powders, Micas, Mother of Pearl Powders, and Thompson's Carefree Lusters (these micas are not metallic lusters). Although these mica products are similar, my personal preference is Thompson's Carefree Lusters or Sepp Leaf's micas.

I first discovered micas about 18 years ago when flipping though one of my mother's *Ceramics Monthly* magazines. I found an article in which a potter was mixing glazes and adding micas to his glaze to obtain a sparkle effect. Subsequent to this, some glass friends introduced me to a company called Sepp Leaf, which specialized in gilding supplies and carried a line of micas which were being marketed as additives to varnishes for painting picture frames. It was this combination of information that prompted me

averyanderson.com

facing upper:
"Tiger" from her Vanishing Links Series, a limited edition began in 2001, 19 in. (48 cm) in. diameter x 2 in. (5 cm) deep. Copper colored mica powder is used for the tiger fur pattern.

facing lower:
"Raven Spirit Vessel" 5 ½ in. (14 cm) H. x 28 in. (71 cm) long x 10 in. (25 cm) W.

below:
"Humming Bird" from her Animal Medicine Series, a limited edition began in 1994, 18 ½ in. (47 cm) diameter x 2 in. (5 cm) deep.

All pieces use Bullseye glass.

to experiment with the application of micas on glass. Reasoning that ceramic glazes were comprised of melted glass, it seemed I should be able to apply these powders to fused glass. After much trial and error, I finally got the results I had hoped for and have used micas in my work ever since.

There are a few basic rules one must know to work with micas. First, micas do not melt. In order for them to stick to the glass, you must fire the glass to a high enough temperature so that it becomes viscous and grabs onto the micas. If you fire the glass too high, the micas will become too faint. Anywhere between 1380 (750° C) and 1415 (770° C) is a good temperature range for micas when working with soft glass. Micas show up best on dark glass, but if you wish to work with clear or light-colored glasses, the metallic colors are the best to use (gold, copper and russet). The interference colors (green, lavender, blue) will all but disappear. The best way to apply micas and to obtain a nice, even, coating is by airbrushing them and building up numerous layers. You should always apply a thick coating of the micas. Once the glass with the mica has been fired, any of the product that does not come into contact with the glass will wash off. This is to be expected. You can reclaim the micas that do not adhere to the glass by simply brushing them back into their original container. Micas do not change their composition after being fired.

There are numerous ways in which to apply micas to glass and to achieve artistic results. Aside from airbrushing (as mentioned previously), micas can be applied by painting, sponging, sifting in a line sifter, squeeze drawing, screen printing, etc. When painting, squeeze drawing, and screen printing, micas should be applied with a mixing agent such as A-13 or Squeegee Oil. Because I personally do not care for the use of oil based products in my studio, I use A-13 which is a thick, water based medium produced by Thompson Enamels. I use this product to mix with regular enamels also. When airbrushing, my choice of a mixing agent is Klyr-Fire, a water based product produced by Thompson Enamels.

Application:
You will need a glass palette which has been lightly sandblasted, causing a tooth - this palette is very useful when mixing enamels, micas, or any dry agent with a medium. You will also need a palette knife for mixing, and an airbrush.

Note on airbushes: my personal preference is the Aztek airbrush, which is a hobbyist tool that was designed to airbrush model airplanes and trains. This airbrush is relatively inexpensive and has no internal mechanisms which can clog. It has interchangeable nozzles, so if you experience a "clog," you simply remove the nozzle, drop it in a jar of water, and apply another nozzle. If you have a sandblaster, you can use the same compressor that powers your sandblast system. If you have no compressor, do not be tempted to purchase one of those small airbrush compressors you find in art supply stores. They are very expensive and do not have the capacity to apply more than 20 lbs. pressure. I'd advise going to Home Depot or a similar store and getting one of the small "mushroom" compressors or something that is rated for about 120 PSI. You will save money and be happy with the results.

When applying micas via airbrush, you need to mix to a heavy, creamy consistency and set your airbrush to about 40 lbs. of pressure. Apply numerous coats (10 to 12) but apply with a higher air to medium setting. In other words, you want to apply the micas so they go on almost dry. If you apply them too wet and thick, you will not get an even coating and the wet spots will be visible on your finished product.

Once applied, fire the micas to about 1400° F (760° C) and hold for 10 minutes. This schedule is for firing on black glass, which is soft. White glass, window glass, etc. will require a higher temp and longer hold. Experiment and keep good records of your firings. Micas are a beautiful, metallic product that can enhance your glass projects. I hope you enjoy using them as much as I have.

Avery F. Anderson

mica techniques with Avery Anderson

(1) A glass tile is covered with sandblast resist. Avery is removing a piece of the clear resist for her gazelle design that she cut out with an Exacto knife.

(2) The finished resist on a glass tile that is ¼ in. (6 mm) thick x 6 in. (15 cm) square and was fused from two ⅛ in. (3 mm) pieces of black Bullseye glass.

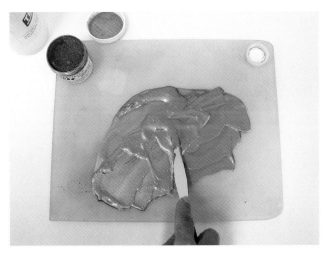

(3) Mica powder is mixed with Klyr-Fire, a water based medium.

(4) Mica powder in Klyr-Fire medium is airbrushed onto the resist covered tile and left to dry.

(5) The resist has been carefully peeled away. Gold luster dots are also applied. This tile is fired at 1400° F (760° C) for 10 minutes.

(6) The finished plate has been slumped into a shallow mold. It took three firings to create this piece.

sandblasted mica coating with Avery Anderson

(1) Mica powder in Klyr-Fire medium is airbrushed onto a tile that Avery fused from two pieces of ⅛ in. (3 mm) x 6 in. (15 cm) square Bullseye Glass.

(2) The mica powder is fired onto the tile at 1400° F (760° C) where it is held for 10 minutes. Mica that does not adhere to the tile can be saved for reuse.

(3) Clear sandblast resist is applied, and the gazelle design is hand-cut with an Exacto knife. Dots of white glue are also applied as a resist.

(4) The mica has been removed with sandblasting and the resist carefully peeled away.

(5) Avery signed her piece with a gold luster pen. The 24 karat gold was fired onto the glass during the slump. Four plastic bumpers act as feet.

(6) The finished piece.

mica flakes and sheet mica

(1) Mica is a mineral found in metamorphic rocks. Purchase mica in a rock shop, split the mica sheets into pieces, and fuse them between sheets of glass.

(2) I use a folded piece of paper to shake the mica flakes onto a piece of glass. Sometimes natural mica flakes can be found at craft stores.

(3) Here is a sample of the mica flakes after fusing the glass together.

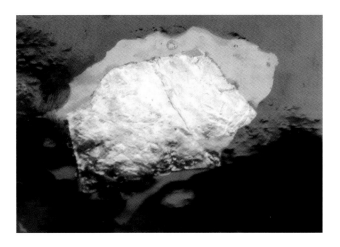

(4) Example of a large 2 in. (5 cm) long piece of natural Muscovite mica in Kyle Kinsey's bowl.

Kyle Kinsey, "Mica Platter" 2004, 12 in. (30 cm) x 16 in. (40 cm), glass enamels, Mason Stains, sheet mica, window glass.

Edwin Walter, "Boomerang Bowl" 10 in. (25 cm) x 8 in. (20 cm) x 1 ½ in. (4 cm) deep, fused window glass, brown enamel, and cut and punched mica pieces.

Part 3: Glass Painting
the history of stained glass

Medieval stained glass windows usually told Bible stories to the illiterate peasants, and the windows' colorful intensity reminded them about the ethereal majesty of god. Stained glass roots can be found in ancient dwellings - whose windows were covered by translucent animal hides - Roman glass windows, alabaster marble windows in early Christian churches, and Moorish wooden lattice windows that were covered with colorful cloth. The Moors also brought their talent for silver staining and vitreous enamels to Europe. Local glass blowers continued the Roman tradition of making clear cylinder glass - broad sheet window glass - and were also making colored sheet glass.

So all the glass pieces fell into place to fill the holes in the walls, in buildings of ever taller cathedrals – each one trying to out do the other. The oldest stained glass windows that are still in their original setting date back to 1140 A.D. and can be seen in the Augsburg Cathedral in Germany. The techniques of leading and glass painting are fairly advanced in these windows, so one wonders what became of earlier stained glass windows. Romanesque stained glass filled simple window shapes, and later fancy stone tracery led to Gothic rose windows, of which Chartres Cathedral is an early example. The continual building of churches has kept glass craftsmen employed ever since, and in Europe after World War Two, stained glass artists rushed to fix the damaged cathedrals and began a new movement – Architectural Glass.

In Victorian America, roughly 1875 to 1910, most middle class houses had to have stained glass. During this time Louis Comfort Tiffany and John LaFarge developed new techniques for windows and lamps, using hand rolled opalescent glass. Later the Great Depression wiped out the demand for stained glass, and by the 1960s only a few church window craftsmen were left. Out of this void, hippie craftsmen started a new stained glass revival. Hand-made glass factories sprang up, and old techniques were rediscovered, but this too peaked during the mid 1980s - killed by too many bad windows and "sun-catchers." Today stained glass and glass painting survives, and glass artists have expanded into glass blowing, bead making, glass fusing, and kiln forming.

facing upper left: "The Prophet Daniel," one of the 5 leaded and painted stained glass windows surviving from the 1140s, Augsburg Cathedral, Germany.

Facing upper right: North Rose Window with five lancet windows in the north transept of Chartres Cathedral. This window was crafted about 1230.

facing lower left: "Jesus," detail of a window in the Rochester Cathedral in England. This panel shows glass painting using black trace on clear, cobalt blue, and purple transparent stained glass, and silver staining on clear glass - the yellow parts.

facing lower right: Chagall's Window at All Saints Church, Tudeley, Kent, England

Bottom: The right third of Louis Comfort Tiffany's "Education," stained glass window at Yale University, New Haven, Connecticut.

Sherry Boyd-Yost b. 1955

Master Glass Painter

As a young girl attending Catholic mass, Sherry Boyd lost herself in the luminous stained glass windows, and this enchantment became her profession. In 1977 a stained glass class led to work at Weiser Art Glass in Bellingham, Washington. Two years later she joined Our Glass Company, and with Deena Matlack, researched and experimented with glass painting using an antique gas-fired kiln.

In 1982 Sherry moved back to Spokane, Washington, where she established her own studio, Lost Art Originals. For her first project she hand-painted 15 center medallions of the life of Christ for the Holy Trinity Episcopal Church, a collaboration with Sauer Stained Glass.

In 1984 Sherry joined a seminar taught by Jochem Poensgen and Lutz Haufschild, along with 16 international architectural glass artists, at the 1st Architectural Glass Seminar held at the Hein Derix Studio in Kevelaer, West Germany. The next year she attended Pilchuck Glass School, studying with Joachim Klos and Lutz Haufschild, and returned in 1987 to manage the Pilchuck store for half the summer.

Settling into her Spokane glass business, Sherry Boyd-Yost has completed many windows for private homes and liturgical commissions. Today she raises her family, works on commissions and speculative pieces that reflect her personal vision, and teaches at her studio.

lostartoriginals.com

facing:
"Beach Glass" 1993,
collaboration with Paula Grayhek who did the casted glass pieces, 50 in. (127 cm) x 34 in. (86 cm) in the collection of Connie Crow, Ashland, Oregon. Photograph by Connie Crow.

left:
"Sea Life" 2007 26 in. (66 cm) H. x 25 in. (63 cm), 2007, Spokane, Washington.

facing: "Annunciation" 1992, 52 in. (132 cm) x 31 in. (79 cm), Carmel of the Holy Trinity, Nuns Cloister, Spokane, Washington.

left: "Moses and Miriam" 1992, 54 in. (137 cm) x 22 in. (56 cm), Central Lutheran Church, Spokane, Washington.

right top: "Christ in Majesty" 1996, 52 in. (132 cm) x 31 in. (79 cm) Carmel of the Holy Trinity, Nuns Cloister, Spokane, Washington.

right bottom: "Roses and Lilies" (detail) 1994, 17 in. (43 cm) H. x 22 in. (56 cm), St. Aloysius Church, Gonzaga University, Spokane, Washington.

Glass Painting Techniques with Sherry Boyd-Yost

Painting or staining glass traditionally allowed the artist to add details to glass vessels and windows by blocking or changing the light that entered the glass. The tools and techniques for this art have developed over the centuries and are very exacting and meticulous. In this section about glass painting you will meet master glass painters and artists who just pick up a brush and "go for it."

You may be able to glean the basics from a book, and here are a couple of classics to start with; *The Art of Glass Painting* by Albinus Elskus, 1980 and *Stained Glass Painting: Basic Techniques of the Craft* by Richard Millard and Anita & Seymour Isenberg, 1979. You might want to buy a few low-fire enamels to try glass painting, but to pursue traditional glass painting, I emphatically recommend that you seek out a competent master glass-painter to learn from.

Many glass paints contain lead and other harmful chemicals. Wear rubber gloves and a good dust mask, clean your area safely, and don't eat or allow young children in your glass painting studio.

(2) Sherry first dry-mixes a Reusche Stainer's Color - Tracing Best Black - with a dusting of Gum Arabic. In the above photo, she is mixing water with the glass paint - using a palette knife - to achieve the right consistency; she has also added a few drops of Reusche Waterbase Medium.

(3) Black Trace is applied onto a piece of "Tsunami" - a large glue chipped textured window glass. She chose this glass to give the painting a watery look, and the painting is done on the smooth side. The glass is laid on a paper pattern that has been placed on the light table. The painted piece is fired to 1275° F (690° C) in a kiln. Notice the "bridge" that keeps her hand out of the paint.

(1) Some of the tools for glass painting include very expensive sable hair tracing brushes, badger-hair blending brushes, many other brushes, a glass muller (pestle), palette knife, and various mediums.

(4) Using an expensive and very fine brush, a thin wash of Best Black is brushed over the previously fired trace. This process is called "matting."

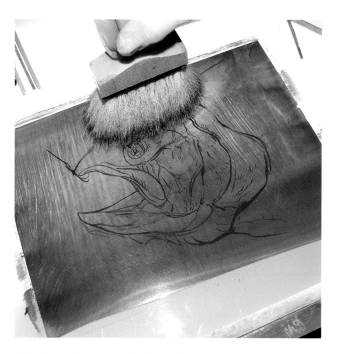

(5) After this matte is allowed to dry, it is then removed and textured with a texturing brush. Wear rubber gloves and a dust mask when doing this as the glass paint contains lead and other harmful metals. Use a HEPA vacuum to clean up the studio area or damp mop the area.

(6) Sherry is further tweaking the matte with a variety of specialized brushes. The piece is then returned to the kiln and fired to 1275° F (690° C). The firing temperature will depend on your kiln, the type of glass, and the type of paint.

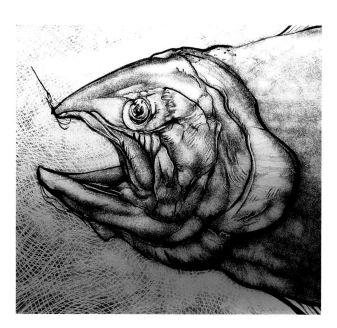

(7) The piece after the "Trace" and "Matte" firings. Some glass painters do this in one firing, using a hardener, such as vinegar to hold the trace, so the matte can be applied on top of it. Sometimes this works, but it is not as controllable as two firings. Further matte layers and firings can build intricacy.

(8) A Reusche Brown Gray Umber paint is applied.

(9) The Umber Matte is brushed off, leaving shading and texture, and fired again to 1275° F (690° C).

(10) Sherry applies Fuse Master Peacock Blue Transparent enamel to the background. This is fired to 1250° F (675° C).

(11) Sherry placed the painting into her kiln. It is a ceramic fiber, top-element with a bottom wall element, for a total of 50 amps (240 volt), single phase, with inside dimensions of 23 in. (58 cm) x 46 in. (117 cm), and uses a programmable controller. I built this kiln for Sherry in 1985 for fusing and glass painting.

(12) After the fourth firing.

(13) Sherry applies more transparent enamels. She brushes Fuse Master Emerald Green and a second color, which she mixes from Fuse Master Fuchsia Pink and Reusche Ruby. This piece is fired for the final time at 1050° F (565° C).

(14) "Salmon Moon" by Sherry Boyd-Yost, 2008, 9 in. (23 cm) x 12 in. (30 cm).

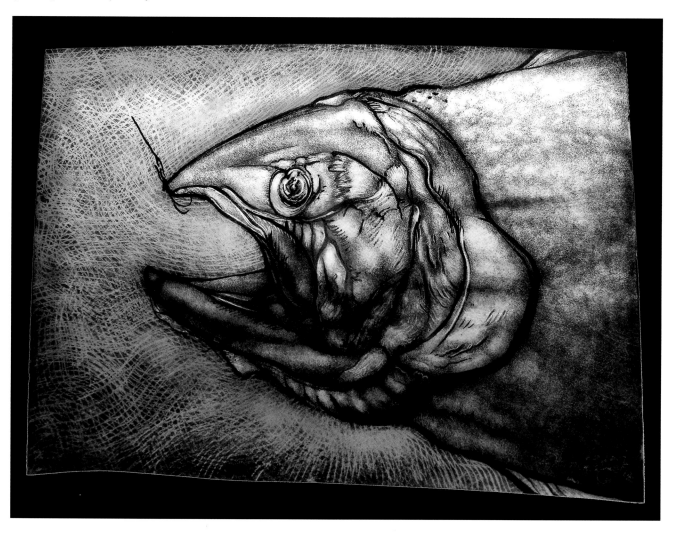

Peter McGrain b. 1956

"Vitri-Fusáille®," is the term that Peter McGrain has coined to describe the technique that he has developed to create his pictorial images. Instead of using lead to assemble individually painted pieces of glass into a traditional stained glass panel, he fuses separate pieces of transparent colored glass into a single tile and then paints directly on top of it.

So far, Peter has lived "the life" - hanging out in Steamboat Springs, Colorado for skiing, sailing his own boat in the Florida keys, and now living near the sailboard Mecca, Hood River, on the Columbia River. Along the way he had to pay his bills. While working for the Forest Service in Colorado, he began playing with copper foil, making stained glass windows. Inspired by the 1970s hippie stained glass book, *New Glass by Otto Rigen*, his glass art skipped traditional and went directly to playful and exuberant.

With no formal art training, and self taught in glass, Peter returned to Rochester, NY, where he set up a glass studio and ventured into the world of architectural glass - completing a huge window for the Strasenburgh Planetarium in 1986. To create his autonomous pictorial panels, McGrain quickly moved through all the techniques of stained glass - leading, foiling, sandblasting, layer carving flashed glass - and in 1993 developed his own tricks for layering dichroic float glass. In 1995 he completed a 25 ft. (7.5 m.) x 100 ft. (30 m.) monumental window for the Rochester International Airport. During that year he studied glass painting with Richard Millard. It seems to have all come together in his new Vitri-Fusáille® technique. Today Peter McGrain makes commissions, creates glass paintings, teaches his techniques, and plays the musical saw - an artist's life.

www.petermcgrain.com

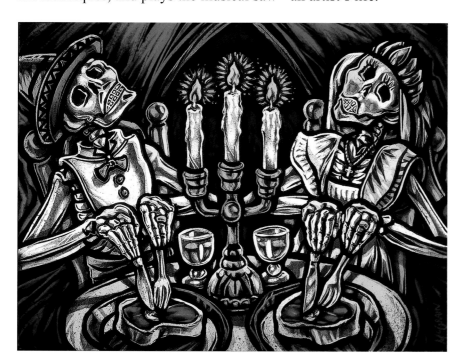

facing:
"Accordion Player" 20 in. (50 cm) x 28 in. (70 cm), 2008 Courtesy of Prairie Glass, Winnipeg.

below:
"Muertos Comiendo" 14 in. (35 cm) x 18 in. (45 cm), 2005 Private Collection.

133

facing:
"Carnival Duo," 20 in. (50 cm) x 28 in. (70 cm), 2008
Courtesy GlassForum / Norway.

upper:
"Crowfight," 20 in. (50 cm) x 30 in. (75 cm), 2008
Courtesy of D&L Glass / Boulder, Colorado.

lower:
"El Cubano," 14 in. (35 cm) x 18 in. (45 cm), 2006
Private Collection.

Peter McGrain - technique for Vitri-Fusáille®

Vitri-Fusáille® is a hybrid glass working technique, combining fusing with glass painting, that Peter McGrain developed for expressive spontaneity in his pictorial imagery. With traditional stained glass, the intruding lead lines can be bulky, and fragment the imagery, but with Vitri-Fusáille®, all the separate colored elements are fused into a single tile free of lead lines, upon which the artist can then paint. This approach allows far more immediacy in the art making procedure, and for anyone who has struggled with the shackles "old School" stained glass technique, it can be truly liberating!

This process begins on paper, and any design style that incorporates a dark line drawing, enhanced with texture shading; isolated color fields can be used. Just like stained glass, a paper pattern for cutting the glass is made. Then Peter cuts ⅛ in. (3 mm) compatible, transparent glass pieces, which are positioned on top of an ⅛ in. (3 mm) piece of compatible clear glass and fired to full fuse 1450° F (790° C) - 1500° F (815° C). The fused tile will have a smooth top surface and clear lines between the colors' fields where the base glass oozed up between the glass pieces.

Peter illustrates the design by painting Reusché Lead Free Tracing Black onto his fused tile, making sure that he covers the seam lines. When the seams are obscured it is impossible to tell how the color is integrated into the design, and this leads to a notable "mysteriousness" as to how the work was made.

After the initial "trace" has been fired, a series of shading "mattes" are applied using more Reusché Tracing Black. The paint is manipulated and fired again to create texture and dramatic shading. Like all glass painters, Peter uses as a variety of brushes, tools, and techniques - secret weapons - to achieve his memorable imagery.

Peter McGrain teaches Vitri-Fusáille® workshops at his home studio and at other world-wide locations. His book, *Peter McGrain - Uncommon Stained Glass,* and demonstration videos are available on his website **www.petermcgrain.com**.

(1) A simple concept sketch begins the design process. Usually this is done on white paper within a perimeter outlining the intended size of the final piece. Generally, it is necessary only to establish the general placement and shape of forms within the composition. Specific details will be more fully developed during the painting stages.

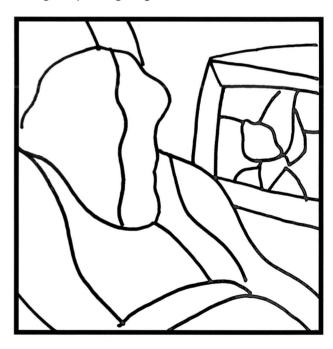

(2) A cutting pattern is then prepared, derived from the initial sketch. Each color field is designated as a separate piece within the design. It's a good strategy to position the edges of the color fields in places where they will be conveniently covered up or "camouflaged" underneath the eventual dark trace lines and shadings of the painted imagery.

(3) All the separate pieces of compatible colored glass in the design are then cut out. Small inconsistencies in cutting accuracy are not much of a problem since they tend to melt together quite tightly when fired to full fuse. All the pieces are then assembled as a complete second layer over a single base of smooth clear ⅛ in. glass.

(4) The fused tile is out of the kiln and ready for painting. Ideally the surface should be completely smooth, free of any valleys or crevices between the colored pieces into which paint could become trapped. Note how the clear/white seams between the individual colored pieces are visible. These seams will be hidden behind paint later on.

(5) Using a narrow ox hair quill and Reusché Tracing Black paint the line work of the image is applied, trimmed, and fired into the tile at approximately 1250° F (675° C). This establishes the "drawing" aspect of the picture. These lines are also used to cover up and hide the seams between the colored areas.

(6) The final texture and shading of the picture is accomplished by applying and firing a series of overlapping mattes directly over the tracing. It is best to adopt a high contrast style of imagery when working with Vitri-Fusáille®, and the resulting work will appear dramatically illuminated with saturated color and a higher degree of apparent depth.

Cappy Thompson b. 1952

Artist Cappy Thompson grew up in Seattle, Washington and graduated in 1976 from the Evergreen State College in Olympia, WA. with a Bachelor of Arts in painting and printmaking. A college internship led to a job at Mansion Glass, a stained glass studio in Olympia, where she experimented with glass painting. During the 1970s in the United States only a few people painted on stained glass, and Cappy learned by trial and error.

In 1984 Thompson returned to Seattle and was an artist in residence at the Pilchuck Glass School with stained glass artist Dick Weiss. Later Cappy inspired Weiss to pick up a brush, and, along with Walter Lieberman, they would get together and paint.

Enchanted by folk art, world mythologies, fables, and tales, Cappy developed her own iconography which she used to narrate her painted stained glass "animal stories." An example is on the following page, which was created in 1982 and is titled "The Lion and the Mouse." Cappy's painting is fired onto stained glass and assembled into a leaded glass panel.

At Pilchuck in 1988, artist Flora Mace gave Cappy a vessel to paint on, which opened a new world of possibilities. A sample of this early work may be seen below. As Cappy put it, "With the change from the flat panel to the vessel came a larger context, environment, or setting—sea and land, heaven and earth, islands, rooms with views, day and night, country and city, etc. With the larger context came the incorporation of aspects of my own life, my personal narrative. I was no longer painting mythological imagery but autobiographical imagery—albeit with mythopoetic allusions. This was a powerful shift in my approach to narrative." It is these delightful vessels that brought her international recognition as a glass painter.

cappythompson.com

below:
"Eve," 1988, 10 in. (25 cm) H. x 12 in. (30 cm) in diameter. Reusche black enamel, fired onto the inside of a translucent blown vessel. Collection of Museum of Arts and Design, New York, NY.

facing: "Lovers Dreaming a Dream," 1996, 16 in. (41 cm) H. x 16 in. (41 cm) in diameter, vitreous enamels painted on the inside of a glass vessel that was blown at Ben Moore's studio. The intimate narrative portrays Cappy's dream.

To create her dream-like narrative vessels, Cappy hires local glass artists to blow the clear or translucent white vessels that she paints on. Today her blanks are produced at Ben Moore studios by artists such as Dante Marioni, Richard Royal, and Paul Cunningham. Even William Morris has contributed blanks to this effort.

Cappy sketches her images with a marking pen on the outside of the glass vessel. Then she lays the vessel on its side, and using short handled brushes she paints the linework with black low-fire enamel (Reusche 8225MB) on the inside of the vase. The vessel is fired to 1100° F (595° C) in an electric kiln.

The next step is called "grisaille" – a gray-tonal painting technique in which a thin wash of the same vitreous black paint is applied. After this dries, it is partially removed using a series of dry brushes chosen to create various textures. The vessel is fired a second time to 1100° F (595° C).

Color is applied using vitreous enamels made from metal oxides which have been pre-mixed with a clear low-melting lead glass called a flux. Fuse Master transparent enamels are one of Cappy's favorites. Colored enamels are painted and then fired on the inside of the vessel, and this process can take up to three applications and firings. As an art piece Cappy's vessels can last for hundreds of years, but, in general, low-fired enamels exposed to water or acid rain over time can deteriorate. This is why colored soda-lime sheet

above: "The Lion and the Mouse," 1982, 24 in. (60 cm) x 24 in. (60 cm), leaded painted stained glass. Collection of Washington State Arts Commission.

facing right: "We Are Sailing in the Sea of Possibilities toward Our Next Bright New Beginning," 2008, 6 ft. (1.8 m.) x 8 ft. (2.4 m.), King County Library Commission in Covington, Washington. Vitreous enamels reverse-painted on mouth-blown sheet glass, laminated with transparent silicone to brushed aluminum panel.

below: "Bee Keepers Journey: The Queen of Heaven Grants a Boon," 2008, 35 in. (89 cm) x 65 in. (165 cm), vitreous enamels reverse-painted on mouth-blown sheet glass, laminated to brushed aluminum.

glass is generally used in stained glass windows, rather than low-fired vitreous enamel coatings on clear glass.

Cappy says, "I was happily painting vessels throughout the 1990s. Then in 2000 I was commissioned to do something I had never done, let alone considered, before—a massively large 33 ft. x 90 ft. (10 m. x 27.5 m.) painted glass window wall at SeaTac International Airport." To do this monumental piece, Cappy turned to Derix Studio located near Frankfurt, Germany. They had the experience, staff, and equipment to produce large painted glass panels - they worked with another factory for tempering glass and had further business connections for fabricating the insulated window units and shipping these units to Seattle. The SeaTac airport job led to a series of other relatively large public and semi-public projects with Derix, which included: the Museum of Glass in Tacoma, Washington; the Montgomery Museum of Fine Arts in Montgomery, Alabama; and the Evergreen State College in Olympia, Washington, where she graduated.

"When I did the big projects at Derix, I painted the grisaille personally and supervised and assisted the fabricator in everything else. In my own studio, I have produced medium-scale wall paintings, using the gluing technique that I learned in Germany. This involves painting sheets of mouth blown glass (manufactured in Seattle at Fremont Antique Glass) and laminating the painted pieces onto reflective surfaces—usually brushed metal sheeting over wood panels. The lamination uses a platinum-based, room-temperature vulcanized two-part ("RTV-2") silicone manufactured by companies such as Wacker, GE, and Silicones, Inc."

Cappy says, "My work is not only about glass but also about telling a narrative or story to people. In my career, I've progressed from narrative paintings that were intimate in scale but public in content, to paintings that are public in scale and intimate in content."

above: "Muses Bestowing Blessings on the Pacific Northwest," 2003, 7 ft. 2 in. (2.2 m.) x 8 ft. 2 in. (2.5 m.). Residential commission for a partition wall, Medina, Washington. Vitreous enamels painted on opalescent sheet glass, laminated to plate glass.

right: "I Imagine Us As a Holy Family Engaging in the Great Work of Increasing the Light," 2006, 10 ft. (3 m.) x 66 ft. (20 m.) The Evergreen State College, Daniel J. Evans Library, Olympia, Washington. Vitreous enamels and silver stain painted on float glass with areas of reverse-laminated stained glass, assembled as insulated glass window units. Fabricated at Derix Glasstudios in Germany. Washington State Arts Commission.

above:
I Was Dreaming of Spirit Animals," 2002, 33 ft. (10 m.) x 90 ft. (27.5 m.) Installation view, SeaTac International Airport, Seattle, Washington. Vitreous enamels painted on float glass with areas of reverse-laminated stained glass, assembled as insulated glass window units. Port of Seattle commission. Fabricated at Derix Glasstudios, Germany.

middle left:
Cappy on the left with her assistant, painting black trace paint onto float glass at Derix in Germany.

lower left:
Cappy texturing the grisaille layer.

lower right:
airbrushing blue transparent enamel.

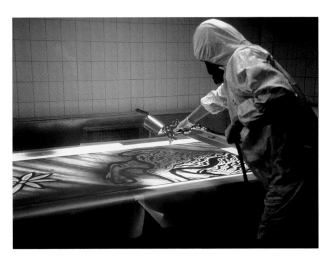

143

Italo Scanga 1932 - 2001

Art vs. Technique

Italo Scanga was born in Italy and emigrated to America in 1947. He pursued art, and received an MA from Michigan State University in 1961, and his first teaching job was at the University of Wisconsin where he met Harvey Littleton. Italo's exhibitions and teaching kept him moving around the US, and in 1978 he relocated to La Jolla, California where he taught at UCLA, San Diego. Italo became a very successful multimedia sculptor and painter; once I saw him on the cover of *Art News.*

In 1967, while lecturing at the Rhode Island School of Design, he met graduate student Dale Chihuly, and later they became very close friends. Italo went to the Pilchuck Glass School in 1973 as a visiting artist and returned there every year until 2001. Several summers at Pilchuck I had opportunities to watch him create. He was a "real artist," not just a "glass artist." Italo would take a tree trunk with branches, and with helpers, paint on it, toss in a piece of glass, and mount it on a pedestal. Quick art, not much technique, very spontaneous, REAL ART – and I didn't get it until years later.

In 1987 Italo telephoned me at my studio in Seattle. He told me that he had been painting on glass vases at Pilchuck and that they had slumped and collapsed when fired in the brick kilns there. He had heard that I had a large, fast, kiln, and would I like to fire his pieces? I would, and maybe some of his spontaneity would rub off on me.

So Italo came to my studio for 5 days and painted about two dozen clear vases, blown by Ben Moore. Leafing through an old Italian children's picture dictionary for inspiration, he outlined figures and objects in black enamel and then told Robbie Miller and Ruth Brockmann, who were assisting him for this project, where to place the colored enamels. Someone at Pilchuck had given him a box containing opened bags of random enamels, mostly Reusche of unknown compatibility and firing temperatures. They were applied using only water, so we had to be careful where we touched as the enamel would rub off.

I stacked them in my kiln, 12 at a time - about $40,000 worth of art - and turned on the electricity. Nervously, I slowly took them up to 1050° F (566° C). My kiln is a fiber kiln and very fast, so after the initial heat up, I kicked it on high, and it jumped to 1350° F (732° C) in about 5 minutes. I peeked through the vent hole, and when the vases began to quiver, I opened the kiln all the way and vented it. I fried the enamels onto the vessel surface, which on some colors left blisters and bumps, which Italo loved. His spontaneity did rub off on me. Italo told me, "Go ahead, Reechard, you can do it!"

www.italoscanga.org

facing:
1987, Italo painting enamels and with the finished pieces. Vases loaded in my kiln for firing.

below:
One of Italo Scanga's poster paint on matte board paintings, 21 in. (53 cm) H. x 15 in. (38 cm) W., 1987.

Low-fire Vessel Painting

Before I begin talking about painting on vessels, I want you to see this Chinese glass snuff bottle that has been blown, cut, and polished. This piece is the same size as the image below, 3 in. (8 cm) high. What's remarkable is that the painting is on the inside of the bottle and was done with tiny brushes, some that probably have only one hair, and painted through a ⅜ in. (9 mm) opening.

Here's how you can get started. In an article in *Glass Studio Magazine* # 37, 1982, Albinas Elskus, one of the foremost American glass painters, eloquently writes about mixing enamels: "One of the basic and most often used mixtures is prepared with ordinary water and gum arabic. Take a full tablespoon of powder paint and place it on a glass palette and, with a palette knife, pound it down to a thickness of approximately ⅛ in.. Now, take gum arabic powder on the tip of your palette knife and, by tapping it lightly, sprinkle the gum over the paint until it looks like freshly fallen snow. You should always see the paint under the gum.

Now, mix the gum and paint together into one heap. Begin to add water in small amounts- say a half teaspoon at a time- stir slowly and carefully with a palette knife. When the mixture reaches the consistency of yogurt, do not add any more water but keep on mixing for a few minutes longer." "The ideal tracing fluidity is attained when the paint flows smoothly from the brush, covering the glass with a thin but opaque coat of paint." Sherry Boyd tells me that a bit of gum arabic acts like a flux for the paint, and Cappy Thompson uses liquid gum arabic that you can buy at an art supply store. When I first tried glass painting I just used straight water, and I had to handle the painted glass very carefully before it was fired as it would rub off easily. I recommend that you use a bit of gum arabic with your paint.

In the late 1980s, Seattle glass painter Walter Lieberman organized a benefit for the Pike Place Market food bank called "101 Glasses of Beer." He got friends, such as Cappy Thompson, Dick Weiss, and Paul Marioni, and other well known artists - some of whom were not necessarily associated with glass, to paint on pint beer glasses, which were then fired. These glasses were filled with beer at the local watering hold, The Virginia Inn, near the Pike Place Market, and sold for $10 each. The drinker got to keep the art-glass. I even painted a few and also fired a bunch in my kiln.

At first I was really intimidated at the idea of painting, but it seemed to work out. I offer the following simple painting exercise to get you started. If you like the process, then take a glass painting workshop. As you have seen in the previous pages, there is a lot that can be done with glass paints and vitreous enamels.

Go to your studio and paint!

To get started, purchase a few colors of "Fuse Master Transparent Enamels" and some "Water Friendly Medium" (www.fusionheadquarters. com). Vases and glasses may be found at thrift stores, but don't buy lead glass. Clean the vase in a dishwasher and wipe with denatured alcohol. Low fire vitreous enamels usually contain lead, so on the drinking glasses, I masked off the rim, so there would be no chance of lip contact. The low fire enamels don't hold up well in dishwashers, so clean them carefully by hand.

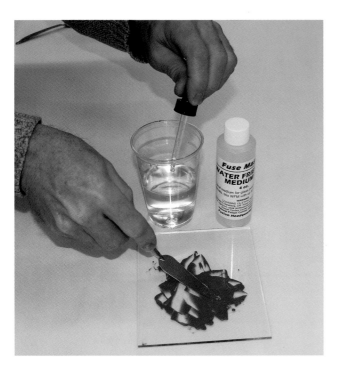

(1) On a piece of window glass, mix a small amount of "Fuse Master - Transparent Enamel" with water and add a couple drops "Fuse Master - Water Friendly Medium" or liquid gum arabic; blend with a steel palette knife to a smooth, creamy consistency. The dried paint can be reconstituted later with water.

(2) Clean your glass in a dishwasher and wipe with denatured alcohol. All oils must be removed, or the paint will not stick. Use a synthetic hair or real sable brush with very fine bristles. Load the brush and paint away! Very thick lines can pop off when fired, so make the strokes moderately thin, but color filled.

(3) Firing schedule for a pint glass: 250° F (140° C) per hour to 1000° F (540° C). As fast as you can to 1150° F (620° C). Vent your kiln to 1000° F (540° C). Anneal at 960° F (515° C) for 1 hour. Cool down 250° F (140° C) per hour to room temperature.

(4) The finished vase inspired by the Islamic Luster painting shown on the next page. Now that you have seen how easy it is to begin, I hope my simple example encourages you to get some vitreous enamels and try glass painting.

Part 4: Metals and Glass

the history of metallic luster on glass

Luster painting is a process using heat, in which liquid metallic ions migrate just below the surface of glass into the molecular structure and produce a permanent stain. The term luster probably refers more to a shiny metallic look on pottery, and the ancient glass pieces that have been found seem to have a dull stain. The term "stained" and "luster painted" are used interchangeably for ancient work. Today, these fired liquid metals can be shiny, but the stained glass technique of silver staining is transparent yellowish and non-lustrous.

To make lustered glass, an object would be blown, and when cool, silver and copper that had been dissolved in a liquid was applied as a paint. These pieces were heated above their annealing point, picked up with a bit of hot glass on a metal rod, and reheated in a furnace - which fused the metallic stain into the glass surface. Luster staining, probably began with Coptic glassmakers in Egypt during the 6th - 7th century, and with the advent of Islam in the mid 7th century, these glassmakers changed their style from post Roman to Islamic, in which realistic imagery was replaced by abstract designs and script. In the Islamic world, metallic stained glass was popular from about 675 - 1,000 A.D. Later, during the European Renaissance, shiny luster painting and gilding was used to embellish glass pieces.

facing: "Cup," 786-787 A.D. from Damascus, Syria, 4 in. (10 cm) H. x 5 in. (13 cm) in diameter, blown glass with dark red-brown and yellow silver stain.

below left: "Drinking Horn," 8th - 9th century, probably Egypt, 8 ½ in. (21.5 cm) H. x 2 3/8 in. (6 cm) diameter, blown glass with brown and yellow silver stain.

below right upper: "Bowl" in transmitted light, 9th century, Egypt, 2 3/8 in. (6 cm) H. x 6 ¼ in. (16 cm) diameter, blown glass with purple, red and orange brown copper stains and yellow silver stain.

below right lower: "Bowl" in reflected light, a true dichroic.

All ancient Islamic luster pieces courtesy of The Corning Museum of Glass.

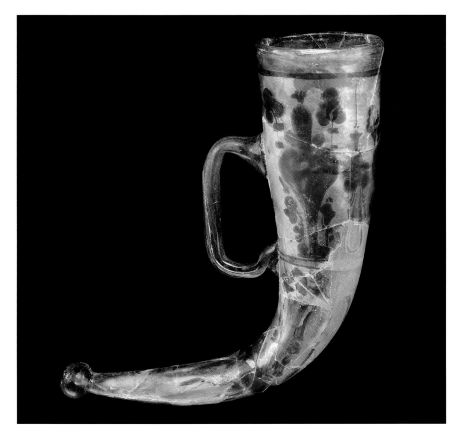

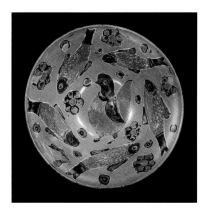

Contemporary Metallic Luster

You may have seen a thin gold band on fancy drinking glasses or shiny gold on a glass ashtray. These are examples of metallic lusters. Commercially, they are screened onto glass and then fired to adhere the metal to the glass surface.

Metallic lusters are precious metals that have been dissolved into a liquid and blended with binders and thinners. Today, they are available in platinum, palladium, glass gold, bright gold, and copper. Mother of pearl, an iridescent luster, and a few colored lusters can also be found. Lusters are usually applied to the glass surface with a brush or pen. Airbrushing, silk-screening, sponges, decals, and other transfer methods can also used. For some applications you might want to dilute the luster with a special luster-compatible thinner, sometimes called an essence.

I prefer using a Kemper Tools Gold Pen to write my signature and make dots and lines in my artwork. I describe this on the next page. Lusters fire at 1050° F (565° C) - 1300° F (705° C),

which makes them perfect to fire onto a vessel without sagging it, or during a slump.

Frances and Michael Higgins used gold luster for signature and line work applied with pens; they also lustered and fired sheets of glass that were later cut into pieces and fused, such as the fish and the lustered plate that Michael Higgins is holding below.

facing upper:
Michael Higgins is holding his 24 in. (61 cm) diameter fused platter that he made from cut gold lustered and enameled glass sheets, 1992. This is one of two that he made at the Dearborn factory in the early 1960s. This plate sold at auction in 2004 for nearly $13,000!

facing bottom:
"Fish," 1995, size of detail shown, 9 in. (23 cm) H. x 12 in. (30 cm) W., Higgins Glass Studio. Prefired gold luster on window glass, cut into pieces and fused with clear and prefired enameled window glass.

below:
This is an example of commercial decorative ware. Georges Briard was the artist pseudonym for Jascha Brojdo, who in the 1950s designed many pieces that were manufactured by the "Bent Glass Company" which made ceiling light fixtures. Georges Briard pieces sold in department stores under his "Glass Guild" label. 22 kt. gold luster and vitreous enamels were screened onto clear window and white flashed glass, which was then fired and slumped into a mold. He also designed many lustered and enameled drinking glasses, ceramic plates, and wooden serving trays. "Apple," 8 in. (20 cm) x 8 in. (20 cm) x ¾ in. (2 cm) deep, circa 1950.

metallic luster pen

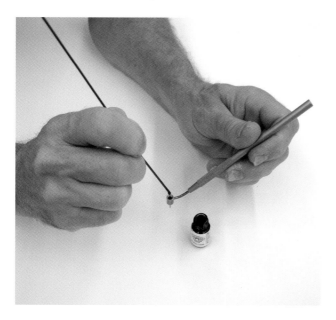

(1) I use a Kemper Tools gold pen, which comes in two sizes, small with a .26 mm tip and large, .49 mm tip. Here I am putting 2 - 3 drops of "liquid bright gold" into the pen, using a glass stringer. Toothpicks will also work. I do not dilute the luster with thinner for this pen.

(2) Clean the glass surface well. I touch and let the tip of the pen glide on the glass surface as I write my name. This tool is also very good at making gold dots and lines on your artwork. The liquid binder has a really noxious smell, so do this in a well ventilated area, or you might get a headache. If you wipe off a mistake, be sure to use lacquer thinner. Smears that you can't see can sometimes show after firing.

(3) After using this pen, clean the metallic luster out of the tip with a paper towel. Use lacquer thinner to help remove the excess liquid and ream the tip out with the thin wire tool provided. It is very important that you clean this tool as soon as you are done. The luster can set up and clog the tiny hole.

(4) This luster fires on between 1100° F (595° C) to 1300° F (705° C) and was photographed on black to show the gold.

halo luster

(1) Clean your glass well and wipe with denatured alcohol. Paint on a thin coat of "halo luster" with a soft brush and do not go back over your strokes. Let it dry for just a few minutes. Here I am using halo gold luster.

(2) Dip the brush back into the halo luster and touch the previous luster surface. A dot will grow into a ring that will move outward depending on the amount of luster applied. Small drops produce small rings, larger drops make bigger rings. Play with this until you create a mottled surface. Too many drops and it will all run away; just experiment.

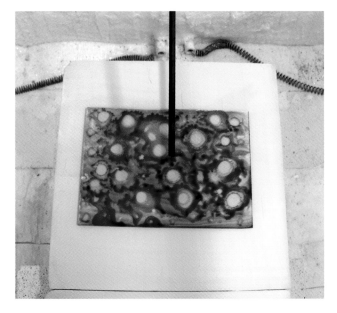

(3) The luster may be fired in a kiln at temperatures between 1100° F (595° C) to 1300° F (705° C). You can also fire luster during a slump. If the luster has not matured and become metallic or doesn't stick, fire a bit hotter. Vent the kiln slightly and the room, too, as luster gives off noxious fumes as it fires. The black temperature thermocouple is about 1 in. (2.5 cm) above the glass.

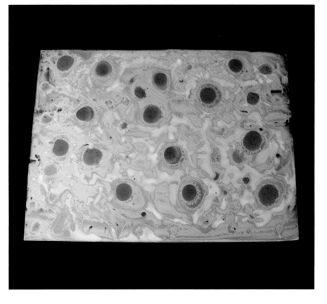

(4) Halo luster after firing, photographed on black. The gold reflects like a mirror and has a great mottled quality. Halo luster can also be applied after the glass has been fused and fired on during the final slump firing. If you fire much hotter than 1400° F (760° C), the luster will burn off and disappear.

Edris Eckhardt 1905 - 1998

Gold Glass and Lost Wax

In 1953, Edris Eckhardt, who was nationally recognized in the ceramic art world, started experimenting with glass to try to rediscover the ancient Roman technique to produce gold images sandwiched in glass, which she had seen in New York City.

Her experiments involved fusing gold between sheets of window glass, which wasn't as successful as she had hoped, so she made her own clear glass in an electric kiln and rolled out small sheets with a wet wooden rolling pin on a marble slab. Edris is believed to be the first artist to mix and melt her own glass batch in her studio in the United States. She later returned to using manufactured glass.

Her efforts produced a number of artworks with designs cut in gold and silver foil. These were sandwiched between and sometimes applied to the surface of sheets of transparent glass that were decorated with enamels and pieces of colored glass and then fused in an electric kiln. Edris usually mounted these in a frame, and sometimes they were backlit in a light box.

In 1954 she traveled to the Corning Museum of Glass in Corning, New York, where her sandwiched gold glass was pronounced to be the first successfully done since ancient Roman times. This led to two Guggenheim Fellowship awards (1956 & 1959) and a Louis Tiffany Foundation Award (1959).

While in Corning, Edris also discussed the lost wax casting of glass with Frederick Carder, the American master of this genre and a founder of Stueben Glass Works. Her ceramics background and mold making led her to create many lost wax glass sculptures, for which she is recognized today. She carved a wax model, which was cast in a mold that she devised from gypsum and clay. The wax was melted out and was replaced with powdered glass, which, upon firing, melted to fill the hollow mold. After the glass was annealed and cooled, the mold was broken away, leaving the glass sculpture.

In 1961, Edris was invited to teach for a year at the University of California in Berkeley where she introduced glass making to the art department. While there, she developed her technique for casting bronze around pieces of glass. By adding zinc, she modified the expansion rate of bronze to fit that of her glass. In 1968 the Corning Museum of Glass honored Edris Eckhardt with a retrospective show, the museum's first solo exhibition of a contemporary artist.

Edris rolled her own sheet glass with a wet rolling pin on a marble slab and made sandwiched gold glass, a technique that had been lost for 1500 years.

above: Ancient Gold Glass from the bottom of a broken vessel. Depicts Eve from the Christian Bible. Courtesy of the Corning Museum of Glass.

facing: "Mother and Child" 1973, 8 ½ in. (22 cm) H. x 4 in. (10 cm) W. x 4 in. (10 cm) D. Signed Edris 73 on the backside.

155

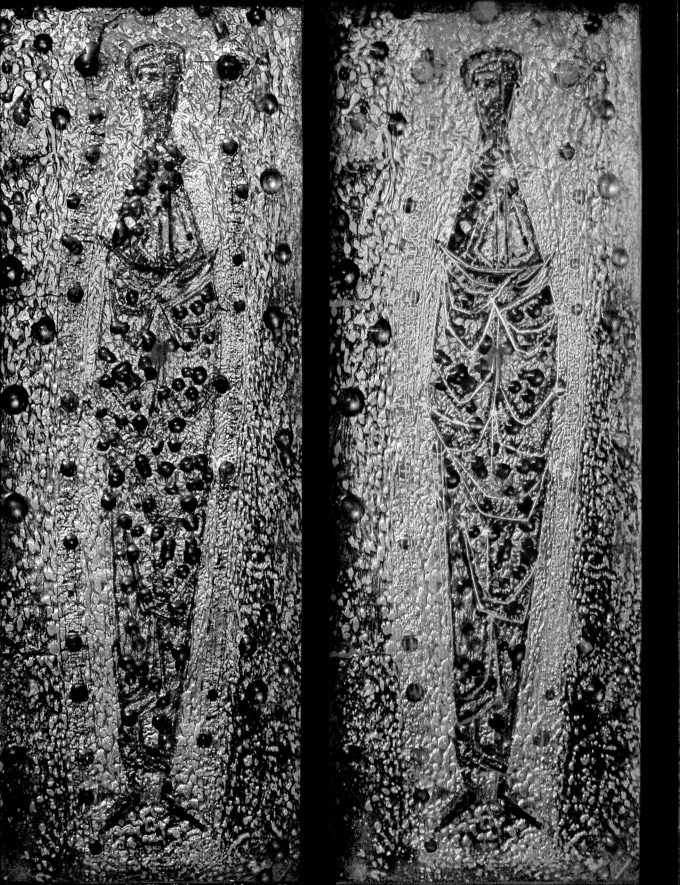

St. Elmo - gold glass light box
artist: Edris Eckhardt

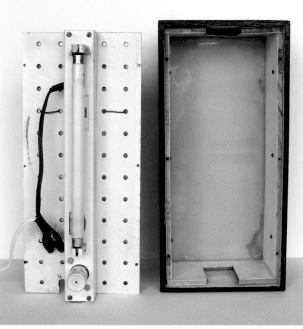

facing: The inscribed gold leaf and enamel panel, "St. Elmo," by Edris Eckhardt. The left panel is in reflected light and the right panel shows transmitted light shining through the glass, highlighting the red glass below the gold leaf surface.

above left: "St. Elmo," circa 1960, 12 ½ in. (32 cm.) H. x 6 in. (15 cm.) W. x 4 in. (10 cm.) D., gold leaf and vitreous enameled glass panel mounted in a black painted plywood lightbox, by Edris Eckhardt.

above right: The back of the light box showing holes for air flow, an exhibition sticker, and the title of the piece written on masking tape, "St. Elmo."

below left: Shows the inside of the light box. Edris glued her fused glass panel onto a piece of white plastic with what looks like a clear Epoxy. Note: she left a ½ in. (12 cm.) space around the glass panel, where light could shine around and highlight the gold surface on the front of the piece. The light also shines through the opaque plastic, clear epoxy, and glass panel; where the gold was cut away, it shows the red enamel. Edris used a fluorescent tube light that does not give off too much heat.

Precious Metal Foil - La Londe Style

I love Edris Eckhardt's gold leaf light box and decided to create my own, using fusible Bullseye glass, and to update my light box with a "Flat-light." The textural quality of her gold glass piece is wonderful, and I thought about using a single firing to achieve a similar effect; however, my interest was piqued when I read a December 1956 *Craft Horizon*'s magazine article, in which Edris describes making a gold under glass piece. I will not exactly replicate her process here, but instead create my vision using the "liquid glass line" technique, which I explain on page 193, and gold foil using two firings. Silver foil is much cheaper but harder to etch and sometimes tears. It usually turns gold when fired and is also worth trying.

(1) I open and dissolve 8 large empty gelatin capsules, used for medicine and purchased at a Health Food Store, in a ¼ cup (50 ml) of almost boiling water.

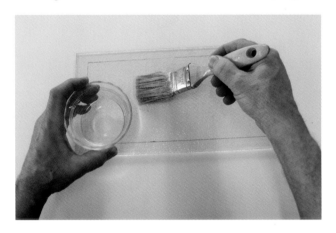

(2) I brush the gelatin sizing onto a piece of ¼ in. (6 mm) piece of clear Bullseye glass. I leave a ½ in. (12 mm) clear border for mounting in a frame.

(3) Japanese gold foil is 8 in. (20 cm) square and expensive. I cut it to size with scissors and then transfer it to the wet glass using a thin piece of cardboard.

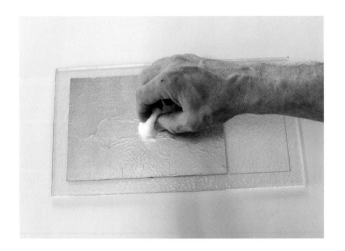

(4) I carefully press and blot out some of the water under the foil. Butt the remaining piece next to the first and stand the glass on edge to dry over night.

(5) When it is thoroughly dry, I burnish with a light circular motion with a cotton ball until it shines. I used a lot of gelatin to stick it well.

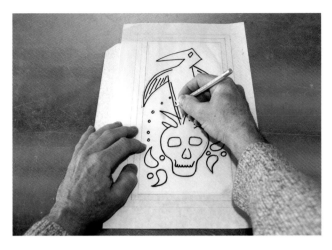

(6) I transfer my design to the foil using a piece of "old-fashion" carbon paper placed between my drawing and the foil.

(7) With a very small diamond bit in a rotary Dremel tool I cut out my design and etch lines into the foil. Wear a dust mask.

(8) Here I place black "liquid glass line," see page 193, over the etched lines to create a black outline.

(9) I use a folded piece of paper and selectively tap various transparent Bullseye powders over the remaining etched lines.

(10) I cover the powders and lines with clear Bullseye 01, a table sugar-sized frit, place it on a primered kiln shelf in my kiln and fuse to stick, about 1310° F (710° C).

(11) I flip the cooled piece over, clean the back, and the piece is ready to full fuse with the backside up, to 1500° F (816° C). See page 195 for more details.

make a "flatlight" panel

(5) I designed my glass piece to be illuminated by a custom "flatlight," which I purchased with its power source, from **www.artisticlightingsolutions.com** for about $100 (see the Materials & Suppliers List on page 237). The light emitting capacitor (LEC) looks like pink paper and is sandwiched between two pieces of plastic. It is as thin as a credit card, flexible, cool to the touch, energy efficient, and produces light when phosphor crystals are excited by an electric current. I designed my gold foil glass piece to be back-lit by this "flatlight," which I will place between a backing board and the glass. It will be held together by a metal frame only ¾ in. (9 mm) deep.

(6) I drill countersunk holes into ¾ in. (20 cm) x ¾ in. (20 cm) mitered aluminum angle that creates a frame for my piece.

bottom right: With the light off. "Rebirth," 12 in. (30 cm) x 6.5 in. (16 cm) x ¾ in. (18 cm) deep, 2009.

facing: "Rebirth" with the light on.
I think that there is a lot of potential for the "flatlight" and also fused glass with etched gold or silver foil.

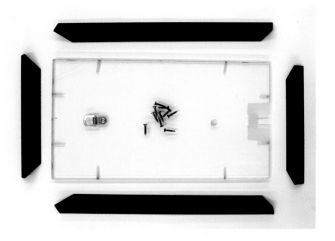

(7) Side mounting screws attach the painted black, aluminum angle and sandwich the glass panel and flat light in-between the frame and a 3/8 in. (9 mm) thick plastic backing board (plywood will also work).

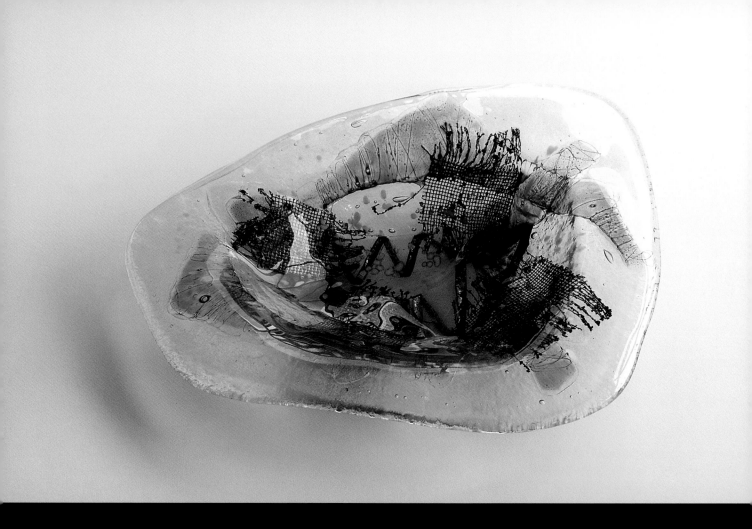

window glass & metal inclusions

The compatibility of metal and glass must be taken into account when fusing them together in-between two pieces of glass. I fuse a small test to see how things might look and to check compatibility issues using a polarizing light.

Platters that have copper fish fused in-between window glass and wall sconces seem popular in craft-art galleries today. Thin sheet copper is fusible with window glass, Bullseye 90 and Spectrum 96. After fusing it is usually a magenta color because the glass contact with the copper creates a reducing condition, producing red cuprous oxide (Cu_2O) on the surface of the copper. When copper is in an oxidation situation, such as when it is trapped within a bubble, it stays bright copper. Applying some types of clear enamels, such as Versa Color clear, can also keep it bright. Copper on the surface turns black when fired and flakes off black cupric oxide (CuO).

Many types of metal can be fused in-between glass, especially when in small amounts and thin, including bronze screen, aluminum screen, aluminum foil, brass, copper, stainless steel wire, nonferrous drill bit shavings, metal dust, steel wire (if not too thick-about 26 gauge or less), and Kanthol element wire. Steel nails fused in glass produce a severe halo under polarizing light and can crack the glass, so I don't use steel. Though non-metallic, you might want to experiment with fiber glass matt and screen. Try other metal products and see what you come up with. Precious metal leaf and foil, such as silver and gold, can also be quite effective when fused on the surface or in-between clear glass. You can put many things into a kiln, but do not heat any material that will give off poisonous fumes or explode!

One of the things that is bothersome when fusing metal between two pieces of glass is trapping air bubbles. You can use small 3/16 in. (1.5 mm), chips of glass on the outside clear corners of your piece. The idea is that the center of the piece will melt down first and as it fuses the air gets pushed out. If you fuse a metal washer with a hole in the center, then expect to trap an air bubble. Design your work so there is a channel for the air to get to the outside edge.

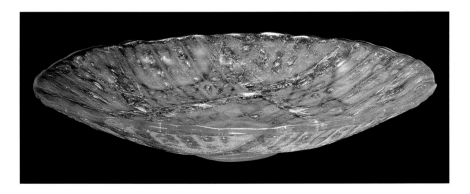

You can become an alchemist creating magic when fusing glass with metals, and you never really know how it will turn out.

You can put many things into a kiln, but do not heat any material that will give off poisonous fumes or explode!

facing upper:
"Bowl with Metal Inclusions" 1970s, 1 ½ in. (4 cm) deep x 9 ½ in. (24 cm) x 7 in. (18 cm), signed WaLᴛer.

This piece contains yellow enameled pieces of thin window glass wrapped with strips of sheet copper; very fine steel wire has also been wrapped around transparent blue enameled pieces of window glass. Also contains metal screen, turquoise frit, and white enamel.

facing lower:
"Erector Set Bowl" by June Fitzpatrick - 10 in. (25 cm) H. x 17 in. (43 cm) x 19 in. (48 cm), 2008.

below:
"Zoe" by Roger Nachman, 1988, 3 in. (8 cm) H. x 18 in. (46 cm) in diameter. Fused window glass with gold and copper leaf. The copper turns into turquoise-colored bubbles when fully fused between glass sheets. Slumped in a second firing.

163

mixed metal fused glass

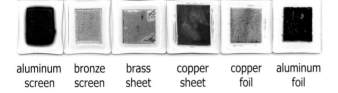

aluminum screen   bronze screen   brass sheet   copper sheet   copper foil   aluminum foil

(1) You can fuse various materials in a kiln as long as they do not give off poisonous fumes or explode. For this project I use black painted aluminum screen and bronze screen, heavy duty aluminum foil, and thin sheet brass and copper. I fuse test pieces to see how the metals react and to check them with polarizing light for compatibility.

(2) Use scissors to cut the metal and screen, and simple pattern punches work well on the thin sheet metals.

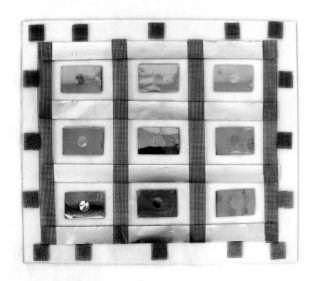

(3) I laid out a geometric pattern on a sheet of "double strength" ⅛ in. (3 mm) clear window glass. I placed small brass circles onto the copper pieces and copper circles onto brass. I hope that this produces an interesting effect. Some air bubbles will be trapped and add to the textural quality of this piece.

(4) Lay a piece of "prefired" ⅛ in. (3 mm) fiber paper onto a kiln-washed shelf and sift a dry layer of alumina hydrate, the releasing agent in shelf primer, onto the fiber paper. You can brush a texture into the powder; this gives a lined and rough texture to the back of the fused glass. Texturing transparent glass moves the light around and creates interest.

164

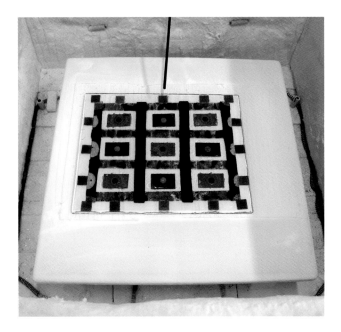

(5) Place the bottom sheet of glass, with the metal (figure 3) onto a textured kiln shelf. Check the top piece of ⅛ in. (3 mm) window glass for the tin side which shows milky white under a short wave UV (Ultra Violet) light. Clean the glass, handling by the edges, place the non-tin side down against the metal pattern, and fire this in a kiln to full fuse.

(6) The full fused piece in my fiber kiln. You can use an overglaze such as Fuse Master "Super Spray" (no lead) or Hotline "Spray A" (contains lead) to prevent devitrification.

(7) "Mixed Metals Bowl," 2008, 13 ½ in. (35 cm) x 11 in. (28 cm) x 3 in. (7.5 cm) deep.

making a welded stainless steel slumping mold

(1) Making a 4 in. (10 cm) wide cardboard pattern the same size as the stainless steel. Cut a 45° angle on four pieces of wood to hold this pattern and then draw the mitered angle with a felt pen. With a protractor this angle measures at 54°.

(2) This cardboard model is 6 in. (15 cm) x 9 in. (23 cm) at the bottom and 11 ½ in. (29 cm) x 14 ½ in. (37 cm) at the rim. I plan to slump a piece of glass 11 in. (28 cm) x 14 in. (35 cm) and after it is shaped the glass will have a 2 ½ in. (6 cm) wall height.

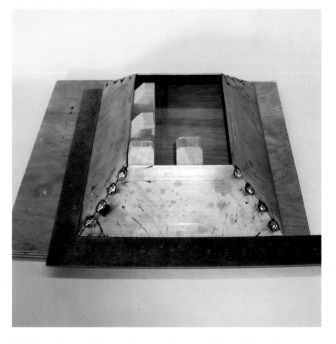

(3) Cutting the 4 in. (10 cm) wide x ⅛ in. (3 mm) thick stainless steel flat bar at a 54° angle, the same size as the cardboard pattern, with a metal cutting band saw. You can also use an abrasive cutoff saw or have it cut in a metal shop. Stainless steel is a very hard metal.

(4) The four 45° angle cut pieces of wood position the metal and a metal square keeps them at a right angle. Weld the corners using 4 spots of weld per seam. This way it does not warp the metal.

166

(5) Heat the mold in a kiln to 300° F (150° C) and place it on wooden slats, outdoors. Wear a dust mask and use an inexpensive Badger brand airbrush to spray shelf primer onto the stainless steel mold. Reheat and apply enough primer to cover the metal. Usually, I can slump a few times before reapplying more primer.

(6) Here is my mixed metals project sitting in the mold, in my kiln. I place the mold on a shelf- primered mullite kiln shelf, which sits on four kiln bricks. My fiber kiln has top and bottom elements. The small black line at the middle of the upper edge of the photo is the tip of my thermocouple. I like it close to my work to get a good reading.

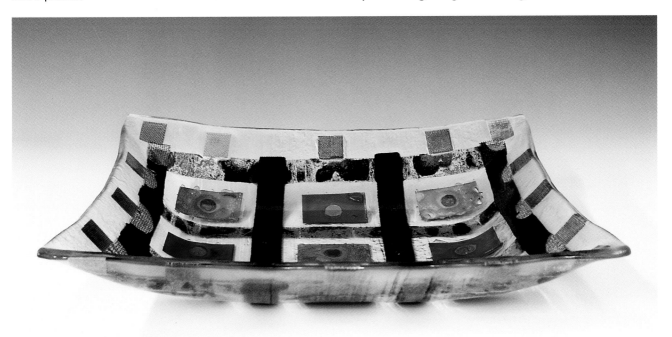

Part: 5 Other Techniques

John Luebtow b. 1944

Enormous Slumped Glass Sculpture

I first met John at the 1992 Glass Arts Society conference in Mexico City where we were both speaking on a panel about kilns. I proudly showed pictures of my 4 ft. (1.25 m.) x 4 ft. (1.25 m.) electric kiln and then ... John came to the podium. His 14 ft. (4.25 m.) x 10 ft. (3 m.) gas fired kiln, which he lifts open with a fork lift, blew me away. I had no idea that anyone was working that big, and he built his first big kiln back in 1976. His kiln is a metal box that is lined with 5 inches of high temperature fiber insulation and sits on fire bricks on the ground.

Disenchanted after three years of engineering studies at UCLA, John changed directions and graduated in 1969 with an MA in ceramics. He found a great first job, working for Koninklijke Porceleyne Fles, one of the oldest earthenware factories in Holland, and soon became the director of their Architectural Ceramics Department. Here John discovered glass through a collaboration with Leerdam Glass in Amsterdam. The glass bug bit, and as they say, "The rest is history."

John puts it this way, "In 1971 I returned to Los Angeles, divorced, got custody of my son, a teaching position, a studio space, and an MFA in glass from UCLA; that began focusing on what would become the dominant medium and artistic concerns of my work …glass and line."

Since then, John has completed over 100 commissions for corporate collections, public buildings, and a few private residences, located throughout the United States and also in Japan and Australia. Since 1971 he has been an art instructor and has inspired students at the Harvard-Westlake School in North Hollywood, California.

below: "Linear Fountain" glass, 7 ft. (2 m.) x 45 ft. (13.75 m.) x 5 ft. (1.5 m.) with a 12 ft. (3.5 m.) x 12 ft. (3.5 m.) reflecting pool, 100 First St (at Mission) in San Francisco, California, 1 in. (2.5 cm) glass, granite, water, and stainless steel.

www. luebtow.com

"John's gas fired kiln is just a big box sitting on the ground, but he opens it with a fork lift and that just blows me away!"

—R. La Londe

facing left:
"Sapientia" 1990, 15 ft. (4.5 m.) x 15 ft. (4.5 m.) x 3 in. (7.5 cm) deep, Nestles' Corporation Building, Glendale, California. Kiln-formed 1 in. thick glass, sandblasted, welded & polished stainless steel.

facing upper right:
LF-13-97/10, glass, steel, 90 in. (230 cm) x 8 in. (20 cm) x 5 in. (12.5 cm), private residence, Los Angles, California, plasma cut galvanized steel I-beam, 1 in. thick, kiln formed & sandblasted glass.

facing bottom right:
"Synchronicity," 25 ft. (7.6 m.) x 4 ft. (1.25 m.) in diameter, Sheraton Bal Harbor Resort, Bal Harbor, Florida, 1 in. (2.5 cm) glass, granite, water, and polished stainless steel.

above: John inside his kiln which is 5 ft. (1.5 m.) H. x 14 ft. (4.25 m.) W. x 10 ft. (3 m.) deep. This kiln is gas fired with burners located outside and at the top right-hand side of the kiln - the hot injected air heats the kiln. This kiln is lifted open with a forklift and supported by safety bars when open.

bottom left: John and a friend loading 1 in. (2.5 cm) thick plate glass into the kiln. Note the back support belts and that they are wearing dust masks to protect against airborne ceramic fibers.

bottom right: John inspecting his slumped glass.

170

above left: Shows the slumped 1 in. (2.5 cm) plate glass laying on thin fiber paper which has been placed over large steel pipes to create a wave form.

below: The "Ventus Vitae" fountain mocked up in John's large studio. This piece is 55 ft. (17 m.) long and is supported by fabricated stainless steel gussets which can be seen at the bottom, perpendicular to the glass pieces. When the sandblasted pattern is viewed through two of the glass pieces it create a moire effect of moving lines.

above right: John sandblasts a linear pattern into the glass. He is shown inside his large sandblast booth, using an industrial pressure pot and aluminum oxide grit. He is wearing a hood with face shield that supplies outside air.

Day and Night Views of the "Ventus Vitae" (Winds of Life) Fountain by John Luebtow, 2008, 11 ft. 6 in. (3.5 m.) H. x 55 ft. (17 m.) W. x 15 ft. (4.5 m.) deep. Located at Held Properties, 1880 Century Park East, Century City, California, 1 in. (2.5 cm) glass, concrete, water, and polished stainless steel.

This fountain project began February 2007 with a competition that included drawings and a model. John won the competition and was awarded the commission. He fabricated the fountain, directed the site concrete work, and installed it May, 2008.

Michael Dupille b. 1955

Michael Dupille's introduction to glass began in the early 1970s at Central Washington State College's glassblowing program. After school, Michael launched his career with surrealistic watercolors and acrylics; he also designed for the textile industry. Wanting to visit Nepal in 1988, Michael pre-sold enough paintings to sponsor his trip to the base camp of Mt. Everest.

I met Michael in 1978 while exhibiting at an outdoor craft show. The adjacent space remained empty until ten minutes before the show opened. Along came this guy with a few cardboard boxes and a folding table; it was Michael. He proceeded to sell two thousand dollars worth of tee shirts before he ran out, folded his table, and left by early afternoon. I liked his style, and Michael and I became friends.

Michael again caught the glass bug, designing T shirts and print ads for Bullseye 1981 - 1985, and spent part of his summers at Camp Colton, where kiln-glass was taught from 1986 - 1993. Boyce Lundstrom, one of the founders of Bullseye Glass Company, had purchased the old Oregon summer camp, and Michael went there to learn, experiment, and teach. During this time, Boyce was writing Books II & III about kiln-glass, and Michael's creative input is featured throughout.

In the early 1990s, Michael's artistic and technical experimentation led him to create what he calls "Fritography." He also developed new techniques for kiln casting frit into a mold material that he invented - called "Castalot." In 2000, Michael and I collaborated on a series of technically challenging glass murals. These large fused frit murals are located outdoors, on a South facing brick wall, for the Pierce County/City Courthouse in Tacoma, Washington.

Michael, always up for a challenge, spent months to develop the technology to kiln cast borosilicate into large hollow supports for granite benches. These are lit from the interior with colored light and are part of the 911 renovation in New York City. Dupille's public commissions also include projects for the The Field Museum in Chicago, Illinois; The Washington State Arts Commission; Oregon State Arts Commission; Amazon.com; and the Seattle Mariners Baseball Organization.

I love to visit Michael at his West Seattle workshop, which is chock full of experiments and art pieces. When he is not on the road teaching, Michael Dupille is constantly turning his dreams into glass realities.

Michael teaches workshops around the county, and both his demonstration video, *"Beginning Fritography,"* and also his **"Castalot"** mold mix are available on his website at **www.michaeldupille.com.**

Michael is known as Mr. Frit.
michaeldupille.com

facing: "Rain Delay" 1997, 36 in. (90 cm) H. x 24 in. (60 cm) W. x 5 in. (13 cm) D., manipulated fused glass & cast glass figures.

bottom: "Michael with his New York City Bench Supports" 2005, 12 in. (30 cm) H. x 24 in. (60 cm) L. x 16 in. (40 cm) W., 1 in. (2.5 cm) thick. The kiln cast borosilicate, hollow bench supports are illuminated and the colors can be changed with the season. Created for the NYC Parks Dept.

above left: "Summer Triangle" 2005, 20 in. (30 cm) H. x 18 in. (45 cm) W. x 14 in. (35 cm) D., kiln formed glass, cast glass, on a steel base.

below: "A Parliament" 2008, 15 in. (38 cm) H. x 25 in. (64 cm) W., one of the pieces in Dupille's "Animal Grouping Series."

above right: "Sea Turtle Detail," 2008 The size of the sea turtle is: 18 in. (45 cm) H. x 36 in. (90 cm) W. x 3 in. (7.5 cm) D., cast glass with frit detailing. The turtle and fish are glued to a 32 ft. (10 m.) tall transparent cast glass, sculptural feature installed in a circular stairway on a custom yacht. This project was a collaboration with GlassStudio, Seattle, WA.

"Castalot" shell mold with Michael Dupille

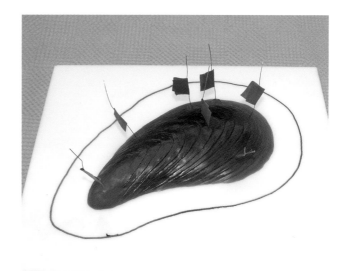

(1) Simple tools are used for mixing Michael Dupille's "Castalot" mold mix. Michale spent years experimenting with various mold mixtures to develop a light-weight, open-face mold mix that would hold up to repeatable firings. His efforts produced "Castalot" mold mix.

(2) A polyurethane mussel shell is attached with silicone sealant to a piece of ¼ in. (6 mm) Plexiglass. A clay or plasticine model also works. Vent hole wires are placed into the model - tape ¾ in. (2 cm) from the model acts as a thickness guide for the mold mix. Vegetable oil (PAM) is sprayed on a paint brush and brushed onto the model and plastic base.

(3) Add 1 part water first and then 2 parts "Castalot" mold mix to the water. Wear a good dust mask or respirator when handling the dry mixture.

(4) Mix thoroughly for 90 seconds mashing the major lumps. "Castalot" has a working time of 7 - 8 minutes, so have your model all set up, and brushed with vegetable oil (PAM) ahead of time. Pour immediately.

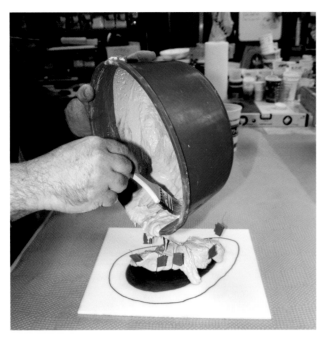

(5) At this point, the mixed material should have the consistency of a milkshake. To create a shell mold, the mixed "Castalot" is poured onto the mussel shell model. A soft bristle brush is first used to spread the mix all over the model.

(6) The "Castalot" is spread around the model to the bottom of the tape guides. If it slides down the model, wait a minute, and it will thicken becoming easier to spread into place. A soft rubber spatula finishes the job – just like icing a cake. When done, clean your tools in water, in a bucket. Do not pour any "Castalot" down your sink drain; it will plug it up.

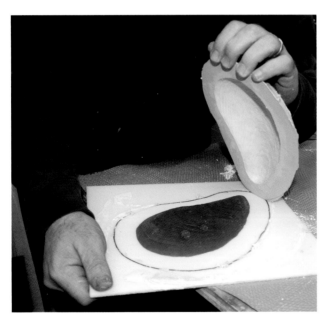

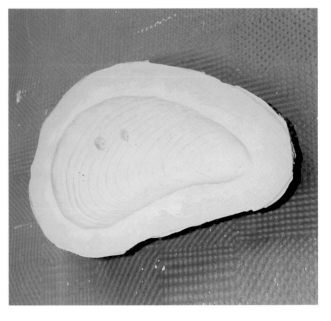

(7) After the mold has set hard, about 30 - 40 minutes, then the vent wires are removed with a pair of pliers. To de-mold, place the plastic over the edge of a table, and pull down slightly while lifting up on the mold. If there are no major undercuts in your model, it should pop loose easily.

(8) The finished mold is then pre-fired, 30 minutes to 190° F (88° C) and held there for 2 hours. This removes excess water as steam. Then fire at 275° F (150° C) per hour to a temperature 50° F (10° C) above your highest firing temperature. Turn off your kiln and cool the mold naturally. For larger molds, fire slower. Coat the mold thinly with shelf primer.

178

(9) A pre-fused shape of a mussel shell has been created by Michael fusing compatible frit onto an ⅛ in. (3 mm) piece of compatible glass. Remember to reverse your pattern if you want the fused surface against the mold.

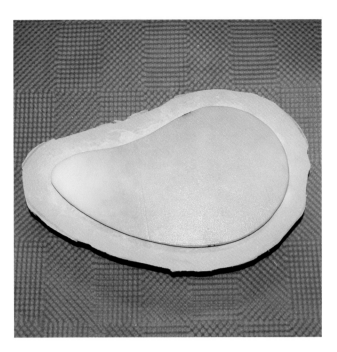

(10) The glass is flipped up-side-down and positioned over the mold. The mold is set on an ⅛ in. (3 mm) piece of pre-fired fiber paper laid on a kiln shelf and propped with pieces of soft fire brick. The fiber paper allows the bottom vent holes to breathe.

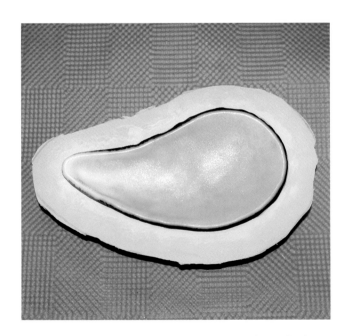

(11) The glass has slumped into the mold at a high enough temperature to pick up the mold detail, which for this project was to 1425° F (775° C), and held for 10 minutes.

(12) The finished glass mussel. You can see two barnacles on the shell, which were prefused and placed into the indentations in the "Castalot" mold. They fused to stick during the slump fire. This piece is about 8 in. (20 cm) long.

"Castalot" box mold with Michael Dupille

(1) Michael modeled the image of a candle with "plasticine" - plastic clay - which is secured to a brown piece of ¼ in. (6 mm) Plexiglass plastic. He built and screwed together a wooden form, which is secured to the plastic with plasticine pressed around the mold to keep the casting mix from leaking out.

2) The tools for mixing "Castalot" mold mix. Note that Michael uses a drill motor that can be plugged in. You do not want to run out of battery power half way through the mixing process. One bucket is filled with water, and the other bucket is for mixing.

(3) Michael eyeballs the amount of mix that he needs to fill his mold and adds water to the mixing bucket. He then dumps in the "Castalot" at a ratio of 2 parts water to 1 part "Castalot."

(4) Michael mixes the "Castalot" with a simple paint mixer by moving the drill around. The mix should be the consistency of thick pancake batter and might be slightly lumpy.

(5) Michael immediately pours the mixed "Castalot" into his box mold. The plasticine candle has a few wires stuck into it where the thickest parts of the casting will be - for vent holes. The "Castalot" is about 2 in. (5 cm) thicker than the highest part of the mold.

(6) The mold is agitated by shaking. This moves the "Castalot" in and around the plasticine model removing air bubbles. Pop the bubbles that rise to the surface with your finger and continue agitating until you get rid of most of the bubbles. The mix sets up fairly quickly in about 10 minutes.

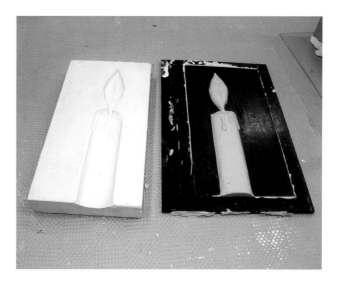

(7) After about 30 - 40 minutes the mold will have set hard, and then the vent wires are pulled out with a pair of pliers. Remove the forms: using a drill, take out the screws and pull the wooden sides away. Round the edges - "chamfer" with a scraper.

(8) To de-mold, place the plastic over the edge of a table, pull down slightly while lifting up on the mold. Pre-fire the mold, 30 minutes to 190° F (88° C), and hold there for 2 hours. This removes excess water as steam. Then fire at 275° F (150° C) per hour, to a temperature 50° F (10° C) above your highest firing temperature. Turn off your kiln and cool the mold naturally. With a larger mold, go slower.

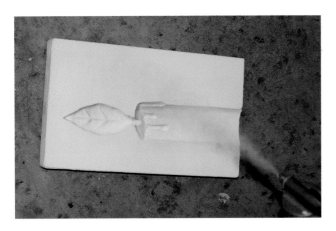

(9) This mold has been prefired to 1510° F (820° C). Shelf primer is airbrushed into the mold and also on the kiln shelf dams that go around the mold.

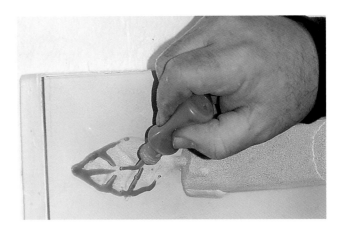

(10) A piece of clear ⅛ in. (3 mm) fusible glass is cut the exact size of the mold and laid on the mold. Liquid glass (CMC and frit) details are applied.

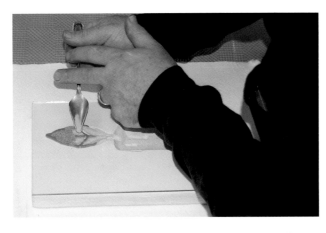

(11) Frit is placed within the squirt glass lines with a tapered spoon. Note: the mold is sitting on a piece of pre-fired, ⅛ in. (3 mm) fiber paper on a kiln shelf.

(12) A dam surrounds the mold, and the rest of the colored frit that makes up the design is placed using the tapered spoon or a folded piece of paper.

(13) A very thin layer of clear 01 fine frit is sifted over the piece. This cushions the clear 02 medium sized frit that is poured to about ¼ in. (6 mm) and built up thicker over the relief areas - the candle cutout.

(14) Firing schedule:
4 hours to 1100° F (595° C), soak 45 minutes.
1 ½ hours to 1475° F (800° C), soak 25 minutes.
Cool to 960° F (515° C), anneal soak 2 hours.
Cool down to room temperature, 8 hours.

carved "Castalot" slab mold with Michael Dupille

(1) "Castalot" has been poured into a wooden mold, sealed to a piece of ¼ in. (6 mm) Plexiglass with plasticine. With a long needle pierce the mix all over when it starts to set to create many small vent holes.

(3) A design is drawn and carved in the damp "Castalot" slab. After carving, the mold is prefired to 1510° F (820° C), as described in the previous section, and coated with shelf primer.

(5) The glass is fired to 1460° F (820° C) where it is held for 30 minutes. After cooling, the glass is removed with a suction cup. The mold is ready to be primered and reloaded with glass.

(2) Unscrew and remove the mold after it has set, about 1 hour.

(4) The carved slab is set on a piece of pre-fired ⅛ in. (3 mm) fiber paper on a kiln shelf with dams that are held with stainless steel clamps. A piece of clear ¼ in. (6 mm) fusible glass is placed in the mold, and then ½ in. (12 mm) pieces of clear glass are added.

(6) The finished ½ in. (12 mm) thick piece shows an almost glossy surface with very fine detail. "Castalot" molds with very little or no undercuts can be re-used many times. Use the same firing schedule as the candle piece.

"Colour de Verre"
Craig Smith, Jayne Persico & Larry Jacobsen

"Colour de Verre" Molds

Craig Smith, a classically trained ceramist turned glass artist, and Jayne Persico, a glass artist and instructor, along with Larry Jacobsen are the founders of "Colour de Verre." They develop, design, and market a line of high quality, open-faced, reusable ceramic molds and accessories for frit casting and "pâtte de verre." Their company is located in an old Victorian house in Portland, Oregon, and their warehouse is in a nearby industrial area. They work with local craft and art potteries to make their molds and pride themselves in producing their products locally, but distributing their products throughout the world.

I first encountered "Colour de Verre" at the Technical Display during the 2008 Glass Art Society conference in Portland, Oregon. At first glance, I thought they were only for the "craft-hobbyist," but after talking to Larry, and really looking at what they were doing, I realized that their molds had real potential for professional glass artists.

I was amazed that with these molds it is possible to fuse very delicate objects such as life-sized pine needles; with their Egyptian mold one can fuse tiny glass ankhs so light that they can be used for earrings. Glass fusers can add dimensional components to their artwork, and even children can enjoy making simple projects with these easy to use molds. My 11-year old son loved making the Egyptian scarabs.

colourdeverre.com

Craig Smith b. 1954 (left)
Jayne Persico (center)
Larry Jacobsen b. 1956 (right)

facing: "Cherry Blossom Lamp" 2007, 11 in. (28 cm), molds and lamp designed and made by artist Craig Smith, blossoms, branches, leaves and bees, fused in "Colour de Verre" molds and then dimensionally fused onto sheet glass covered with frit, then slumped. The lamp was assembled with components Colour de Verre design and sells.

below left: "Summer Floral Plates" 2007, 9 in. (23 cm) across, "pâte de verre" pieces created by artist Jayne Persico using "Colour de Verre" molds.

below right: "Scarabs & Ankhs," largest scarab 1 ½ in. (6 cm) mold designed by Craig Smith.

"Colour de Verre" pine cone lamp designed & demonstrated by Craig Smith

(1) The mold is coated with "Hotline Primo Primer™," filled with colored frit, and topped with clear frit. For COE 96 glass, fire 300° F (165° C)/hour to 1325-1350° F (715-730° C). For COE 90, add 25° F (15° C).

(2) Fused branches. Check www.colourdeverre.com for the exact weight of frit to add and firing schedules. Weigh frit with an inexpensive digital scale.

(3) Mold, fused glass, needles, and pine cones.

(4) Branches, needles, and cones laid out.

(5) Here, the dimensional branch, along with a border strip, is stuck to a sheet of ripple glass with glue. For COE 96, fire slowly to 1260° F (680° C); add 25° F (15° C) for COE 90. Anneal well and cool slowly.

(6) The dimensionally fused panel is slumped over a "Colour de Verre," 10 in. (25 cm) ceramic, oval panel former. Again, don't rush your firing, and glass that is both thick and thin needs extra annealing.

(7) A second piece of glass, with or without more branches and cones, is slumped to make the 2-piece lamp. "Colour de Verre" sells the lamp parts kit used.

(8) Attaching the electrical cord and finishing the lamp.

(9) "Pine Cone" lamp, 2007, 11 in. (28 cm) H. designed and made by Craig Smith using "Colour de Verre" molds and lamp parts.

Roger Nachman b. 1953

Crystal Clear Adhesive

Roger Nachman, a graduate of University of Colorado, was so artistically inspired while attending school in Japan his Junior year that he moved back to Kyoto in 1975, and lived an artist's life for 8 years. Roger blew glass and created stained glass commissions, which include an 8 ft. (2.5 m.) x 24 ft. (7 m.) stained glass mural for the Okuzawa Health Sciences building in Kameoka, Japan. In 1983, Nachman co-founded the Miasa Glass Program, a creative Glass Arts Workshop in the Japan Alps, that became a vital part of the Japanese Studio Glass Movement. Roger exhibited in solo gallery shows in Japan and the U.S. and has taught workshops around the country and abroad.

During 1985, Roger returned to the U.S. and helped set up a group studio in Seattle, Washington. He became friends with one of the studio artists, Richard La Londe, whom he commissioned to build what was at the time a large 22 in. (56 cm) x 44 in. (112 cm) bell kiln. With this, he created kiln-formed, copper leaf and gold leaf dinnerware and subsequently his series of large scale "beetle" wall sculptures.

In 2004, Roger purchased an old industrial building in Seattle and added a 4 ft. (1.5 m.) x 6 ft. (2 m.) kiln. Currently, he specializes in "Art for Architecture," creating glass commissions for the home and public environments. His art is installed in colleges, public schools, health care facilities, the Washington State Patrol Crime Lab, and Seattle Children's Hospital. Roger Nachman's sculptural glass room divider, "Stand In Light," 12 ft. (3.5 m.) x 18 ft. (5.5 m.) can be seen in the lobby of the Elliott Grand Hyatt Hotel in Seattle.

nachmanglass.com

facing upper left: "Ocean Bottom" 2007, 5 ft. (1.5 m.) H. x 4 ft. (1.25 m.) W. fused glass glued to tempered/laminate - two pieces of ¼ in. (6 mm) tempered glass that were laminated together. The back sheet was shattered and coated with crystal clear polyurethane to maintain glass integrity. Light is diffracted by the multitude of broken pieces, making the artwork dance.

facing upper right: Detail from a series of over 300 fused glass panels for patients' rooms in the Pediatric ICU, Children's Hospital, Seattle, WA. 1999.

facing lower: This series represents three sets of 4 vertical windows between the Biology Labs in the new Life Sciences Building of Foothill College, Los Altos, CA. 2007.

lower left: Detail, "Bee on Echinacea Flower."

lower right: Detail, Panel between Marine Biology and Anatomy/Physiology Labs.

left: "Seaweed Wall", 2007, 7 ft. (2 m.) H. x 8 ft. (2.4 m.) W. Children's Hospital, Norfolk, Virginia, fused glass panels glued to ½ in. (12 mm) tempered plate glass.

crystal clear adhesive - Roger Nachman

(1) Tools for gluing which include - Loctite E-05CL Crystal Clear Epoxy, low tack tape, glass cleaner, razor blades, and plastic glue spreader.

(2) Roger's fused and kiln cast pieces are laid out on the tempered ½ in. (12 mm) window glass strips that they will be glued to.

(3) The clear glass panels are laid onto the original pattern, and the fused and cast elements are outlined with a washable marking pen.

(4) Low tack tape is laid over the lines, the fused elements are traced again, the tape is cut with a razor knife and removed where the glass will be glued.

(5) Barrier cream is rubbed onto hands. Epoxy adhesive is sticky, can be absorbed through the skin, and is toxic. <u>Work in a well ventilated room as the fumes are also poisonous. Wear safety glasses!</u>

(6) The two part Loctite E-05CL, 5 minute set Epoxy, is mixed in the special nozzle of the glue gun, and a dollop about ½ the area is squeezed out and spread with the plastic spreader.

(7) The glass surface needs to be level! The fused element is placed, the self-leveling Epoxy is squeezed out, and a razor blade scrapes the excess glue away. Tape the glass in place to keep it from moving. When the glue has set, the tape is removed.

(8) Detail of the kiln cast apricots and fused leaves, glued to the ½ in. (12 mm) tempered glass panels.

"Orchard" 2008, 10 ft. 6 in. (3.2 m.) H. x 6 ft. (1.8 m.) W. mounted floor to ceiling, Foothill College, Los Altos, California.

"Dreamer Awaken"
Richard L. Smith
1994

Part 6: More Fused Glass
liquid glass line

In 1993 I developed this technique in order to create an outline that could be filled in with colored frit. Many years later, I realized that this is similar to the wire and enamel technique used for cloisonné.

Make the Liquid Glass Goop

To get started, go to a ceramic supply place, such as Seattle Pottery Supply, and purchase a one-pound bag of CMC (carboxy methyl cellulose). This product is used for ceramics and also as a food additive (check the ingredients list for tortillas).

Boil water and then pour one pint of the hot water into a heat proof container. Add five heaping tablespoons of powdered CMC and stir for about thirty seconds. You will have to experiment with the amount of CMC because it differs between manufacturers and comes as either granules or flakes. Mash the lumps, but don't worry about those chunks that don't seem to want to break down. After the mixture cools and sits, say overnight, it will be a clear gel; the chunks should have dissolved. As with a good cup of coffee, I prefer to make it thicker rather than thinner. You can always thin it with water, but you can't make it thicker; if it's too thin, start over.

To create the "liquid glass," I mix a ratio of about ⅓ CMC goop to ⅔ glass powder (I use 08 Bullseye powder) in a squeeze bottle. Experiment with this ratio to get the right proportions until you can lay a nice even round line onto a piece of glass. A mixture that is too thin will flow and spread out. A mixture too thick will be too hard to squeeze through the nozzle. You can achieve some nice effects by spreading this mixture with a pallet knife or smearing it with a paintbrush. Fusing the line to stick will produce a dimensional line, and, of course, full fuse will make it flat. Either way, the CMC burns off clean.

Liquid Glass Line Tool Kit

(1) **squeeze bottle** - a bottle over 3 in. is too hard to squeeze.
(2) **stir rod with handle** - use a round shaft Phillips screwdriver.
(3) **small paint brush** - sharpen the end and use it to push the line around.
(4) **flat bottomed spoon** - used for tamping the frit down.
(5) **straightened paper clip** - use to clean out the nozzle.
(6) **folded card** - tape one end closed and use for applying frit.
(7) **razor blade** - use to cut and remove the liquid glass line.
(8) **ultra fine Sharpie marker** - use for drawing on the glass; it burns off in the firing.
(9) **paper towels** - use for cleaning the liquid glass off of the stir rod.
(10) **CMC goop -** for mixing with fine glass powder.
(11) **glass powder** - I use size 08 or finer.

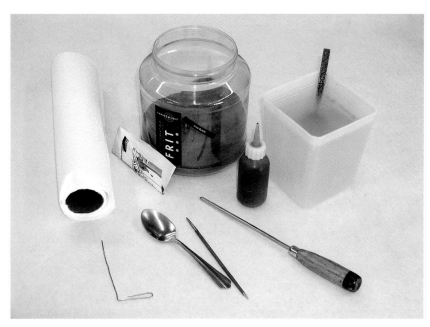

facing:
"Dreamer Awaken," 1994, 41 in. (104 cm) H. x 26 in. (66 cm) W., fused glass with the liquid glass line, dichroic glass, silver and gold leaf, artist Richard La Londe.

(1) Drizzle about $^1/_3$ CMC goop to $^2/_3$ glass powder (size 08) into the squirt bottle and mix with a stir rod. Wrap a piece of paper towel around the bottle neck and withdraw the rod. This keeps the liquid glass in the squirt bottle. Some people premix in a jar and then put it into the bottle or a small pastry bag. You will have to restir occasionally as the powder will separate with time.

(2) Working in reverse, place ¼ in. (6 mm) glass on your drawing that has been flipped over. Squeeze and touch the liquid glass to the clear sheet, lift up ½ in. and let the glass line drop into place. It should flow easily but not expand sideways. If this occurs, add more glass powder and restir. The clear glass is ¼ in. (6 mm) thick to prevent the huge bubbles discussed in the volume control section.

(3) I mix 50/50 size 01 fine frit with 08 powder, which makes a mixture that flows easily from the tapper. I take a folded piece of postcard about 1 ½ in. (4 cm) H. x 4 in. (10 cm) long and tape one end closed. I place the frit mix into it with a spoon and tap with my finger allowing a controlled and steady flow of glass powder.

(4) I clean up the spillover with a vacuum pen. I describe how to make this in the equipment section.

194

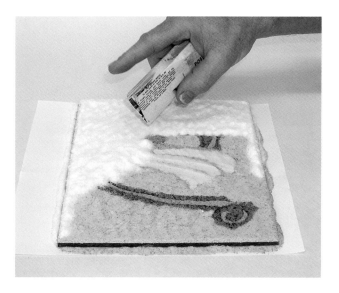

(5) I tap the frit down with the back of a spoon. You must apply at least ⅛ in. (3 mm) of frit (as it is about 50% air and fluffed up), so that after it full fuses it is about ⅛ in. (1.5 mm) thick. Crushed glass frit is much less dense in color than glass enamels and it takes more volume to cover an area. Place the light and transparent colors last.

(6) I cover all of the previously applied frit with a 50/50 mix (size 01 & 08) of white frit for a wall piece or clear for a bowl. This layer keeps all the different colors from pulling up and leaving exposed areas as I discussed in the section about volume control. Tap it all down flat with the back of a spoon. I fuse the frit so it sticks to the glass but does not full fuse, about 1310° F to 1380° F, depending on your kiln.

(7) After the first firing I take the piece out of the kiln, flip it over, and clean the surface with glass cleaner and a rag. In the past I sandblasted this surface, but now I just apply a very thin layer of "Spray A" with a foam brush, which takes care of any extraneous junk picked up from the first firing. The "Spray A" should be applied thin enough to see through. Put the piece back into the kiln and full fuse the glass to 1500° F - 1550° F.

(First Firing) fused to stick
225° F (130° C) /hr. to 1100° F (593° C).
800° F (448° C) /hr. to 1310° F (710° C) 1 min.
ASAP to 960° F (516° C) 1 hr. soak.
The kiln cools on its own.

(8) The finished tile after firing to a full fuse. There will probably be a clear line around the tile because the volume is a bit thicker than the magic ¼ in. (6 mm). This can be prevented by placing a dam made from a sawed mullite kiln shelf around the tile and then grinding and polishing the edge.

(Second Firing) full fused
225° F (130° C) /hr. to 1100° F (593° C).
800° F (448° C) /hr. to 1500° F (816° C) 3 min. ASAP to 960° F (516° C).
The kiln cools on its own.

artist's gallery - liquid glass line

I asked artists who had tried the "liquid glass line" to send me photos, and from among the responses I chose 12. It is interesting to see how they interpret this technique. Some people used it as the "flip technique," described on the previous page that I reprinted from my first book. Others used the line and covered it with clear frit, and still others used it on the top surface. I am pleased to learn that it has traveled world-wide.

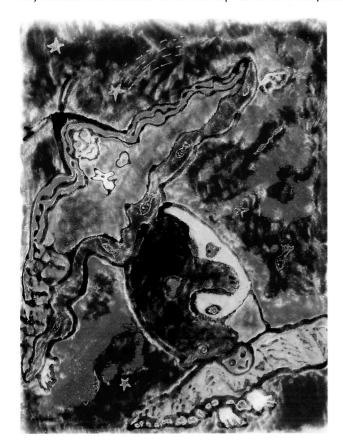

facing page:
Alex Sutton (Washington) "Vajrapani"
21 in. (53 cm) x 16 in. (40 cm) 2008.

above:
Martha Saly (California) "Blaze"
8 in. (20 cm) x 10 in. (25 cm) 2008.

left:
Martha Saly (California) "Animal Woman Dream"
14 in. (35 cm) x 11 in. (28 cm) 2007.

below:
Dan Urban (Colorado) "Capricious"
9 in. (23 cm) x 16 in. (40 cm) x 14 in. (35 cm) 2007.

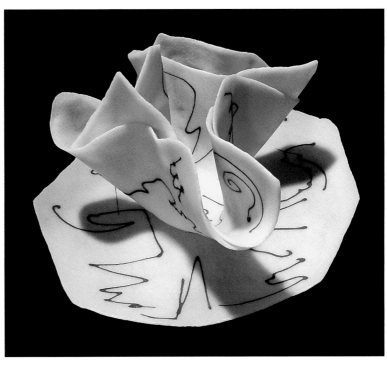

Alex Sutton (Washington) "Great Horned Owl" 22 in. (56 cm) x 15 in. (38 cm) 2008.

Rebeca Gilad (California) "Fruits from Home" 25 in.
(63 cm) x 25 in. (63 cm) 2008.

top right: Irene Sippel (Germany) "Abraham"
40 in. (1 m.) x 60 in. (1.5 m.) 2008.

right: Shoshana & Gideon Shapira (Israel)
"The Spiral" 9 in. (22 cm) in diameter 2008.

below: Pat Walsh "This One"
10 in. (25 cm) x 17 in. (43 cm) 2008.

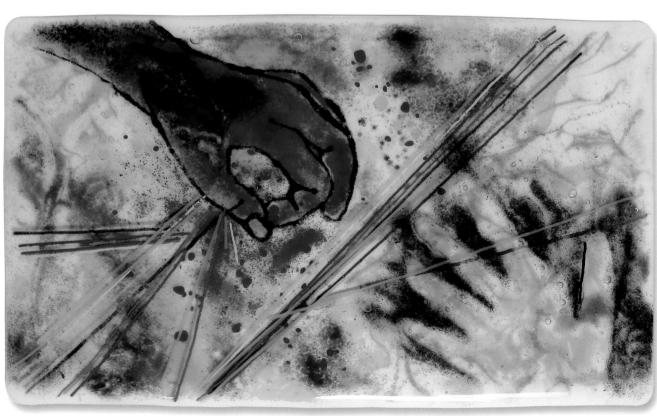

Rachel Shoham (Pennsylvania) "A New Day" 36 in.
(92 cm) x 36 in. (92 cm), located at the Erie Avenue
Ronald McDonald House in Philadelphia, Pennsylvania
2008 (shown without frame).

Shoshana & Gideon Shapira (Israel) "Mainly Red"
9 in. (22 cm) in diameter 2008.

Peggy Shashy (Florida) "Cock-Of-The-Rock - A Male
Displaying" 7 in. (18 cm) x 7 in. (18 cm) 2009.

above: Angie Dixon (Washington) "Deer and the Moon" 8 in. (20 cm) x 12 in. (30 cm) 2008.

below: Cindy Durant (Australia) "Navajo Blanket Wira"
3 in. (7.5 cm) H. x 24 in. (62 cm) x 9 in. (23 cm) 2007.

below: Cindy Durant (Australia) "Serpentine" Detail of
wall piece, 16 in. (40 cm) H. x 47 in. (120 cm) 2007.

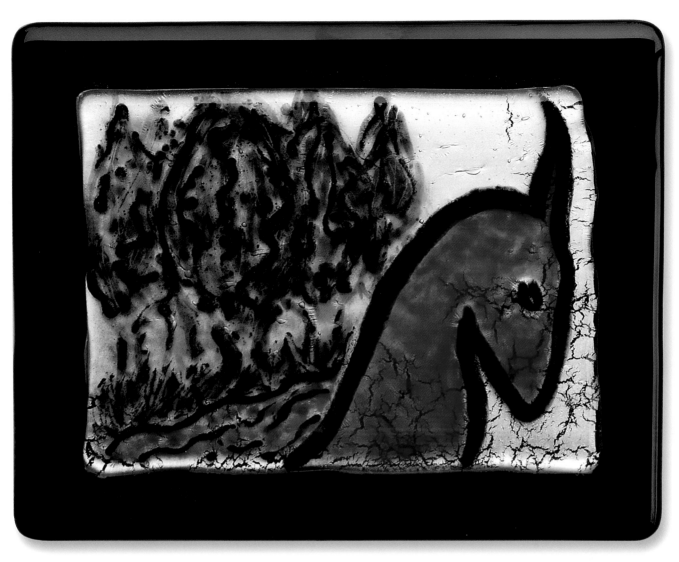

above: Angie Dixon (Washington) "By the River"
7 in. (19 cm) x 8 ½ in. (22 cm) 2008.

below: Stacey King (Washington) "Steelhead"
10 in. (25 cm) x 22 in. (55 cm) 2007.

Botanicals: Multi-layer Technique

I originally made 24 "botanicals" between 1985 - 1986. This was my favorite vessel series; they were created from cut pieces of sheet glass, glass threads and chunks of crushed glass. These pieces were very tricky to make. I used my large kiln with an inside dimension of 44 in. (112 cm) x 44 in. (122 cm) x 24 in. (61 cm) deep to fuse and then slump into my large fluted metal mold. I lost a few pieces during this process and felt that they pushed me to my technical edge, at that time.

For over twenty years I revisited this series and tried to recreate it using my latest technique. I tried with frit and then later with the liquid glass line. They just didn't look quite right and didn't have the magic of the original series, and I never exhibited these experiments. Then during the summer of 2007 I created six botanicals using silver foil and ripple glass. Once again, they are the most technically challenging pieces that I have done. It takes three firings to make them.

I am very excited about my new "botanicals." They use just about every technique that I have developed and written about in my first book, **Richard La Londe: Fused Glass Art and Technique.** I use "frit on the shelf," the "liquid glass line," "multi-layer technique," silver foil, flipping the piece over, and slumping in my handmade fluted stainless steel mold. This chapter in this book is an extension of my first book, and I thought that you might like to see the steps that it takes to make one of these babies.

facing:
"Botanical #4," 2008, 10 in. (25 cm) H. x 19 in. (48 cm) x 23 in. (58 cm), artist Richard La Londe.

bottom:
My original botanicals, "Tropical Moon" (left) 1986, 13 in. (33 cm) H. x 21 in. (53 cm.) W. x 19 in. (48 cm) D. and "Saturn's Serenade" (right) 1986 14 in. (35 cm) H. x 19 in. (48 cm) W. x 21 in. (53 cm) D.

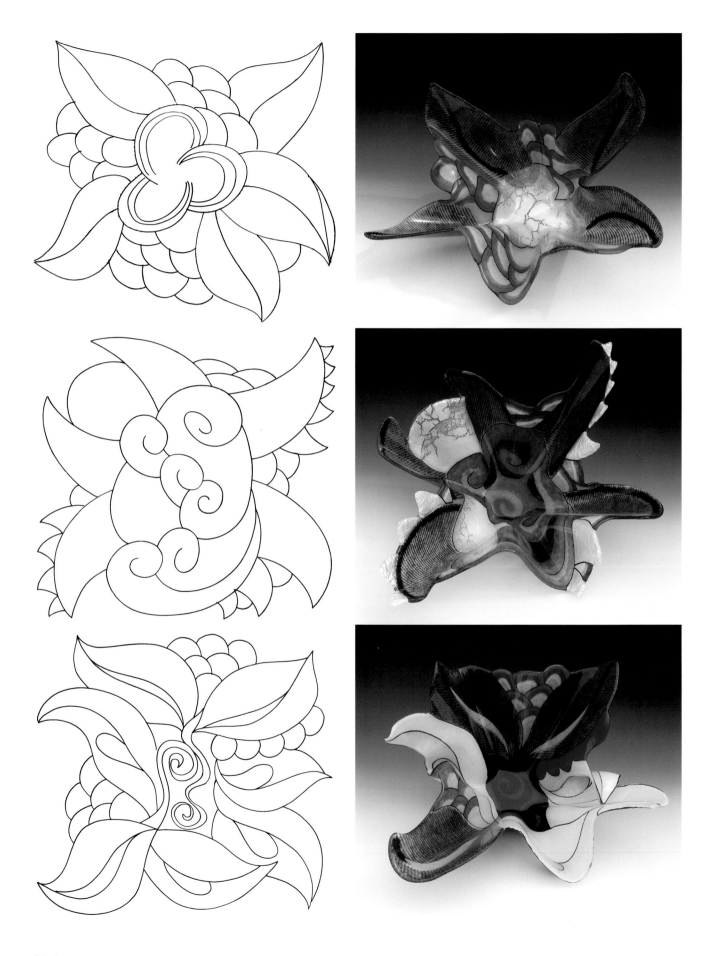

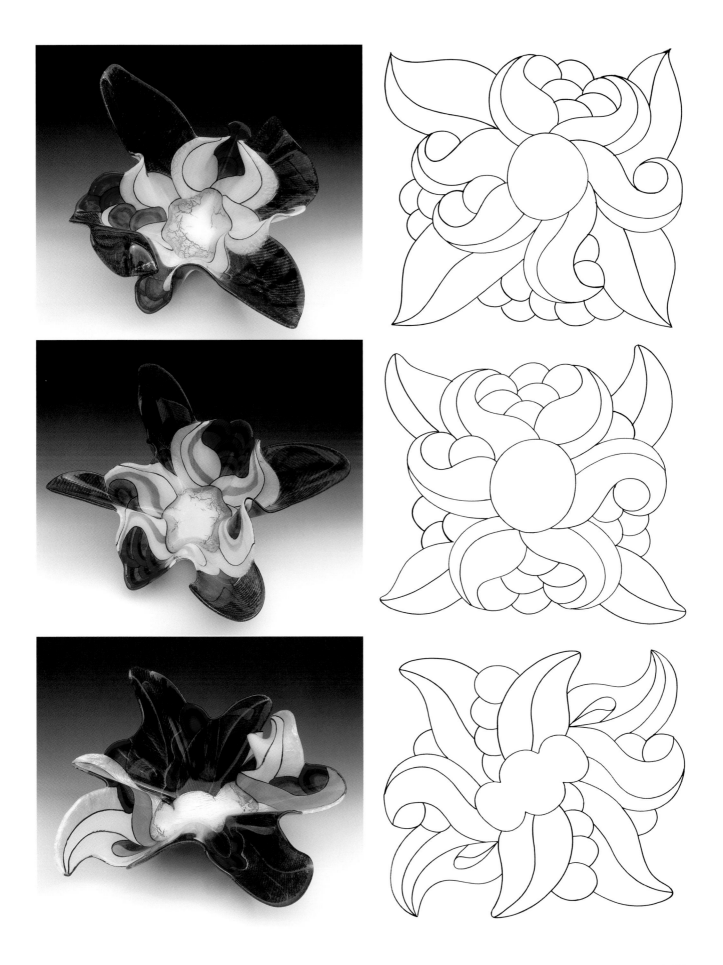

205

1) I drew a pattern using a "Sharpie" marker pen. It is designed to fit on a 24 in. (60 cm) x 24 in. (60 cm) kiln shelf.

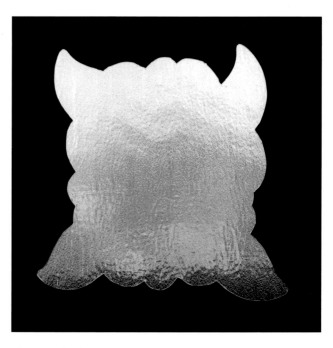

2) I cut the bottom piece of ⅛ in. (3 mm) Bullseye glass using a glass cutter for the easy cuts. I used an 8 in. (20 cm) circular diamond saw to make the inside cuts that would have been very complicated for a glass cutter to do.

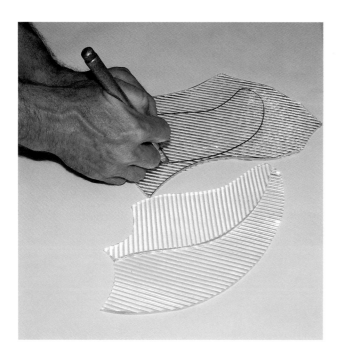

(3) I cut the leaf shapes in Bullseye ⅛ in. (3 mm) "Prismatic" ripple glass. I cut on the non-ridged back-side of the glass.

(4) Using a paper pattern I made little felt pen dots on a sheet of Japanese real silver foil. I laid this onto a sheet of paper for support and cut both the foil and paper together with scissors. With a brush, I applied a sizing, which is gelatin from empty medicine capsules dissolved in warm water, to the glass. I then laid the foil onto the glass that had been sized.

206

(5) I squeezed black size 08 Bullseye powder mixed with CMC "goop" and created a "liquid glass line" on some parts of my design. I let this air dry, but I could have dried it quickly with a hair dryer.

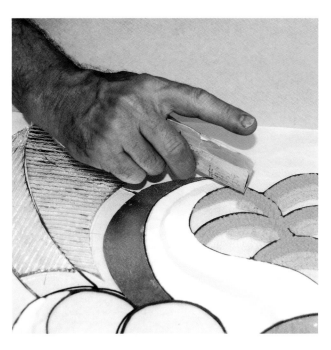

(6) I placed size 08 Bullseye powder in-between the "liquid glass" lines that I drew.

(7) I used my vacuum pen to extract unwanted powder from my design.

(8) I tamped the powder down gently with the back of a spoon.

(9) I sprinkled a mixture of different colors of size 01 Bullseye frit into the grooves of the ridged prismatic glass. You will be able to see a pattern of lines after it has fused.

(10) I sprayed hair spray onto the frit to hold it in place.

(11) The leaves are placed and the finished frit piece is ready to cover with a layer of clear. Notice that I have also covered the silver foil with turquoise powder, which will show through when the foil crackles.

(12) I covered the whole piece with a very fine layer of size 01 clear frit. I keep this to a minimum - just enough to cover the black liquid glass lines and colored frit. If you make this layer too thick, then you will see many tiny trapped bubbles, and it will appear translucent.

208

(13) I sprinkled size 02 clear frit all over the back. This is a thicker layer and should cover the whole piece. This total coverage acts as one layer, builds up the volume to about ¼ in. (5 - 6 mm), and keeps the different areas of color from separating.

(14) I sprinkled size 02 frit onto the shelf, and I placed the frit piece on top. This lets the air out and keeps trapped air from blowing giant holes into the piece before it fuses together.

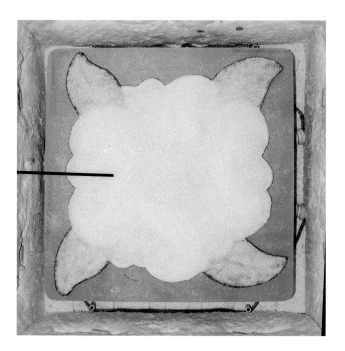

(15) Here is the finished frit piece, ready to fire to a full fuse.

(16) This is the piece after it has been fired.

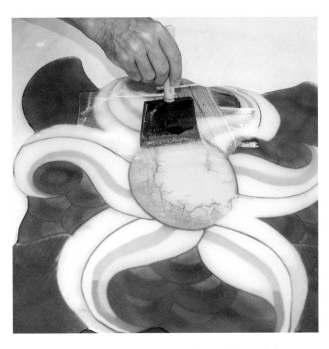

(17) I flipped the piece over and sandblasted the back to knock off any impurities from the kiln wash or devitrification. I then brushed it with a thin layer of Hotline "Spray A" overglaze. This is then fused a second time.

(18) Here the piece is shown after the second firing to almost a full fuse, about 25° F (14° C) less than the first firing. I used two kinds of silver foil. The thinner one turned a nice yellow and crackled, and the thick kind became a very light silvery yellow.

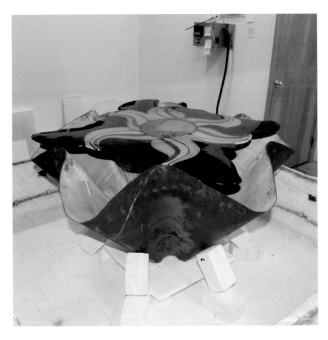

(19) On a third firing, I placed the piece at the top of my fluted stainless steel mold.

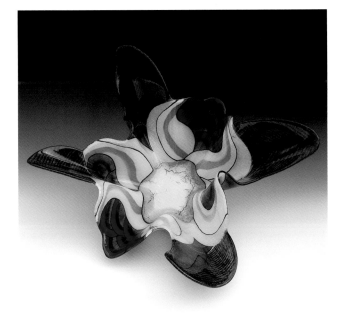

(20) This is the finished "botanical" piece, 10 in. (25 cm) H. x 19 in. (48 cm) x 23 in. (58 cm).

Firing Schedule for the Botanical Piece

Temperatures will vary with different kilns, placement of pyrometers, and whether the kiln is high temperature fiber or brick. The multi-layer piece is 22 in. (55 cm) x 22 in. (55 cm) on a 24 in. (60 cm) x 24 in. (60 cm) x 5/8 in. (160 mm) mullite kiln shelf. **hr. = hours   min. = minutes**

(First Firing) Full Fuse

85° F (47° C) /hr. to
1100° F (593° C)
1 min. soak

200° F (112° C) /hr. to
1500° F (816° C) - 1550° F (845° C)
(Wherever your kiln will Full Fuse flat)
1 min. soak

ASAP to
960° F (516° C)
2 hr. soak

100° F (55° C) /hr. to
700° F (375° C)
1 min. soak

120° F (70° C) /hr. to
150° F (65° C)
1 min. soak

Off

(Second Firing) Almost Full Fuse

85° F (47° C) /hr. to
1100° F (593° C)
1 min. soak

200° F (112° C) /hr. to
1435° F (780° C) - 1475° F (800° C)
(About 25° F [14° C] less than the first full fuse)
1 min. soak

ASAP to
960° F (516° C)
2 hr. soak

100° F (55° C) /hr. to
700° F (375° C)
1 min. soak

120° F (70° C) /hr. to
150° F (65° C)
1 min. soak

Off

- -

(Third Firing) Slump

85° F (47° C) /hr. to
1100° F (593° C)
1 min. soak

ASAP to 1290° F (700° C) - 1330° F (720° C)
(You must watch the slump and vent your kiln
when desired bending has been achieved)

ASAP to
960° F (516° C)
4 hr. soak

70° F (40° C) /hr. to
600° F (315° C)
1 min. soak

100° F (55° C) /hr. to
130° F (55° C)
1 min. soak

Off

a public art commission

In 1974 Washington state was one of the first states to establish an Art in Public Places Program, which provided that ½ of 1% of the construction budget for state-owned buildings could go for the acquisition of artwork. Since then, many cities and states have followed with commission programs. My first public commission was for the Washington State Arts Commission in 1984, and since then I have completed 15 public commissions for various agencies. Also during this time, I have never had the opportunity to see another artist's art proposal, and so I trudged along by myself. I thought that you might like to see my latest art proposal and follow a public commission from the beginning to installation.

The first step is getting a job, and today the internet is a good place to start. On the internet, you can google search "public art commission" and you will find many listings for public art agencies and "calls for artists." Sometimes you can submit images and a resume to be included into an artist's registry, and other times you submit a proposal and compete for a specific job.

The Washington State Arts Commission, WSAC, maintains an image roster of juried artists. The Mount View Elementary School committee viewed hundreds of images and chose me. In January 2007, I was selected to meet with them and visit the site. The committee included the school principal, a facilities manager, an art teacher, interested teachers, and a person from outside the school. They were advised by a representative from the arts commission. The committee told me about the art that they wanted and the site, and I showed them examples of my glass. They agreed that I should proceed with a proposal.

facing:
"One World" center panel, 80 in. (203 cm) H. x 60 in. (152 cm) W., Mount View Elementary School, Washington State Arts Commission, 2007, artist Richard La Londe.

left:
The Art Commission site at the Mount View Elementary School, White Center, Washington. This brick wall is in the main entry hall and contains decorative concrete elements from the previous school, dated 1942. I would have to work around these decorations and also attach my glass mural to the brick.

Design and Proposal

I signed a "Proposal Development Contract" with the WSAC and would be paid for my proposal. Here I am working on the design, which is ½ the size of my glass wall piece. I used a light table to transfer my drawings to the final composition, and my local copying service reduced them to fit onto an 8 ½ in. (21 cm) x 17 in. (43 cm) piece of paper.

Richard
La Londe

Art Proposal for the
Mount View Elementary School

White Center, Washington

sponsored by the
Washington State Arts
Commission

May 29, 2007

Richard La Londe
www.richardlalonde.com

4651 Melody Lane   Freeland, WA. 98249
(360) 730-2166   Email: lalonde@whidbey.com

Art Proposal for the
Mount View Elementary School in White Center, Washington
sponsored by the Washington State Arts Commission
May, 29, 2007

I propose to create a triptych consisting of (2) 60" high by 40" wide and (1) 80" high x 60" wide, fused glass art panels.

The left and right panels will each contain (4) 23" x 20" and (2) triangular 14" high x 20" fused glass narrative sections. The center section will consist of (6) 23" x 20" and (3) rectangular sections with a tapering top with an additional Sun piece mounted on top, for a total height of 80".

The sections of the triptych will be mounted on the brick entry wall. There will be a 16" space between each of the three sections and they will cover an area 14' 3" long by 6' 8" high. Included in this proposal is a diagram showing the mural location on the entry wall, a mounting system diagram, and (3) designs, one for each section.

My pictorial designs include realistic images and fantasy. My hope is that this can lead the viewer to see new things and develop ideas that emerge over time. Here are a few of my basic ideas:

Left Panel This design shows our ties to the nature, the native peoples who lived here before us, and petroglyphic drawings suggest past mythology. There are salmon eggs in the gravel representing children waiting to emerge into Mount View school and community. Hearts are planted like seeds, ready to take root. There are juvenile salmon and a returning salmon illustrating the cycle of life.

Center Panel This design represents the tree of life. The bottom left corner illustrates the Autumn, the beginning of the school year. Clockwise and above that is Winter, then Spring, and Summer. Children from all lands surround our earth and from left to right, cycle through the seasons and end up on the golden path toward the future. All of the different children link hands in cooperation and community.

Right Panel This design represents the future which is heralded by trumpet blowers flying on the back of a bird. There are hands holding unknown energy and hands shaking in cooperation. We must choose which path we follow. The golden path leads to a bright star and a cornucopia of abundance.

It is my hope that these artworks will enhance, bring enjoyment, create discussion and further the development of the children attending Mount View.

Mount View Elementary School
White Center, Washington
Washington State Arts Commission
May 2007

Richard La Londe - artist
4651 Melody Lane
Freeland, WA. 98249
(360) 730-2166
www.richardlalonde.com

One World (working title)
Left Panel
Fused Glass 60" high x 40" wide

Mount View Elementary School
White Center, Washington
Washington State Arts Commission
May 2007

Richard La Londe - artist
4651 Melody Lane
Freeland, WA. 98249
(360) 730-2166
www.richardlalonde.com

One World (working title)
Center Panel
Fused Glass 80" high x 60" wide

Mount View Elementary School
White Center, Washington
Washington State Arts Commission
May 2007

Richard La Londe - artist
4651 Melody Lane
Freeland, WA. 98249
(360) 730-2166
www.richardlalonde.com

One World (working title)
Right Panel
Fused Glass 60" high x 40" wide

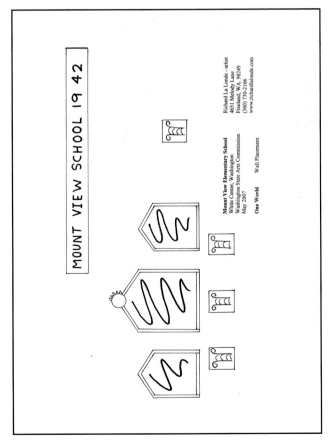

MOUNT VIEW SCHOOL 19 42

Richard La Londe - artist
4651 Melody Lane
Freeland, WA. 98249
(360) 730-2166
www.richardlalonde.com

Mount View Elementary School
White Center, Washington
Washington State Arts Commission
May 2007

One World   Wall Placement

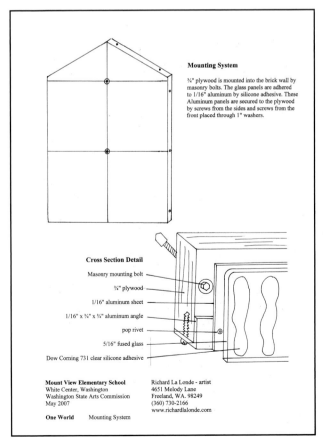

Mounting System

¾" plywood is mounted into the brick wall by
masonry bolts. The glass panels are adhered
to 1/16" aluminum by silicone adhesive. These
Aluminum panels are secured to the plywood
by screws from the sides and screws from the
front placed through 1" washers.

Cross Section Detail

Masonry mounting bolt
¾" plywood
1/16" aluminum sheet
1/16" x ¾" x ¾" aluminum angle
pop rivet
5/16" fused glass
Dow Corning 731 clear silicone adhesive

Mount View Elementary School
White Center, Washington
Washington State Arts Commission
May 2007

Richard La Londe - artist
4651 Melody Lane
Freeland, WA. 98249
(360) 730-2166
www.richardlalonde.com

One World   Mounting System

Budget and Art Committee

One of my favorite forms is the triptych. I had
seen these in museums as picture frames dating
from the Renaissance period. The paintings were
OK, but I just loved the frames. I thought about
using the triptych form for my wall piece.

I had a budget and a big wall. I wanted to fill
the space well and also get paid for my effort.
I started by measuring the wall and making a
scale drawing of the triptych form that I thought
that I could financially build. I had an idea for
mounting the glass to pieces of aluminum that
would screw to a plywood background. This
would then be bolted to the brick wall. I also
measured the inside of my car and designed the
mounting system so that I could get the sections
into my car for delivery to the site.

I met with the art committee, March 2007. During
this meeting I spoke about my proposed artwork,
showed an example of my fused glass, presented
a mounting model, and handed out my seven page
proposal. The committee debated, and my proposal was approved with a few minor changes.

I signed a "Contract for Commission of Artwork"
with the WSAC. This contract spells out the who,
what, and when it needs to be done. It discusses
liability and sets out a schedule of 6 payments -
listing the requirements to get paid at each stage.

The first hurdle was a structural engineer's
approval of my mounting system. That
accomplished, I returned to the copy service and
blew up my drawings full size. Next I cut out
pieces of clear 6 mm Bullseye Tekta glass. My
basic module is 20 in. (50 cm) x 23 in. (58 cm).

Budget for "One World"
Mount View Elementary School
White Center, Washington 2007
Washington State Arts Commission

Proposal Development & Design Fee
Paid for proposal, budget and timeline;
separate from the commission fee $ 2000
(whether accepted or not by the art committee)

Fabrication Budget
Structural Engineer
Approval and Stamp $ 350

Fabrication
Materials (glass, aluminum, bolts, silicone,
rivets, plywood) $ 2400
Equipment (kiln electricity) $ 200
Artist Labor ($35 per hour) $ 8400
Studio Costs $ 2200
Insurance $ 600

Installation
Artist Labor ($35 per hour) $ 420
Assistant For Installation ($30) $ 240
Travel Cost (art transport, gas, ferry) $ 190
Meals During Installation $ 120
Installation Equipment (buy rotary drill) $ 230

Completion
Artist Office Time ($35 per hour) $ 700
Photography $ 450
Plaque $ 65
Dedication Transportation, Meals, Ferry $ 90

Miscellaneous
Artist Fee $ 2019
Contingency (10 %) $ 2282

Washington State Sales Tax $ 1865

Total commission fee $ 22,821

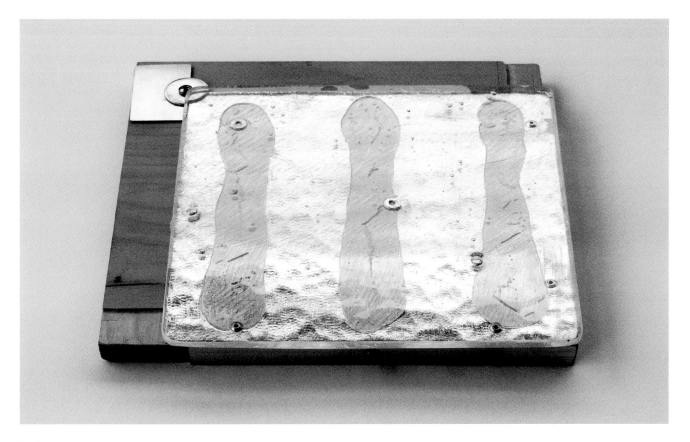

facing:
My full sized drawings, after blowing them up at the copy service. There would be 18 in. (46 cm) between each of the triptych panels when mounted.

above:
My 10 in. (25 cm) x 10 in. (25 cm) mounting system model, demonstrating how the glass mural would be attached to the wall.

constructing "One World"

(1) I am using the "Liquid Glass Line" technique that I previously described. First I flip the pattern over and then place clear 6 mm Bullseye Tekta glass pieces on top of that. For this piece I put a ¾ in. (2 cm) wide, white 3 mm thick, glass border piece along the edge and stuck it down with liquid hair spray. I also outlined the design with powdered black glass mixed with a CMC binder using a squeeze bottle. I am now laying crushed colored glass into my glass outline using a folded piece of paper. I use Bullseye Glass.

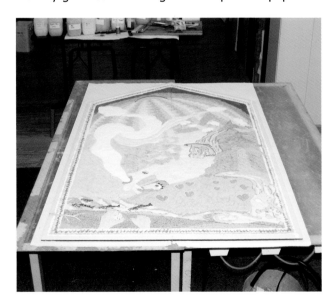

(2) View of the mural section after all of the crushed glass has been laid down.

(3) I am covering the whole piece with a layer of white crushed glass, which helps keep the previous layer of frit from separating during the firing, and it also makes it opaque.

(4) A section of the white frit backed piece ready to put into the kiln for the first firing. I fuse the frit just enough to stick to the glass, so that I can flip the piece over for a second firing.

(5) Each frit covered section is placed on a kiln shelf and fused to stick. Then the piece is flipped over, painted with Hot Line "Spray A" overglaze, and put back onto a kiln shelf. Mullite dams are placed and wedged, and the piece is fired a second time to full fuse.

Firing Schedule for the One World Mural

Temperatures will vary with different kilns, placement of pyrometers, and whether the kiln is high temperature fiber or brick. These pieces are 20 in. (50 cm) x 23 in. (58 cm) on a 24 in. (60 cm) x 24 in. (60 cm) x ⅝ in. (160 mm) mullite kiln shelf. **hr. = hours   min. = minutes**
Better to go too slow than to break the piece by thermal shock!

(First Firing) Fuse to Stick

70° F (40° C) /hr. to
1100° F (593° C)
1 min. soak

600° F (333° C) /hr. to
1300° F (705° C) - 1345° F (730° C)
(Where the frit will not fall off when flipped over)
1 min. soak

ASAP to
960° F (516° C)
2 hr. soak

50° F (28° C) /hr. to
700° F (370° C)
1 min. soak

100° F (55° C) /hr. to
150° F (65° C)
1 min. soak then Off

(Second Firing) Full Fuse

70° F (40° C) /hr. to
1100° F (593° C)
1 min. soak

600° F (333° C) /hr. to
1500° F (816° C) - 1550° F (845° C)
(Wherever your kiln will full fuse flat)
1 min. soak

ASAP to
960° F (516° C)
2 hr. soak

50° F (28° C) /hr. to
700° F (370° C)
1 min. soak

100° F (55° C) /hr. to
150° F (65° C)
1 min. soak then Off

fusing, grinding & gold

(6) I am wet grinding the sharp edges that were fused against the dams. I found it better to let the water from the hose flow across the edge than from the grinder. I use a series of diamond disks: 70 for rough cutting, then 220; I finish with diamond im-pregnated rubber pads; 800, 1500, and then 3000.

(8) After grinding and polishing with the series of diamond pads, I bring the edge to a final polish with a felt wheel, cerium oxide powder, and water. When you are shaping and polishing an edge, be really careful not to scratch the top surface of the tile. It is very hard to smooth and polish a flat surface with these hand tools.

(7) Above is my wet grinder, which is protected from shocking me with a "GFI" - ground fault interrupter. I also check to see if the receptacle is properly wired, with a hardware store "ground check meter," the yellow device above. Wear rubber gloves and rubber boots. You can get electrocuted and killed if you and your grinder are not insulated and GFI protected.

(9) Here I have polished the left and upper edge, which were fused against a dam so that they would be straight. They will be placed directly adjacent and touching an-other tile. The bottom and right white border edges do not touch any other tiles, and so I do not dam them. I let these edges expand and round naturally in the kiln.

(10) Here is my wet belt sander that I made. You can grind and polish edges with a series of belts, but I prefer the hand tools on larger tiles, which are heavy to hold up to and against the belt. A set of rollers to support the edge would help.

(11) For shaping I use a 60 grit silicon carbide wet belt. I then change the belts and progress through 120, 220, 400. I then bring the glass almost to a polish with a used 600 grit belt. I finish with the cerium and felt wheel.

(12) Sometimes I leave a transparent or clear area in my tiles that I later back with real silver or gold leaf. I use pharmaceutical gelatin capsules dissolved in water as a sizing to hold the leaf. I pick up the fragile leaf with a "gilder's tip" brush and touch it to the sized glass, to which it sticks.

(13) I place pieces of leaf on the back of the glass, let them dry, and then burnish with a cotton ball. I seal the leaf with spray enamel plastic as the gelatin is water soluble. I recommend the book **Gold Leaf Techniques** by Kent Smith; taking a class can also be a big help. Leafing is an art and takes practice to master.

221

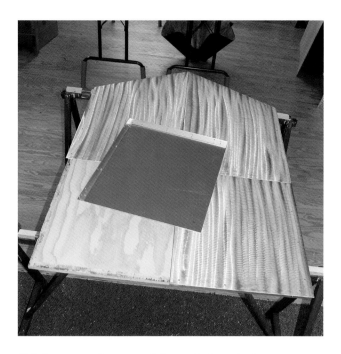

(14) I create 16 gauge, $^1/_{16}$ in. (1.5 mm) aluminum backing plates for my glass. I cut them $^1/_8$ in. (3 mm) narrower than the finished glass size and rough up the surface with a grinder. These will be screwed to a $^3/_4$ in. (2 cm) piece of plywood that will be bolted to the brick wall.

(15) I pneumatically pop-rivet $^3/_4$ in. (2 cm) x $^3/_4$ in. (2 cm) aluminum angles to the edges of the aluminum backing and you can also use a manual hand pop-rivet tool. I will use screws on the edges to hold the backing plates to the plywood. The imported rivet tool is relatively inexpensive when purchased at a discount tool store.

(16) I glue the glass tiles to the roughened aluminum with Dow Corning 732 clear silicon sealer. I make vertical strips of silicone which have spaces between them, allowing the silicone to dry, and I use $^1/_{16}$ in. (1.5 mm) spacers to hold the glass slightly away from the aluminum, so that I don't squeeze all of the silicone out, decreasing its holding strength.

(17) My friend Don drills a hole into the brick with a rotohammer drill. I do as much of the installation setup in my studio as I can, so the on-site work is kept to a minimum. It is good to have a helper with the larger plywood pieces, moving everything into the school, and keeping kids away; extra hands for holding is also much appreciated.

(18) The plywood has been bolted to the wall, and I am mounting mural sections to it. I screw the aluminum along the edges and also at the joints where the panels meet. This holds the glass to the wall. The mural was installed March 2008.

(19) Don & I finished the installation, and we collapsed on the green couch opposite the mural. I shot this photo just as the kids first saw the mural. The high ceiling, scattered light, and people remind me of tourists viewing art in a European cathedral.

(20) "One World," 2008, Mount View Elementary, White Center, WA in conjunction with the Washington State Arts Commission, fused glass triptych 7 ft. (2.1 m.) x 16 ft. (5.3 m.) Dedicated April 2008, a 16 month project.

Part 7: Appendix
studio equipment & kilns

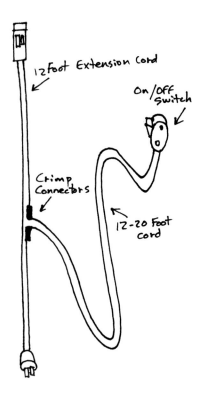

Make a switch extension
(left) Cut only one wire, the hot wire coming from the smaller prong of the male end of a 12-foot extension cord. Cut off the ends of a second 12 - 20 foot extension cord, or use a piece of equivalent wire, and splice it into the first wire with crimp butt connectors, as in the diagram. Tape over these connections with duct tape. Place a switch on the end.

Build a vacuum pen
(bottom) Neck down the hose from a shop vac with a plastic PVC pipe reducer and attach a smaller diameter hose. Adding a plastic nozzle further reduces the hose – this time I used a plastic ballpoint pen case. I place the shop vac outside of my studio to eliminate the noise and glass dust; I turn the vacuum off and on with a switch on a longer cord.

facing upper:
using the vacuum pen to clean up the spillover of frit. The glass project is on the light table to help illuminate the frit.

Build a light table
(facing lower left) Use metal or wood and place inexpensive shop fluorescent lights 6 in. (15 cm) below the table top and no more than 6 in. (15 cm) apart. I put all of my tables on wheels, so I can reconfigure my studio easily.

(facing lower right) Place a surplus tempered glass shower door on top of the frame and run the glass all the way to the edge. I place a thin piece of Lasco "Crystalite" flat fiberglass reinforced acrylic on top of the tempered glass to protect it from nicks because they will weaken the glass. I cut my glass right on top of this sheet of plastic.

Build a polariscope
(bottom right) This small light box has a bulb inside. I've placed a 10 in. (25 cm) x 10 in. (25 cm) piece of polarizing plastic under a piece of window glass. View your test glass through another piece of polarizing plastic.

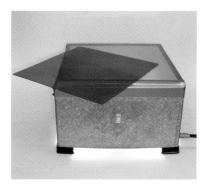

fiber kilns

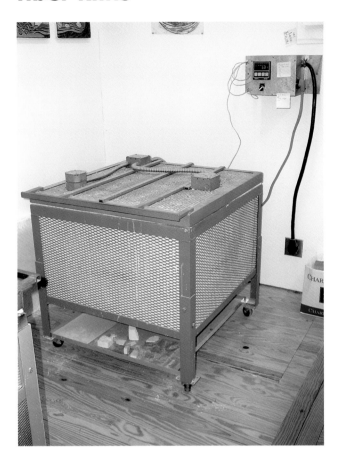

The top load kiln, my favorite kiln design today, has an inside dimension of 28 in. (71 cm) x 28 in. (71 cm) x 17 in. (43 cm) deep. It takes a 240 volt, 50 amp receptacle. This kiln has both top and bottom elements which help give it a more even heat. This is an easier kiln to load than the front loading kiln. I call this kiln the "geriatric kiln" because I use an overhead block and tackle hoist to load my kiln and save my back for my golf game.

above right: 60 amps of elements on 1 in. mullite ceramic tubes and the high-temperature fiber blanket lining.

bottom left: in 1984 I added a 30 amp ring with side elements for a total of 90 amps, 240 volts. It runs on (3) 30 amp breakers.

bottom right: shows the kiln lid lifted and my stainless sheet mold for slumping my bowls.

compatibility

The bigger your piece, the more effect compatibility has. You might successfully fuse a tiny earring, but compatibility is more critical in a huge wall panel. Multiple firings can also alter the compatibility. If I have a problem or I suspect a color shift or reaction color change, I fuse a quick test.

Most materials expand when heated and shrink when cooled. When different glasses are heated in a kiln and fused together, they need to cool – to shrink and contract – at the same rate, or incompatibility stress will build up during cooling, and the glass will crack.

above: Breakage caused by incompatible glass.

The clear has a higher expansion rate than the yellow samples on either end; as it cooled, the clear shrunk more than the yellow, shattering the clear.

The clear has a lower expansion rate than the red sample in the center; as it cooled, the red shrunk more than the clear and pulled away, causing a break in the clear all the way around the red.

Today, most people, including me, just buy fusible glass and don't test for incompatibility; however, I know how to do it, and occasionally when something doesn't work or I need to know about the properties of the glass, I use a "polariscope" to test my glass. This is also a good method for glass blowers to check compatibility or to set up a palette from a glass company such as the German glass GNA that is not listed as compatible.

When in doubt, test it out!
Use a "polariscope" and the "Stressometer Test," originally described in *Glass Fusing Book One* by Lundstrom and Schwoerer, Vitreous Publications, 1983.

This test will show you:
(1) **Compatibility**
(2) **Color Change** -some glass changes color after firing.
(3) **Devitrification** - the surface of some glass looks scummy from surface crystal growth.
(4) **Relative viscosity** of the glass, hard vs. soft, or which melts sooner.

This is how I do the "Chip Test" to set up a compatible pallet of glass.

Cut a 2 in. (5 cm) x 18 in. (46 cm) strip of clear glass. This is the base glass to test against.

Cut a triangle off one corner and place it on the clear strip. This is to indicate whether the strip has been properly annealed.

Cut pieces about ½ in. (12 mm) x ½ in. (12 mm) from the glass to be tested and place them on the clear strip with 1 in. (2.5 cm) between the chips.

Label the chips with a felt tipped paint marker, which will fire onto the glass.

Fire this strip in a kiln to a full fuse flat and then anneal.

Place this fused strip between two pieces of a polarizing film. You can buy a "Stressometer" or make a "polariscope" by purchasing a sheet of polarizing film from Edmund Scientific and cutting it in two pieces.

Take a light source, place one piece of polarizing film over it, and place the fused glass test strip on top of that.

View the fused glass test strip through a second piece of polarizing film. Rotate the upper film until it is at its darkest position.

Check to see that no annealing stress shows on the cut corner fused on itself. If there is stress, it will show up as a halo of light, affecting your compatibility test, giving you a false reading.

Next check for incompatibility, which will show up as a halo of light on the corners of the chips. No halo, no stress. I fuse glass that shows no

halo or just a slight hint of light – see the chip test photo below; more than that can produce problems in large fused pieces. You can get away with more incompatibility, more halo, in a very small piece of jewelry.

The idea is that if chip A of the glass being tested is compatible to the clear base, and chip B is also compatible to the base clear, then chip A should be compatible to chip B. The beauty of this test is that "Stressometer Test" replicates glass fusing. Additional tests can indicate if the glass has a higher or lower expansion rate than the base clear, but I don't find such tests necessary for the fusing that I do. If you do another compatibility test, place a piece of the original base clear on it to see if the new base that you are testing remains the same. Label your glass fusible and put it in a separate rack away from all other glass in your studio. Besides compatibility, this test shows color change, devitrification, and relative viscosity.

Chips above are viewed under natural light, full fused onto a strip of a base of Bullseye 1101 clear glass.

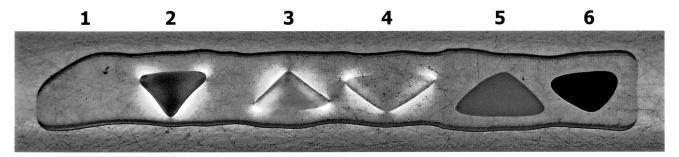

Chips above are viewed through crossed polarizing filters; stress shows as halos.

1 The corner or the base clear is cut off and fused onto itself to check for annealing stress.
2 Mystery glass shows way too much halo - not compatible to the base.
3 Window glass shows some devitrification and is not fully fused - not compatible to the base.

4 Spectrum Clear also shows too much halo - not compatible to the base glass.
5 Mystery White, no halo - compatible to the base.
6 Bullseye black 0100, no halo - compatible to base.

#5 & #6 are fusible to each other and also to the base clear, giving me three glasses to probably successfully fuse, indicated by this test.

volume control

The most important and least understood of "The Big Three" is how to make the glass do what you want it to do! This has to do with the different thicknesses that you work with – in other words, controlling the volume of glass. As you will see, most of my technical developments and breakthroughs involved Volume Control.

Various glasses have different viscosities, so they act differently as they are heated; for example, window glass needs a higher temperature than Bullseye to full fuse. You'll also find fusing temperature differences within the Bullseye palette. Another factor is that dark opaque glass absorbs heat faster than a transparent light-colored glass.

Time and Temperature
Glass has a chance to absorb more heat in a soft brick kiln, which tends to fire slower than a fiber kiln; firing schedules will reflect this difference. Consequently, full fuse in a brick kiln will occur at a lower temperature than in a faster fiber kiln.

My fiber kiln, with a 21 in. (53 cm) x 21 in. (53 cm) x ⅝ in. (16 cm) thick shelf and a piece of 20 in. (51 cm) x 20 in. (51 cm) x ¼ in. (6 mm) glass, goes from 1100 – 1550° F (595 – 845° C) full fuse in fifteen minutes. The same glass and shelf in a Paragon brick GL24 full fuses at 1500° F (815° C) and might take thirty-five minutes or more to get there. You need to know, for the kiln that you use, at what temperatures your glass does what it does. Variables are many.

What Glass Does

Temperatures will vary with:
(1) different types of glass
(2) different kilns
(3) soak times
(4) transparent vs. opaque glass
(5) where you place the thermocouple that measures the temperature in the kiln.

These temperatures are based on my experience with Bullseye Glass.

1200° – 1300° F (650° – 705° C)
Begins to slump.
Glass starts to move slowly, bending under its own weight.

1300° – 1350° F (705° – 730° C)
Slumps and begins to tack fuse.
Sharp edges may round slightly.

1350° – 1450° F (730° – 790° C)
Fuses to stick and semi-fuse.

Devitrification Range
An ⅛ in. (3 mm) thick piece of glass begins to pull up. The glass is moving and the viscosity is decreasing. The surface tension is greater than the pull of gravity. Trapped air between the shelf and glass may create large bubbles.

1450° – 1500° F (790° – 815° C)
Semi fuse to full fuse.
The glass is less viscous, movement increases and as the pull of gravity overtakes the surface tension, the glass begins to flatten. Bubbles between the shelf and glass pop and make holes.

1500° – 1550° F (815° – 845° C)
Full fuse flat.
When full fused, the surface tension and gravity reaches an equilibrium at the magic thickness of just a little over ¼ in. (6 mm).

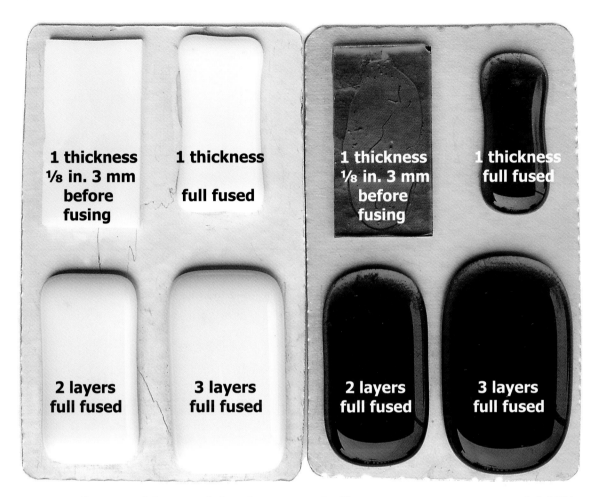

Bullseye white opal 0113 **Bullseye green transparent 1107**

The above glass samples are from my 1983 teaching kit and show the effect of volume control. The white and green samples were fired in the same kiln, right next to each other at the same time. You will see the original size in the upper left hand corner for both the white and green glass.

Observe the effect of surface tension and gravity.

One thickness tries to pull up to the magic ¼ in. (6 mm) - plus thickness and, in the process, rounds the corners and thins the middle. The surface tension is greater than the pull of gravity and, consequently, pulls on glass.

Two layers, stacked one on top of the other, full fuse to almost the same size as the original piece except the corners are rounded. Surface tension and gravity are equal.

Three layers stacked on top of each other, full fuse to a larger size than the original piece, trying to achieve that ¼ in. (6 mm) - plus thickness. Gravity is greater than surface tension, and the glass flows until tension and gravity are equal.

Note that the green transparent is more rounded and that it moved more than the white; the green glass is less viscous than the white.

231

annealing

Ideas and definitions about annealing glass are prolific. Get a group of scientists, engineers, and artists together, and you'll likely get a variety of different explanations: the scientific definition, an economic definition, and then...the La Londe version.

Personally, as an artist, I like to think of annealing as more of a philosophy than a science. Simply put, glass is a viscous material and gets stiffer as it cools. For our discussion, annealing is a controlled cooling through the zone where the glass goes from being plastic to solid.

Trying to understand annealing has always been a brain puzzler for me, so I devised an oversimplified literary picture to describe it.

Annealing occurs when the glass is cooled slowly enough to allow the inside and the outside of the glass to pass from a plastic state to a rigid state at roughly the same time so that stress is minimized. My mental picture is that the outside surface, which cools first, will "lock" and for all practical purposes become a rigid solid. Next the inside continues to shrink, pulling on the locked surface as it cools, until it "locks" as a rigid solid. If the stress between the outside and the inside is too great, the glass will crack. The idea is to slow this cooling so that the inside and outside become rigid at roughly the same time.

You can get real technical – or philosophical – about annealing, but what you really need to know is how to do it to get your glass out of the kiln in one piece – and keep it that way.

Your annealing will take longer if:
(1) Your piece is thick.
(2) Your kiln doesn't cool evenly.
(3) You use a dam, a thick shelf, or a mold – the time increases if these are insulating (for example, a fiber shelf).
(4) The shape of your piece is intricate with lots of sharp angles and internal cutouts.
(5) Your piece varies dimensionally and is thick and thin or tack fused.
(6) You have a transparent glass fused right next to opaque color – sometimes they lose heat at different rates, so allow a longer annealing time.

Also, if glass is poorly annealed, it's more susceptible to breaking if extra stress is added by other outside forces, such as heat (for example, placing a thick piece of poorly annealed glass in a hot window or dishwasher). Incompatibility also adds to the stress.

For most of my work I use the anneal soak temperature recommended by Bullseye Glass Company for their glass: 960° F (516° C).

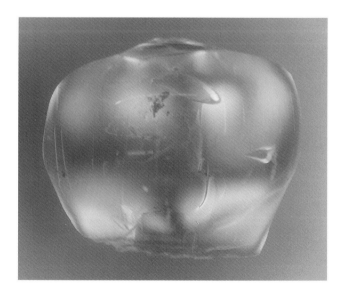

above:
this is what clear glass that has not been annealed looks like under polarized light. This piece is about the size of a golf ball, and I picked it up from the floor of a blowing studio. You can check your clear glass for annealing with a polariscope, "stressometer."

I don't have too much trouble with annealing because: my kilns cool very evenly; my work is usually regular in shape with very few sharp angles; my glass is generally no more than ½ in. (13 cm) thick and is fused on ⅝ in. (16 mm) or 1 in. (25 mm) mullite shelves; and I slump in very thin stainless steel molds. The only problem that I have had is in transparent areas of glass that extend all the way to the shelf, next to an opaque color; under these circumstances, I have to slow my annealing down or end up with a broken piece.

So let's get a bit more technical. A solid has an arranged characteristic order. For example, the molecules of water, frozen into ice, are lined up into a lattice structure and act like a solid. When ice is heated and its atoms absorb enough energy to overcome their lattice bonds, they collapse into a liquid. As water freezes back into ice, its molecules reorganize in the lattice structure again.

On the other hand, glass is so viscous and its kinetic energy is so low that as it cools, glass rarely has a chance to set up a lattice structure and become an ordered solid. Some people refer to glass as a liquid, but I prefer to talk about glass as a plastic; it exhibits some of the properties of a solid and some of the properties of a liquid.

As glass cools, at a certain temperature it begins to change from being plastic to solid. This beginning transition point is called the *"annealing point"* and is located at the upper temperature end of the *"annealing range."* The lower temperature end is referred to as the *"strain point,"* where glass begins to become rigid and behaves like a solid.

The *"annealing range"* is a transition zone where glass goes from being plastic to solid and occurs over approximately a 100° F (38° C) interval; it is where annealing takes place. The molecules of the glass are moving faster at the upper temperatures of this zone; consequently, glass anneals much faster than at the lower end of the annealing range. A temperature of 960° F (516° C) for Bullseye Glass seems to be the most economical place to soak the glass. But you still

have to get through the lower end of the zone and that requires slow cooling.

To make it more complicated, different glasses have different annealing ranges. By doing an anneal soak at 960° F (516° C), we are trying to average the relief of stress for the different glasses that have fused together. Some glasses such as the gold-containing Bullseye 0334, 1334 or 1311 have an even lower annealing range, and when I use a substantial amount of these, I do a second anneal soak at 890° F (477° C).

Even after an anneal soak in which you have allowed the inside and the outside of the glass to reach the same temperature of 960° F (516° C), you still have a long way to go to get out of the annealing zone. A continued slow cooling is still needed to get out of the annealing range without putting intolerable stress back into the glass.

Once below the strain point, you still need to cool very slowly for the next 100° F (38° C). And then you get into the *"thermal shock zone"* where the glass can break either during the heat up or cool down – whenever the temperature difference between the inside and outside puts too much stress on the glass. It's like putting a glass plate (non-Pyrex) into a hot oven or taking a hot piece of glass from your kiln and running cold water on it to cool: "KaBoom."

You really can't anneal something too long, so the idea is to:

• Soak at 960° F (516° C) for a sufficient time: see Bullseye Annealing Thick Slabs chart (appendix).

• Really slow cool to 800° F (427° C).

• Cool slowly to room temperature – that point where you can hold your hand on the piece before you take it out of the kiln.

Don't Rush It!

bibliography (books in my library)

Richard La Londe, *Richard La Londe: Fused Glass Art and Technique*, Ozone Press, Freeland, WA. 2006; of course, it's in my library; available at glass shops or on my website at www.richardlalonde.com.

historical

Stefano Carboni & David Whitehouse, *Glass of the Sultans*, published by The Metropolitan Museum of Art, New York, NY, 2001. An historical book including Islamic lusters and enamels, many photos.

Stefano Carboni, *Glass From Islamic Lands*, Thames & Hudson, New York, NY, 2001. Many photos of ancient Islamic glass including lusters and enamels.

Verlag Gerd Hatje, *Early Glass of the Ancient World : Ernesto Worlf Collection*, distributed by D.A.P. New York, NY, 1994. Glass from 1600 B.C. - 50 A.D., core vessels and fusing.

Florence Dunn Friedman, *Gifts of the Nile, Ancient Egyptian Faience*, Thames and Hudson, New York, NY, 1998. A fabulous book with many color photos of ancient faience, some very amazing pieces included.

Paul Nicholson, *Egyptian Faience and Glass*, Shire Publications, Buckinghamshire, England, 1993.

Harry Stewart, *Egyptian Shabtis*, Shire Publications, Buckinghamshire, England, 1995.

A. Lucas & J.R. Harris, *Ancient Egyptian Materials and Industries*, Dover Publications, Mineola, NY, 1999, Fourth Edition, first published in 1962.

Jutta-Annette Page, *The Art of Glass - Toledo Museum of Glass*, Toledo Museum of Glass, Toledo, OH, 2006.

1950s - 60s enamels on window glass

Harriette Anderson, *Kiln-Fired Glass*, Chilton Books, Radnor, PA, 1970. A good classic book for your library, talks about sifted enamels, interesting for pre-Bullseye compatibility testing and annealing,

Kay Kinney, *Glass Craft*, Chilton Book Company, Philadelphia, PA, 1962. If you want to fuse wind chimes out of wine bottles, this is the book for you.

Donald-Brian Johnson & Leslie Piña, *Higgins Adventures in Glass*, 1997 and *Higgins Poetry in Glass*, 2005, Schiffer Publishing Ltd., Atglen, PA. Lots of photos of Higgins' artwork, their studio, promotional material, and interviews with Frances and Michael Higgins.

vitreous enamels on glass & gold leaf

Kay Bain Weiner, *Contemporary Glass Enameling*, Eastman Publishing, Carlsbad, CA, 2005. Good ideas, written for the hobbyist.

Bettina Eberle, *Creative Glass Techniques*, A & C Black, London, England, 1997. Projects that teach about beginning fusing, painting, and lampworking and also contains a nice section about lusters and enamels.

234

Peggy Karr, *Artistry of Peggy Karr Glass*, Schiffer Publishing Ltd., Atglen, PA, 2005. The story and photos of her production company that makes collectible plates - fusing enamels in-between window glass.

Kent H. Smith, *Gold Leaf Techniques*, ST Publications, Cincinnati, OH, 1998. A great book about precious metal leafing, under and on top of glass.

glass painting and stained glass

Albinas Elskus, *The Art of Painting on Glass*, Charles Scribner's Sons, New York, NY, 1980. The classic on traditional glass painting for windows, out of print, and used copies are expensive, but worth it.

Richard Millard , and Anita & Seymour Isenberg, *Stained Glass Painting: Basic Techniques of the Craft*, Chilton Book Co., Radnor, PA, 1979. A good basic primer by master painter Richard Millard.

Otto B. Rigan, *New Glass*, Ballantine Books, New York, NY, 1976. The classic book about hippie stained glass that changed the way we make colored glass windows.

basic fusing

Boyce Lundstrom & Daniel Schwoerer, *Glass Fusing Book One*, Vitreous Publications, Colton, OR, 1983. The best book written about fusing basics; really covers annealing, compatibility, and volume control. The "classic."

Brad Walker, *Contemporary Warm Glass,* Four Corners International, Clemmons, NC. 2000. A very good contemporary book about basic fusing.

Philippa Beveridge, Ignasi Domenech, and Eve Pascual, *Warm Glass*, Lark Books, New York, NY, 2005. This book has great photos and graphics and an easy to understand "how to."

kiln forming techniques

Boyce Lundstrom, *Advanced Fusing Techniques: Glass Fusing Book Two*, and *Glass Casting and Moldmaking: Glass Fusing Book Three*, Vitreous Group - Camp Colton, OR, 1989. Book Two - information about glory holes, slumping, enamels, and lusters. Book Three - mold making and kiln casting.

James Kervin, Dan Fenton, *Pâte de Verre and Kiln Casting of Glass*, GlassWear Studios, Livermore, CA, 1997. One of the most comprehensive and detailed books about modeling and *pâte* verre.

Susanne K. Frantz, *Particle Therories: International Pâte de Verre and Other Cast Glass Granulations*, Museum of American Glass at Wheaton Village - exhibition catalogue / book, Milleville, NJ, 2005. Contains a short history of Pâte de Verre and examples of pieces, past to present.

Keith Cummings, *Techniques of Kiln-formed Glass*, A & C Black, London, England 1997. Has a good section about ancient glass history and kiln casting.

Keith Cummings, *A History of Glass Forming*, A & C Black, London, England 2002 & University of Pennsylvania Press, USA. Discusses the history of mechanical forming of vessels and window glass.

books & pamphlets about the artist

Edris Eckhardt: Visionary and Innovator in American Studio Ceramics and Glass, Henry Adams & Joseph Kisvardai, Cleveland Artists Foundation, Lakewood, OH, Feb. 18 - Apr. 15, 2006 exhibition pamphlet.

Earl McCutchen: Craftsmanship in Ceramics and Glass, Ashley Callahan, Georgia Museum of Art, Athens, GA, Oct., 19, 2002 - Jan. 12, 2003 exhibition pamphlet.

Peter Grain Uncommon Glass, The Glass Press, Briston, PA, 2002. A great history about Peter Mc-Grain with lots of color photos.

studio glass art

Ray & Lee Grover, *Contemporary Art Glass*, Crown Publishers, New York, NY, 1975. A wonderful book about the early studio glass pioneers; includes Edris Eckhardt, Maurice Heaton, and Frances and Michael Higgins.

Bonnie J. Miller, *Out of the Fire*, Chronicle Books, San Francisco, CA, 1991. A great book about 30 Northwest Glass artists in the early 1990's and a nice history of Pilchuck and NW glass.

Suzanne K. Frantz, *Contemporary Glass*, Harry N. Abrams Inc. New York, NY, 1989. Documents the contemporary glass in the Corning Museum of Glass.

Dan Klein, *Glass A Contemporary Art*, Rizzoli International Publications, Inc. New York, NY, 1989. A worldwide survey of 1989 artists working with glass.

Tina Oldknow, *Pilchuck: A Glass School*, Pilchuck Glass School, Seattle, WA, 1996. A History of Pilchuck.

glass technology

Frank E. Wolley, *Glass Technology for the Studio*, The Studio of the Corning Museum of Glass, Corning, NY, 1999. A spiral bound collection of lecture notes about glass science, annealing, glass composition, expansion, and so on.

Henry Halem, *Glass Notes: A Reference for the Glass Artist*, Franklin Mills Press, Kent, OH, 2006. Glass batching and chemistry, blowing equipment, and a real nice section about "pâte de verre" by Alicia Lomne.

Johnathon Schmuck, *The Joy of Coldworking*, Four Corners International, Clemmons, NC, 2009. A guide to grinding and polishing blown and fused glass.

videos

Beginning Fritography - **Michael Dupille**, 2006, DVD www.michaeldupille.com.
Paul Marioni - Artist, 2007, DVD
Dudley Giberson's Core Vessel Video, Dudley Giberson, VHS only, www.joppaglass.com
Higgins Glass: a Visit with Frances and Michael Higgins, 1996, DVD, www.edandmarthabigger.com
Kiln Fired Glass Updated, Harriette Anderson, 1993, VHV only, www.thompsonenamel.com
Traditional Glass Painting - Lesson One, Traditional Glass Painting - Lesson Two, &
Traditional Glass Painting - Vitri-Fusáille, Peter McGrain's techniques, www.petermcgrain.com.

Richard's material & suppliers list

enamels & supplies

Thompson Enamels & Supplies
Thompson Enamel
PO Box 310
Newport, KY 41072
(800) 545-2776
(859) 291-3800
www.thompsonenamel.com

Fero Sunshine Enamels
Warm Glass
2575 Old Glory Road
Suite 700
Clemmons, NC 27012
(336) 712-8003
www.warmglass.com

Fuse Master Transparent & Non-Lead Opaque Enamels Mediums, Fusing Supplies
Fusion Headquarters, Inc.
15500 NE Kincaid Road
Newberg, OR 97132
(503) 538-5281
www.fusionheadquarters.com

Reusche Glass Paint, Enamels, & Metalic Lusters
Reusche & CO.
1299 H Street
Greeley, CO 80631
(970) 346-8575
www.reuscheco.com

Float Fire 82 enamels & tin scopes
Armstrong Glass Company
1025 Cobb International Blvd.
Kennesaw, GA 30152
770 919-9924
www.armstrongglass.com

Wrinkle Cream, Devit Flux, Fusing and Mold Supplies

Fusing Farm
at Laguna Clay Company
14400 Lomitas
Industry, CA 91746
1-800-452-4862 ext 223
www.fusingfarm.com

glass manufacturers

Bullseye Glass Company
3722 SE 21st
Portland, OR. 97202
(503) 232-8887
www.bullseyeglass.com

Spectrum Glass Company
PO Box 646
24105 Sno-Woodenville Rd.
Woodenville, WA. 98072-0646
(206) 483-6699
www.spectrumglass.com

Uroboros Glass
2139 N. Kerby Ave
Portland, OR. 97227
(503) 284-4900
www.uroboros.com

glass fusing supplies

Bullseye Resource Center
3610 SE 21st Ave.
Portland, OR. 97202
1-888-220-3002
www.bullseyeglass.com

Ed Hoy's International
27625 Diehl Road
Warrenville, IL. 60555-3838
(630) 836-1353
1-800- 323-5668
www.edhoy.com

international fusing supplies & enamels

Creative Glass AG
Geerenstrasse 12 / Kindhausen
8604 Volketswil
Switzerland
0041 44 908 11 55
www.creative-glass.com

Creative Glass
12 Sextant Park
Medway City Estate
Rochester K ME2 4LU
England
0044 1634 735 416
www.creative-glass.com

GlassForum AS
Kvernes 6530 AVERØY
Norway
47 71514100
www.mamut.net/glassforum

suppliers

Casting & Pâte de Verre Molds
Colour de Verre
3216 SE 8th Ave.
Porttland, OR 97202
(503) 232-3629
www.colourdeverre.com

Flatlite Lightsource
Artistic Lighting Solutions
Howard Moore
4620 South Arville Suite F
Las Vegas, NV 89103
(888) 233-9996
(702) 914-4444
artisticlightingsolutions.com

Castalot Mold Mix
Sunset Grove LLC
(206) 248-6233
www.michaeldupille.com.

Dow Corning silicone #732
Atlas Supply
611 S. Charleston St.
Seattle, WA. 98108-5239
1-800-347-5767
(206) 623-4697

Refractories / fiber paper
EJ Bartells Co.
700 Powell Ave. SW
Renton, WA. 98057
1-800-468-9528
(424) 228-4111
www.ejbartells.com

Belts & Diamond Equipment
Covington Engineering
PO Box 35
Redlands, CA. 92373
1-877-793-6636
www.covington-engineering.com

Diamond Pads & Supplies
His Glassworks, Inc.
91 Webb Cove Road
Asheville, NC. 28804
1-800-914-7463
www.hisglassworks.com

Diamond Bits & Equipment
Lortone Inc.
12130 Cyrus Way
Mukilteo, WA. 98275
(425) 493-1600
www.lortone.com

Art Supplies
Daniel Smith
4150 First Ave. S.
Seattle, WA. 98124-5568
(206) 223-9599
www.danielsmith.com

CMC, Kilns, Chemicals, Etc.
Seattle Pottery Supply
35 South Handford St.
Seattle, WA. 98134
1-800-522-1975
(206) 587-0570
www.seattlepotterysupply.com

Sandblast Equipment
Tip Equipment
PO Box 649
Canfield, OH. 44406
1-800-321-9260

Gold & Silver Foil
Olympic Color Rod
818 John Street
Seattle, WA. 98109
(206) 343-7336
1-800-445-7742
www.glasscolor.com

Gold Leaf, Mica, Supplies,
Sepp Leaf Products
381 Park Ave South
New York, NY. 10016
1-800-971-7377
www.seppleaf.com

Polarizing Film
Edmund Scientific
60 Pearce Ave.
Tonawanda, NY. 14150
1-800-728-6999
www.scientificsonline.com

Gloryhole Fans
Johnstone Supply
www.johnstonesupply.com

Grainger Industrial Supply
www.grainger.com

Kiln Elements & Glory Hole Parts
Joppa Glassworks, Inc.
PO Box 202
Warner, NH 03278
(603) 456-3569
www.joppaglass.com

resources

Pilchuck Glass School
Administration
430 Yale Ave N
Seattle, WA 98109
(206) 621-8422

Campus
1201-316th St NW
Stanwood, WA 98292
(360) 445-3111
www.pilchuck.com

Glass Art Society
6512 23rd Ave NW, Suite 329
Seattle, Washington 98117 USA
Phone: (206) 382-1305
www.glassart.org

Corning Museum of Glass & Corning New Glass Review
1 Museum Way
Corning, NY 14830
(800) 732-6845
www.cmog.org

American Craft Magazine
72 Spring St, 6th Flr,
New York, New York 10012
(212) 274-0630
www.americancraftmag.org

A
Adamson, Rob 45, **46-49**, 100
Anderson, Avery **117-120**
Anderson, Harriette **31**, 234, 236
Annealing 149, 186, 229, **232-233**
Apache Tears **15**
Australites **10**
B
Boyd-Yost, Sherry **124-131**
Bubble powder 86-87
Bullseye Glass Company 32, **45**, 95, 101, 175, 232, 237
C
Calcium carbonate 18, **24**, 52
Castalot 175, **177-183**
Ceramic fiber 39, 56, 57, **60-61**, 63, 84
Chip test **34**, 229
Clay mold 23, 33, 51, 54, **58**, 65
CMC 24, 87, 182, **193-194**, 207, 218 238
Colour de Verre molds **184-187**
Colloidal silica 59, **60-63**, 81, 84
Compatibility **31-36**, 95, 99, 145, 163, 164, **228-229**
Core vessel **16-18**, 27, 236
D
Devitrification 15, **36-38**, 40, 65, 67, 86, 115, 165, 210, 228-230
Devit prevention **37**
Dreisbach, Fritz 7, 45, **46-49**, 100
Dropout 58, 71, 76, **81-85**
Dupille, Michael **174-183**, 236, 238
E
Eckhardt, Edris **154-157**, 158, 236
Egyptian faience (see faience)
Enameled Glass 16, 17, **19**, 95, 97, 109, 114, 151, 157
Epoxy 157, **190-191**
F
Faience 15, 16, **18**, 21, **22-25**, 234
Fiber blanket 56, 57, **60-63**, 227
Fiber paper 39, **54-57**, 164, 171, 179, 182, 238
Float glass 36, **42**, 43, 44, 133, 142, 143
Fulgurite 9, **11**
Fuse Master enamels **41**, 54, 67, 89, 130, 131, 140, 147, 237
Fuse-slump 51, **67**
Fusing Farm 37, **38**, 41, 237

Fusing Ranch **7**, 105
G
Glass painting **122**, 124, 132,138,
Gold foil **158-161**
H
Heaton, Maurice 31, **70-71**, 72, 73
Higgins, Frances & Michael 31-33, **80-81**, 86, 88, 112, 150, 234, 236
I
Indochinites **8-9**
Islamic glass 19, **27-28**, 234
K
Kanthol **25**, 163
Kinney, Kay 31, **234**
Kinsey, Kyle **91-93**, 121
L
Lead hazard **31-32**, 37, 39, 95-96, 128, 129
Libyan desert glass **8-9**
Liquid glass line **193-195**, 196-201
Lost wax **155**
Luebtow, John **168-173**
Lukens, Glen **50-53**, 54-55
Luster 19, 33, 41, 117, 119, 120, **148-153**, 234
M
Mapelli, Liz 31, **94-97**
Marioni, Paul **98-105**, 146, 236
MacLeod, Meredith 31, **106-111**
McCutchen, Earl 31, **88**, 236
McGrain, Peter **132-137**, 236
Mica 43, 93, **121**
Mica powder 41, **117-120**
Moldavite **8-9**
N
Nachman, Roger 63, 163, **188-191**
Natron 18, **21**, 23
O
Obsidian 9, **12-15**, 16, 17,
Overglaze 35, **37**, 41, 59, 67, 165, 210, 219
P
Paradise enamels 32, **104-105**, 107, 113
Pliny **21**
Pilkington **42**, 44, 45
Polariscope **34, 225,** 228, 229, 232
Pop rivet 76, **78**
Pumice 9, **12-14**
R
Reusche enamel **41**, 91, 95, 96,

128, 131, 132, 139, 140, 145,237
Roman glass **43**, 123
Rondel **43**, 46, 48
S
Sag 53, 76, 69, **81-83**, 85
Scanga, Italo **144-145**
Sgraffito **65**, 67, 71, 72, 95, 97
Shabti (see ushabti)
Shelf primer 21, 39, **56-57**, 58, 59, 62, 66, 84, 164, 167
Silica 9, 11, 13, **16-18**, 23, 25, 52, 96
Silicone 79, 101, 141, 142, 177, 217, **222**, 238
Silver Foil 38, 41, 69, 82, 155, 158, 203, **206**, 208, 210, 240
Sizing **158**, 206, 221
Soda Ash 17-19, **23-25**, 42
Sodium bicarbonate **86-87**
"Spray A" **41**, 54, 55, 89
Stained glass 16, 27, 32, **45**, 117, 122-123, 125, 133,
Stainless steel mold 21, 59, 72, **76-79**, 85, **166-167**, 210
Steatite 16, **18**, 23
Stressometer **34**, 228, 229, 232
Sunshine enamels 31, 41, **105**, 107, 113
Squeegee oil 41, 105, **108**, 114
T
Tektite **8-10**
Thompson, Cappy 5, **138-143**, 146
Thompson enamels 31, 32, **40-41**, 58, 67, 69, 73, 75, 82, 95, 99, 101, 103, 115, 118, 237, 240
Tin scope **36**, 237
Trintinite **9**
U
Ushabti **23-24**, 25,
V
Vacuum pen 194, 207, **224-225**
Viscosity 18, **228-230**
Vitri-Fusáille **133-137**, 236
Volume control 194-195, **230-231**
W
Wet felt **60-61**, 63, 69
Walter, Edwin 31, 38, **64-65**, 66, 68-69, 112, 121, 163,
Wrangel, Margaret von **90-92**

Our Children Are Our Future

Rainbow Clouds

The clouds look like a blanket
that covers the world,
and unravels in the wind,
revealing a rainbow moon
in the clear sky.

"Four Faces" & "Rainbow Clouds"
by Antoine La Londe (5th grade) 2008. The
glass is 9 in. (23 cm) x 6 in. (15 cm) Bullseye
Glass with silver foil and dichroic.

"Painted Horse" by Amanda
Dixon (6th grade) 9 in. (23
cm) x 13 in. (33 cm) Thompson Enamels between two
pieces of window glass, 2009.

240